ORIGINAL PLAYS

BY

W. S. GILBERT

FIRST SERIES

CONTAINING

THE WICKED WORLD, PYGMALION AND GALATEA
CHARITY, THE PALACE OF TRUTH
THE PRINCESS, TRIAL BY JURY
IOLANTHE

LONDON
CHATTO & WINDUS
1925

NOTE.

The Story upon which "The Palace of Truth" is founded is probably as old as the "Arabian Nights." "The Princess" is a respectful parody of Mr. Tennyson's exquisite poem. It has been generally held, I believe, that if a dramatist uses the mere outline of an existing story for dramatic purposes, he is at liberty to describe his play as "original."

W. S. GILBERT.

CONTENTS.

THE WICKED WORLD.

AN ORIGINAL FAIRY COMEDY,

IN THREE ACTS.

DRAMATIS PERSONÆ.

FAIRIES.

ETHAIS	...	...	...	...	MR. KENDAL.
PHYLLON	...	...	...	...	MR. ARNOTT.
LUTIN, *a Serving Fairy*	...	...	...	MR. BUCKSTONE.
SELENE, *a Fairy Queen*	...	...	...	MISS MADGE ROBERTSON
DARINE	...	...	...	...	MISS AMY ROSELLE.
ZAYDA	...	...	...	...	MISS M. LITTON.
LEILA	.	...	..	...	MISS HARRISON.
NEODIE	..	...	...	...	MISS HENRI.
LOCRINE	...	...	...	...	MISS FRANCIS.

MORTALS.

SIR ETHAIS ...	...	...	...	...	MR. KENDAL.
SIR PHYLLON	...	...	...	MR. ARNOTT.
LUTIN, *Sir Ethais's Henchman*	...	...	MR. BUCKSTONE.

SCENE: IN FAIRY LAND.

⁎ The action is comprised within the space of twenty-four hours.

PROLOGUE.

Spoken by MR. BUCKSTONE.

THE Author begs you'll kind attention pay
While I explain the object of his play.
You have been taught, no doubt, by those professing
To understand the thing, that Love's a blessing :
Well, *he* intends to teach you the reverse—
That Love is not a blessing, but a curse!
But pray do not suppose it's his intent
To do without this vital element—
His drama *would* be in a pretty mess!
With quite as fair a prospect of success,
Might a dispensing chemist in his den
Endeavour to dispense with oxygen.
Too powerful an agent to pooh-pooh,
There will be Love enough I warrant you:
But as the aim of every play's to show
That Love's essential to all men below,
He uses it to prove, to all who doubt it,
How well all men—but he—can do without it.
To prove his case (a poor one, I admit),
He begs that with him you will kindly flit
To a pure fairy-land that's all his own,
Where mortal love is utterly unknown.
Whose beings, spotless as new-fallen snow,
Know nothing of the Wicked World below.
These gentle sons and daughters of the air,
Safe, in their eyrie, from temptation's snare,
Have yet one little fault I must confess—
An overweening sense of righteousness.
As perfect silence, undisturbed for years,
Will breed at length a humming in the ears,
So from their very purity within
Arise the promptings of their only sin.

Forgive them ! No ? Perhaps you will relent
When you appreciate their punishment !

But prithee be not led too far away,
By the hack author of a mere stage-play :
It's easy to affect this cynic tone,
But, let me ask you, had the world ne'er known
Such Love as you, and I, and he, must mean—
Pray where would you, or I, or he, have been ?

THE WICKED WORLD.

ACT I.

Scene—*Fairy Land. A beautiful, but fanciful landscape, which is supposed to lie on the upper side of a cloud. The cloud is suspended over the earth, a portion of which (representing "a bird's eye-view" of a mediæval city), is seen, far below, through a rent or gap in the cloud.*

As the curtain rises Zayda *is discovered standing in a thoughtful attitude, contemplating the world at her feet. To her enters* Darine.

Dar. My sister, Zayda, thou art deep in thought,
What quaint conjecture fills thy busy brain?
Zay. Oh, sister! it's my old and favourite theme—
That wonderful and very wicked world
That rolls in silent cycles at our feet!
Dar. In truth a fruitful source of wonderment!
Zay. Fruitful indeed—a harvest without end!
The world—the wicked world! the wondrous world!
I love to sit alone and gaze on it,
And let my fancy wander through its towns,
Float on its seas and rivers—interchange
Communion with its strange inhabitants:
People its cities with fantastic shapes,
Fierce, wild, barbaric forms—all head and tail,
With monstrous horns, and blear and bloodshot eyes,
As all should have who deal in wickedness!

Enter Phyllon.

Oh, Phyllon! picture to thyself a town
Peopled with men and women! At each turn,

Men—wicked men—then, farther on, more men,
Then women—then again more men—more men—
Men, women, everywhere—all ripe for crime,
All ghastly in the lurid light of sin!

Enter SELENE.

Phyl. In truth, dear sister, if man's face and form
Were a true index to his character,
He were a hideous thing to look upon ;
But man, alas ! is formed as we are formed.
False from the first, he comes into the world
Bearing a smiling lie upon his face,
That he may cheat ere he can use his tongue.
   Zay. Oh ! I have heard these things, but heed them
       not.
I like to picture him as he should be,
Unsightly and unclean.   I like to pair
Misshapen bodies with misshapen minds.
   Sel. Dost thou not know that every soul on earth
Hath in our ranks his outward counterpart?
   Dar. His outward counterpart!
   Sel.   'Tis even so;
Yes, on that world—that very wicked world—
Thou—I—and all who dwell in fairy land,
May find a parallel identity:
A perfect counterpart in outward form ;
So perfect that, if it were possible
To place us by these earthly counterparts,
No man on earth, no fairy in the clouds,
Could tell which was the fairy—which the man !
   Zay. Is there *no* shade of difference ?
   Phyl.   Yes, one ;
For we are absolutely free from sin,
While all our representatives on earth
Are stained with every kind of infamy.
   Dar. Are *all* our counterparts so steeped in sin ?
   Phyl. All, in a greater or a less degree.
   Zay. What, even mine ?
   Phyl.   Alas !
   Zay.   Oh, no—not mine
   Phyl. All men and women sin.
   Dar.   I wonder what
My counterpart is doing now ?

Sel.   Don't ask.
No doubt, some fearful sin!
 Dar.   And what are sins?
 Sel. Evils of which we hardly know the names.
There's vanity—a quaint, fantastic vice,
Whereby a mortal takes much credit for
The beauty of his face and form, and claims
As much applause for loveliness as though
He had designed himself! Then jealousy—
A universal passion—one that claims
An absolute monopoly of love,
Based on the reasonable principle
That no one merits other people's love
So much as—every soul on earth by turns!
Envy—that grieves at other men's success,
As though success, however placed, were not
A contribution to one common fund!
Ambition, too, the vice of clever men
Who seek to rise at others' cost; nor heed
Whose wings they cripple, so that they may soar.
Malice—the helpless vice of helpless fools.
Who, as they cannot rise, hold others down,
That they, by contrast, may appear to soar.
Hatred and avarice, untruthfulness,
Murder and rapine, theft, profanity—
Sins so incredible, so mean, so vast,
Our nature stands appalled when it attempts
To grasp their terrible significance.
Such are the vices of that wicked world!

   Enter ETHAIS, LOCRINE, NEODIE, LEILA, *and*
      other Fairies.

 Eth. My brother, sisters, Lutin has returned,
After a long delay, from yonder earth :
The first of all our race who has set foot
Upon that wicked world. See! he is here!

     Enter LUTIN.

 Sel. Good welcome, Lutin, back to fairy land!
So thou hast been to earth?
 Lut.   I have indeed!
 Sel. What hast thou seen there?

Lut. Better not inquire.
It is a very, very wicked world !
I went, obedient to our King's command,
To meet him in mid-earth.   He bade me go
And send both Ethais and Phyllon there.
      Eth. Down to mid-earth ?
      Lut.   Down to mid-earth at once.
He hath some gift, some priceless privilege
With which he would endow our fairy world ;
And he hath chosen Phyllon and thyself
To bear his bounty to this home of ours.
      Zay. Another boon ?   Why, brother Ethais,
What can our monarch give that we have not ?
      Eth. In truth, I cannot say—'twould seem that we
Had reached the sum of fairy happiness !
      Sel. But then we thought the same, before our King
Endowed us with the gift of melody ;
And now, how tame our fairy life would seem
Were melody to perish from our land !
      Phyl. Well said, Selene.   Come, then, let's away,
                                                    (*going*)
And on our journey through the outer world
We will take note of its inhabitants,
And bring you fair account of all we see.
Farewell, dear sisters !   [*Exeunt* PHYLLON *and* ETHAIS.
      Sel.   Brothers, fare-you-well.
            (*To* LUTIN).
And thou hast really met a living man ?
      Lut. I have indeed—and living women too !
      Zay. And thou hast heard them speak, and seen their
            ways,
And didst thou understand them when they spake ?
      Lut. I understand that what I understood
No fairy being ought to understand.
I see that almost everything I saw
Is utterly improper to be seen.
Don't ask for details—I've returned to you
With outraged senses and with shattered nerves,
I burn with blushes of indignant shame.
Read my experiences in my face,
My tougue shall wither ere it tell the tale.
It is a very, very wicked world !
      Dar. But surely man can summon death at will ;
Why should he live when he at will can die ?

Lut. Why, that's the most inexplicable thing
I've seen upon that inconsistent globe—
With swords and daggers hanging at their sides,,
With drowning seas and rivers at their feet,
With deadly poison in their very grasp,
And every implemont of death at hand—
Men live—and live—and seem to like to live!

[*Exit* Lutin

Dar. How strangely inconsistent !
Sel.   Not at all.
With all their misery, with all their sin,
With all the elements of wretchedness
That teem on that unholy world of theirs,
They have one great and ever glorious gift,
That compensates for all they have to bear—
The gift of Love !   Not as we use the word,
To signify mere tranquil brotherhood;
But in some sense that is unknown to us.
Their love bears like relation to our own,
That the fierce beauty of the noonday sun
Bears to the calm of a soft summer's eve.
It nerves the wearied mortal with hot life,
And bathes his soul in hazy happiness.
The richest man is poor who hath it not,
And he who hath it laughs at poverty.
It hath no conqueror.   When death himself
Has worked his very worst, this love of theirs
Lives still upon the loved one's memory.
It is a strange enchantment, which invests
The most unlovely things with loveliness.
The maiden, fascinated by this spell,
Sees everything as she would have it be:
Her squalid cot becomes a princely home ;
Its stunted shrubs are groves of stately elms ,
The weedy brook that trickles past her door
Is a broad river fringed with drooping trees :
And of all marvels the most marvellous,
The coarse unholy man who rules her love
Is a bright being—pure as we are pure;
Wise in his folly—blameless in his sin;
The incarnation of a perfect soul ;
A great and ever-glorious demi-god!
Dar. Why, what have we in all our fairyland
To bear comparison with such a gift ?

Zay. Oh! for one hour of such a love as that;
O'er all things paramount! Why, after all,
That wicked world is the true fairy land!

Loc. Why, who can wonder that poor erring man
Clings to the world, all poisoned though it be,
When on it grows this glorious antidote?

Zay. And may we never love as mortals love?

Sel. No; that can never be. Of earthly things
This love of theirs ranks as the earthliest.
'Tis necessary to man's mode of life;
He could not bear his load of misery
But for the sweet enchantment at his heart
That tells him that he bears no load at all
We do not need it in our perfect land.
Moreover, there's this gulf 'twixt it and us:
Only a mortal can inspire such love;
And mortal foot can never touch our land.

Zay. But—is that so?

Sel. (surprised).   Of course.

Zay.   Yet I have heard
That we've a half-forgotten law which says,
That when a fairy quits his fairy home
To visit earth, those whom he leaves behind
May summon from the wicked world below
That absent fairy's mortal counterpart;
And that that mortal counterpart may stay
In fairy land and fill the fairy's place
Till he return. Is there not some such law?

Sel. And if there be, wouldst put that law in force?
(horrified).

Zay. No; not for all the love of all the world!
(equally horrified.)

Sel. A man in fairy land! Most horrible!
He would exhale the poison of his soul,
And we should even be as mortals are,
Hating as man hates!

Dar. (enthusiastically). Loving as man loves! (SEL.
looks reproachfully.)
Too horrible! Still—

Sel.   Well!

Dar.   I see a trace
Of wisdom lurking in this ancient law.

Sel. Where lurks this wisdom, then? I see it not.

Dar. (with emphasis). Man is a shameless being,
steeped in sins

At which our stainless nature stands appalled ;
Yet, sister, if we took this loathsome soul
From yonder seething gulf of infamy—
E'en but for one short day—and let him see
The beauty of our pure, unspotted lives,
He might return to his unhappy world,
And trumpet forth the strange intelligence :
" Those men alone are happy who are good."
Then would the world immediately repent,
And sin and wickedness be known no more !

   Loc. Association with so foul a thing
As man must needs be unendurable
To souls as pure and sinless as our own :
Yet, sister dear, it has occurred to me,
That his foul deeds, perchance, proceed from this—
That we have kept ourselves too much aloof,
And left him to his blind and wayward will.

   Zay. Man is everything detestable—
Base in his nature, base in thought and deed,
Loathsome beyond all things that creep and crawl!
Still, sister, I must own I've sometimes thought
That we who shape the fortunes of mankind,
And grant such wishes as are free from harm,
Might possibly fulfil our generous task
With surer satisfaction to himself
Had we some notion what these wishes were !

   Neo. We give him everything but good advice,
And that which most he needs do we withhold.

   Dar. Oh ! terrible, dear sister, to reflect,
That to *our* cold and culpable neglect,
The folly of the world is chargeable !

   Sel. To *our* neglect !
   Zay.   It may in truth be so.
   Lei. In very truth I'm sure that it is so.
   Sel. Oh, horrible ! It shall be so no more.
A light breaks over me ! Their sin *is* ours !
But there—'tis easy still to make amends.
A mortal *shall* behold our blameless state,
And learn the beauties of a sinless life !
Come, let us summon mortal Ethais.

   Dar. But—
   Sel.   Not a word—I am resolved to this.
   Neo. But sister—
   Sel.   Well ?

Neo. (timidly).   Why summon only one?
Sel. Why summon more?
Neo.   The world's incredulous ;
Let *two* be brought into our blameless land,
Then should their wondrous story be received
With ridicule or incredulity,
One could corroborate the other.
Dar.   Yes—
Phyllon has gone with Ethais.   Let us call
The mortal counterpart of Phyllon too—
Sel. Two mortals—two unhappy men of sin
In this untainted spot!
Loc.   Well, sister dear,
Two Heralds of the Truth will spread that Truth
At the least twice as rapidly as one.
Sel. Two miserable men !   Why, *one* alone
Will bring enough pollution in his wake,
To taint our happy land from end to end !
Zay. Then, sister, two won't make the matter worse !
Sel. There's truth in that.   (*After a pause*). The two
        shall come to us.
We have deserved this fearful punishment ;
Our power, I think, is limited to two ?
Lei. Unfortunately.
Sel.   Yes—more might be done
Had each of us a pupil to herself.
Now then to summon them.   But, sisters all,
Show no repugnance to these wretched men ;
Remember that, all odious though they be,
They are our guests; in common courtesy
Subdue your natural antipathies ;
Be very gentle with them, bear with them,
Be kind, forbearing, tender, pitiful.
Receive them with that gentle sister love,
That forms the essence of our fairyhood ;
Let no side-thought of their unholy lives
Intrude itself upon your charity ;
Treat them as though they were what they will be
When they have seen how we shall be to them.
What is the form ?
Dar.   Two roses newly plucked
Should each in turn be cast upon the earth ;
Then, as each rose is thrown, pronounce the name
Of him whose mortal self it typifies.

Here *are* two roses plucked from yonder tree.

Sel. (taking them). Well then, fair rose, I name thee
    Ethais!—
Go, send thy mortal namesake to our cloud;
                       (throws rose to earth)
'Tis done; conceal yourselves till they appear!

    [*The fairies conceal themselves. Hurried music; to
      which enter* SIR ETHAIS *and* SIR PHYLLON,
      *hurriedly, over the edge of cloud, as if impelled by
      some invisible and irresistible power from below.*
      SIR ETHAIS *and* SIR PHYLLON *have their swords
      drawn. They are dressed as barbaric knights,
      and, while bearing a facial resemblance to their
      fairy counterparts, present as strong a contrast as
      possible in their costume and demeanour.*

Sir Eth. Why, help, help, help!

Sir Phy.   The devil seize us all!
Why, what strange land is this? How came we here?

Sir Eth. How came we here? Why, who can answer that
So well as thou?

Sir Phy.   As I?

Sir Eth.   Yes, cur; as thou!
This is some devil's game of thy design,
To scare me from the task I set myself
When we crossed swords.

Sir Phy.   I use no sorcery.
A whirlwind bore me to this cursed spot;
But whence it came I neither know nor care.

Sir Eth. There—gag thy lying tongue; it matters not,
Or here or there we'll fight our quarrel out.
Come! call thy devils; let them wait at hand
And when I've done with thee I'll do with them.

*(They fight. The fairies watch the combat unobserved with
    great interest.)*

Dar. What are they doing?

Sel.   It's some game of skill.
It's very pretty.

Dar. Very. *(Knights pause.)* Oh, they've stopped.

Phy. Come, come—on guard. *(Fight resumed.)*

Zay.   Now they begin again

Eth. (Sees fairies, who have gradually surrounded them.)
Hold! we are overlooked. (ETHAIS, *who has turned for
    a moment in saying this, is severely wounded by*
    PHYLLON.)

Sel.   You may proceed.
We like it much.
Dar.   You do it very well—
Begin again.
Eth.   Black curses on that thrust!
I am disabled. Ladies, bind my wound;
And if it please you still to see us fight,
We'll fight for those bright eyes and cherry lips
Till one or both of us shall bite the dust.
Phy. Hold! call a truce till we return to earth—
Here are bright eyes enough for both of us.
Eth. I don't know that! Well, there—till we return
    (*Shaking hands.*)
But once again on earth, we will take up
Our argument where it was broken off,
And let thy devils whirl me where they may,
I'll reach conclusion and corollary.
Dar. (*looking at* PHYLLON). Oh, fairyhood!
How wonderfully like our Phyllon!
Sel. (*looking at* ETHAIS).   Yes.
And see—how strangely like our Ethais.
Thou hast a gallant carriage, gentle knight. (*Sighing.*)
Zay. How very, very like our Ethais.
Eth. It's little wonder that I'm like myself;
Why, I am he.
Sel.   No, not *our* Ethais. (*Sighing.*)
Eth. In truth, I am the Ethais of all
Who are as gentle and as fair as thou.
Sel. That's bravely said; thou hast a silver tongue;
Why! what can gods be like if these be men.
(*During this dialogue,* DARINE *shows by her manner that
    she takes great interest in* ETHAIS.)
Say, dost thou come from earth or heaven?
Eth. (*gallantly putting his arm round them*).   I think
I've come from earth to heaven.
Sel. (*to* DARINE *with delight*).   Oh! didst thou hear?
He comes from earth to heaven! No, Ethais,
We are but fairies—this, our native home.
Our fairy-land rests on a cloud which floats
Hither and thither, as the breezes will:
At times a mighty city's at our feet,
At times a golden plain, and then the sea,
Dotted with ships and rocks and sunny isles.
We see the world; yet saving that it is

A very wicked world, we know it not—
We hold no converse with its denizens;
But on the lands o'er which our island hangs,
We shed fair gifts of plenty and of peace—
Health and contentment—charity—goodwill;
Drop tears of love upon the thirsty earth,
And shower fair waters on the growing grain.
This is our mission.
    Eth.   'Tis a goodly one!
I'd give my sword—aye, and my sword-arm, too,
If thou wouldst anchor for a year or so
O'er yonder home of mine. But tell me, now,
Does every cloud that hovers o'er our heads
Bear in its bosom such a wealth of love?
    Sel. Alas! Sir Ethais, we are too few
To work the good that we could wish to work.
Thou hast seen black and angry thunder-clouds
That spit their evil fire at flocks and herds,
And shake with burly laughter as they watch
The trembling shepherds count their shrivelled dead?
These are our enemies, sir knight, and thine.
They sow the seeds of pestilence and death—
May heaven preserve thee from their influence!
    Eth. Amen to that!
    Phy.   But tell us, gentle maid,
Why have you summoned us?
    Sel.   Because we seek
To teach you truths that now ye wot not of;
Because we know that you are very frail,
Poor, blind, weak, wayward mortals—willing reeds,
Swayed right and left by every tempting wind;
And we are pure, and very, very brave,
Having no taste for trivial solaces (*taking* Ethais' *hand*);
Scorning such idle joys as we have heard
Appeal most strongly to such men as you;
And we have cherished earnest hope that we,
By the example of our sacred lives,
May teach you to abjure such empty joys,
May send you back to earth, pure, childlike men,
To teach your mothers, sisters, and your wives,
And those perchance (*sighing*) who are to be your wives!
That there are fairy maidens in the clouds,
Whose gentle mode of thought and mode of life
They would do well to imitate. We would

That every maid on earth were such as we !   (*Placing her
    arms round his neck.*)
    Eth. In truth we would that every maiden were,—
(*Aside*) Except our mothers, sisters, and our wives!
    Sel. If you will be our pupils, you must give
Some token of submission to our will.
No doubt you have some form of fealty ?
    Eth. When man desires to show profound respect—
To indicate most forcibly his own
Inferiority, he always puts
His arm round the respected object's waist,
And drawing her (or him) towards him, thus.
Places a very long and tender kiss
On his (or her) face—as the case may be.
    Sel. That form is not in vogue in fairy land ;
Still, as it holds on earth, no doubt 'twill have
Far greater weight with you poor sons of earth,
Than any formula we could impose.
    Phy. Its weight is overpowering.   (*About to kiss.*)
    Sel.   But stay !
We would not *wrest* this homage from you, sir ;
Or give it willingly, or not at all.
    Eth. Most willingly, fair maid, we give it you.
    Sel. Good!   Then proceed.
                    (ETH. *kisses* SEL. *and* PHYL. *kisses* ZAY.)
    Eth.   There ! does it not convey
A pleasant sense of influence ?
    Sel.   It does.
Some earthly forms seem rational enough.
Why Ethais, what ails thee?   (ETHAIS *staggers.*)
    Eth.   Why, I'm faint
From loss of blood.   My wound—here, take this scarf,
And bind it round my arm—so—have a care!
There, that will do till I return to earth ;
Then, Lutin, who's a fairly skilful leech,
Shall doctor it.
    Sel. (*amazed*). Didst thou say Lutin ?
    Eth.   Yes,
He is my squire—a poor, half-witted churl,

Enter Lutin *unobserved.*

Who shudders at the rustling of a leaf;
A strange, odd, faithful, loving, timid knave;
More dog than man, and, like a well-thrashed hound,
He loves his master's voice, and dreads it, too.
Why, here he is! (*In intense astonishment.*)
 Lut.   Who is this insolent,
A mortal here in fairy land?
 Loc.   Yes, two!
 Lut. Oh, this is outrage!
 Eth. (*crossing to him*). Why, thou scurvy knave,
How cam'st thou here? Thou didst not come with us!
What is the meaning of this masquerade?
        (*Alluding to* Lutin's *dress.*)
Be off at once; if I could use my arm,
I'd whip thee for this freak, but as it is,
I'll hand thee over to that wife of thine;
Her hand is heavier than mine. (*To Sel.*) This churl
(So rumour saith) is mated to a shrew;
A handsome, ranting, jealous, clacking shrew;
And he, by means of this tom-fool disguise,
Has 'scaped his home to play the truant here;
 Lut. Who are these men?
 Sel.   The mortal counterparts
Of Ethais and Phyllon. Look at them!
        (*Crosses to* Lutin.)
Dost thou not love them?
 Lut. (*indignantly*). No!
 Sel.   How very strange!
Why we all loved them from the very first.
 Lut. Is this indeed the truth?
 Dar.   It is indeed.
Obedient to our queen's command, we have
Subdued our natural antipathies.
 Zay. They are our guests, all odious though they be,
       (*Takes* Phyllon's *hand*)
And we must bid them welcome to our home,
As if e'en now they were what they will be
When they have seen what we shall be to them.
       (*Kissing his hand.*)
 Lut. Be warned in time, and send these mortals hence;
Why, don't you see that in each word they speak,
They breathe of love?

Sel. (*enthusiastically*). They do!

Lut.   Why Love's the germ
Of every sin that stalks upon the earth :
The brawler fights for love—the drunkard drinks
To toast the girl who loves him, or to drown
Remembrance of the girl who loves him not!
The miser hoards his gold to purchase love.
The liar lies to gain, or wealth, or love ;
And if for wealth, it is to purchase love.
The very footpad nerves his coward arm
To stealthy deeds of shame by pondering on
The tipsy kisses of some tavern wench !
Be not deceived—this love is but the seed ;
The branching tree that springs from it is Hate !

   Dar. (*to* ETH.) Nay, heed him not. There is a legend
     here—
An idle tale, that man is infamous,
And he believes it. So, indeed, did we,
Till we beheld you, gallant gentlemen !

   Lut. Why, they are raving ! Let me go at once
And join my brothers at our monarch's court ;
While they are here this is no place for me.

   Zay. (*eagerly* to SEL.) Let him depart ; then we can
     summon here
His mortal counterpart. (*Fairies delighted ;* SELENE *ex-
     presses indignant surprise,* ZAYDA *changes her
     manner.*) A poor frail man
No doubt, who stands in very sorest need
Of such good counsel as we can afford.

   Sel. Thou speakest wisely. Lutin, get thee gone

   Eth. Be off at once.

   Phy.   Begone, thou scurvy knave !
Thy wife shall hear of this—*she'll* punish thee.

   Lut. Oh, moral plague ! oh, walking pestilence !
Oh, incarnation of uncleanliness !
You call me knave ! Why, harkye men of sin.
You've kings and queens upon that world of yours
To whom you crawl in apt humility ;
Well, sir, there's not an emperor on earth
Who would not kiss the dust I tread upon,
And I'm the meanest here. Good day to you.

                       [*Exit* LUTIN.

   Eth. (*following him angrily, is restrained by* SELENE).
     The fellow's crazed—heed not his rhapsodies,

Thou dost not credit him ?
   Sel.   And if I do,
What matters it ?   Be all he says thou art,
And I will worship thee for being so ;
Thou art my faith—whate'er my Ethais does
Is ever hallowed by his doing it ;
Thy moral law is mine—for thou art mine :
Rob, and I'll scoff at honour ; kill—I'll kill ;
Be perjured, and I'll swear by perjury ;
Aye, be thou false to me, and I'll proclaim
That man forsworn who loves but one alone !
My soul is thine—whate'er thy faith may be,
I'll be its herald ; if thou hast no faith,
I'll be the high priest of thine unbelief !
Thy wisdom's mine ; thy folly's thine—
   Eth.   Hush ! hush !
Why this is madness !
   Sel.   Yes, for this is love !
                (SELENE *kneels at* ETHAIS' *feet.*)

ACT II.

SCENE, *same as Act I.*

DARINE, ZAYDA, LEILA, LOCRINE, *other Fairies, and*
NEODIE *discovered anxiously watching the entrance to*
SELENE'S *bower.*

   Dar. Still, still Selene watches Ethais !
For six long hours has she detained the knight
Within the dark recesses of her bower,
Under pretence that his unhappy wound
Demands her unremitting watchfulness !
(*Indignantly.*) This, fairies, is our queen !—the sinless
     soul
To whose immaculate pre-eminence
We pure and perfect maidens of the air
Accord our voluntary reverence !
   Zay. Her conduct is an outrage on her sex !
Was it for *this* that we proposed to her
That we should bring these mortals to our land ?
Is *this* the way to teach this erring man
The moral beauties of a spotless life ?

To teach him truths that now he wots not of?
Surely this knight might well have learnt on earth
Such moral truths as *she* is teaching him.

Enter SELENE *from bower,* DARINE *retires up.*

   Lei. At last she comes! (*To* SELENE.) We are well
     pleased to find
That, after such a lengthy vigil, thou
Canst tear thyself away from Ethais!
   Sel. Yes, dearest sister, he is calmer now.
(*To* ZAY.) Oh! this has been a fearful night for him;
Not for one moment have I left his side!
   Zay. Poor Ethais! Believe us, sister dear,
He has our heartfelt pity.
   Sel.   All night long
He tossed and raved in wild delirium;
Shouting for arms, and, as it seemed to me,
Fighting his fight with Phyllon o'er again.
At length, as morning broke, he fell asleep,
And slept in peace till half an hour ago.
I watched him through the long and troubled night,
Fanning the fever from his throbbing brow,
Till he awoke. At first he gazed on me
In silent wonderment; then, suddenly
Seizing my hand, he pressed it to his lips,
And swore that I had saved him from the grave—
Mark that—the grave! I—I had saved his life!
He told me that he loved me—loved me well;
That I was fairer than the maids of earth—
That I had holy angel-eyes, that rained
A gentle pity on his stubborn heart—
(He called it stubborn, for he knew it not);
That I was fairer, in his worldly eyes,
Than all the maids on earth or in the clouds!
     (DARINE, *who has listened with intense anxiety to this*
      speech, goes off silently, but in an agony of grief.)
   Zay. (*spitefully*). Could any words more eloquently show
The recklessness of his delirium?
   Sel. (*surprised*). Nay, he was conscious then.
   Neo. (*very kindly*).   Of course he was!
No doubt, Selene, thou hast gained his love.
Be happy in it, dearest sister; but
In thy proud triumph, love, pray recollect

He had not seen *us !*
    Zay.   Thou hast wisely done
To keep him from *our* sight.   Cage thou thy bird,
Or he may fly to fairer homes than thine.
    Sel. *(amazed).*   What mean you, sisters ?   Nay, turn
        not away—
What have I done ?
    Loc. *(very spitefully).* Indeed we do not know ;
But, lest we should affect his love for thee,
We will at once withdraw.
                   [*Exit* LOCRINE, *bowing ironically.*
    Lei. *(with freezing politeness).* Good day to you !
    Neo. Good day !
    Zay.   Good day.   Remember—cage thy bird !
                           [*Exit.*
    Sel. How strangely are my sisters changed to me !
Have I done wrong ?   No, no, I'm sure of that.
The knight was sorely stricken—he had died
But for my willing care.   Oh ! earthly love,
Thou mighty minister of good or ill,
Is it for good or ill that thou art here ?
Art thou an element of happiness,
Or an unwieldy talisman that I,
In heedlessness, have turned against myself ?
"He had not seen *them*,"—so my sister spake ;
Yes, truly, there are fairer forms than mine.
He shall *not* see them !   Oh ! I am unjust.
Hath he not told me that I have his love ?
There is no treachery in those brave eyes ;
There is no falsehood in that gallant heart !
But still—he had *not* seen them.   Oh, for shame !
Can love and doubt reign ever side by side ?
No, Ethais, love is the death of doubt.
I love thee, Ethais, and doubt thee not !
Still it were better that he saw but me.
     (ETHAIS *has entered unperceived from bower and over-*
        heard the last three lines. He is very pale and
        weak, and his arm is in a sling.)
    Eth. Selene, I am weak—give me thine hand.
    Sel. My love, thou shouldst not yet have left thy couch !
Come—thou hast need of rest.
    Eth.   No, let me stay,
The air revives me—I am strong again.
And so, thou trustest me ?

Sel.   In truth I do! (*Sits by his side.*)
Although I cannot tell thee whence proceeds
This strange, irrational belief in thee—
Thee, whom I hardly know.
    Eth.   Is that so strange?
I see no marvel!
    Sel.   Nay, my love, reflect,
I am a woman, and thou art a man;
Well, thou art comely—so, in truth, am I:
We meet and love each other—that's to say,
I am prepared to give up all I have,
My home, my very fairyhood, for thee;
Thou to surrender riches, honour, life,
To please the fleeting fancies of my will.
And why?
Because I see in thee, or thou in me,
Astounding virtue, brilliant intellect,
Great self-denial, venerable years,
Rare scholarship, or godly talent? No!
Because, forsooth, we're comely specimens—
Not of our own, but Nature's industry!
    Eth. The face is the true index of the mind,
A ready formula, whereby to read
The lesson of a lifetime in a glance.
    Sel. (*in wonder*). Then, Ethais, is perfect comeliness
Always identified with moral worth?
    Eth. The comeliest man is the most virtuous—
That's an unfailing rule.
    Sel.   Then, Ethais,
There is no holier man on earth than thou!
My sisters, Ethais, are sadly changed
By the strange power that emanates from thee.
They love thee as I love thee!
    Eth. (*aside*).   Do they so!
I' faith they shall not love their love in vain!
    Sel. I tell thee this that thou mayst shun them, lest
By crafty scheme and subtly planned device,
They steal thee from thy mistress unawares.
    Eth. (*laughing*). No fear of that! Laugh all their
        schemes to scorn,
Treat them with the contempt such jades deserve.
I do not seek *them.*
    Sel.   Does the miser treat
The thief who seeks his treasure with contempt,

Because his treasure does not seek the thief?
No, Ethais, I'll hide my gold away!
Take thou this ring—it is a pledge of love. (*Giving him a
    ring.*)
Wear it until thy love fades from thy soul.
    Eth. 'Twill never fade while thou art true to me.
    Sel. (*amazed*). Are women ever false to such as thou?
    Eth. Are women ever true? Well, not to me.
(*Aside.*) Nor I to them; and so we square accounts!
    Sel. Then thou hast been deceived?
    Eth.   A dozen times.
    Sel. How terrible!
    Eth.   Yes, terrible indeed!
Ah, my Selene, picture to thyself
A man—linked for his life to one he loves.
She is his world—she is the breath he breathes;
In his fond eyes the type of purity.
Well, she is false—all women are—and then
Come tidings of his shame, the damning words,
"I love another, I have cheated thee."
At first it cannot be, it is a dream;
And when by slow procession, step by step,
He sees in it the *waking* from a dream,
His heavy heart stands still—he dies a death,
A momentary death—to wake again
Into a furious life of hot revenge;
His hand against all men; his maddened tongue
Calling down curses on his cheated self;
On him who stole her love, on all but her
Who has called down this crowning curse on **him**!
To find *her* love a lie, *her* kiss a jest,
Her cherished byewords a cold mockery—
Oh, there are words
For other agonies, but none for this!
    Sel. And thou hast suffered this?
    Eth. (*bitterly*).   I have indeed!
    Sel. And how long does this bitter anguish last?
    Eth. Well, in a very serious case, all night!
Next day a fairer face, a nobler form,
A purer heart, a gentler maidenhood,
Will set him dreaming as he dreamt before
Until the time for waking comes again;
And so the round of love runs through our lives!
    Sel. But these are earthly maidens, Ethais—

My love is purer than a mortal's love.

 Eth. Thine is no mortal love if it be pure.

 Sel. (*horrified*). Then, mortal Ethais, what love is thine?

 Eth. (*taken aback*). I spake of women—men are otherwise.

 Sel. Man's love is pure, invariably?

 Eth.   Pure?

Pure as thine own!

 Sel.   Poor, trusting, cheated souls!

        [*Exeunt together into bower.*

Enter DARINE, *who has overheard the last few lines.*

 Dar. She leads him willingly into her bower!
Oh! I could curse the eyes that meet his eyes,
The hand that touches his hand, and the lips
That press his lips! And why? I cannot tell!
Some unknown fury rages in my soul,
A mean and miserable hate of all,
       [*Enter* PHYLLON *unobserved.*
Who interpose between my love and me!
What devil doth possess me?

 Phy.   Jealousy!

 Dar. Perhaps—what matters how the fiend is called?

 Phy. But wherefore art thou jealous? Tell me, now,
Have *I* done ought to cause this jealousy?

 Dar. Thou! Dost *thou* love me?

 Phy.   Love thee? Tenderly!
I love all pretty girls, on principle.

 Dar. But is thy love an all-possessing love?
Mad, reckless, unrestrained, infuriate,
Holding thy heart within its iron grasp,
And pressing passion from its very core?

 Phy. (*surprised*). Oh, yes!

 Dar.   Alas! poor stricken, love-sick knight!
Phyllon, my love is such a love as thine,
But it is not for thee! Oh, nerve thyself,
I have ill tidings for thee, gentle knight!
I love thee not!

 Phy.   Indeed?

 Dar.   Is it not strange?

 Phy. Most unaccountable.

 Dar. (*disappointed*).   But tell me, now,
Art thou not sorely vexed?

Phy. (*quietly*). Unspeakably.

Dar. But thou'lt forgive me? Tell me, Phyllon, now,
That I am pardoned!

Phy. That, indeed, thou art.

Dar. (*hurt*). Phyllon, hast thou despised *my* proffered
  love,
I'd not have pardoned *thee!*

Phy. No, women don't.

Dar. (*impatiently*). But dost thou understand? I love
  thee not.
I, whom thou lovest, Phyllon, love thee not—
Nay, more, I love another—Ethais!
Thou hast a rival, and a favoured one.
Dost thou not hear me?

Phy. (*surprised*). Yes; I'm deeply pained.

Dar. (*delighted*). Thou art?

Phy. Of course. What wouldst thou have me do?

Dar. Do? Hurl thyself headlong to yonder earth,
And end at once a life of agony!

Phy. Why should I!

Dar. *Why?* Because I love thee not!
Why if *I* loved and found my love despised,
The universe should ring with my laments;
And were I mortal, Phyllon, as thou art,
I would destroy myself!

Phy. Ha! ha! If all
Heartbroken lovers took that course, the world
Would be depopulated in a week!
And so thou lovest Ethais?

Dar. (*enthusiastically*). I do!

Phy. But still (I may be wrong) it seems to me
He's taken with Selene—

Dar. (*furiously*). Name her not!
He feigns a love he does not feel, because
She is our queen. He dares not anger her!

Phy. But art thou sure of this?

Dar. (*bitterly*). Oh! am I sure!
Look in these eyes—they do not burn for *thee;*
Behold this form—that *thou* shalt never clasp—
Gaze on these lips—*thou* shalt not press them, sir!
And tell me, now, that Ethais loves me not!
Oh! had I but the power to heal his wound,
And free him from her hated company!

Phy. Were Lutin here, he would assist thy plan.

Dar. Lutin ?

Phy.　　　　His henchman, and a cunning leech;
He has a charm—a potent talisman—
A panacea that will heal all wounds;
Fetch him, and Ethais is healed again.

Dar. (aside). The gods have heard me! (*Aloud, suddenly.*) Oh; insensate knight,
Thou counsellest me how to gain his love;
And yet thou lovest me?

Phy.　　　　　　Oh, pardon me,
That was ten minutes since—an age ago!　　　　[*Exit.*

Dar. Here comes the miserable, mincing jade,
With a fair speech upon her lying lips,
To meet the sister whom her base-born arts
Have robbed of more than life! Oh, hypocrite!

Enter SELENE *from bower.*

Sel. Darine!

Dar. (changing her manner). My sister—my beloved one,
Why, thou art sad; thine eyes are dim with tears!
Say, what hath brought thee grief?

Sel. (with great joy).　　　　Darine, my own.
Thou dost not shun me, then?

Dar. (aside).　　　　Oh, hypocrite!
(*Aloud.*) Shun thee, my own Selene? No—not I!

Sel. Bless thee for that! I feared to meet thy face,
For all my loved companions turned from me
With scornful jest and bitter mockery.
Thou—thou—Darine, alone art true to me!

Dar. True to Selene while Selene breathes!
Come—tell me all thy woes.

Sel.　　　　　My Ethais—
He whom I love so fondly—he is ill,
And I am powerless to heal his wound.
Darine, my love may die!

Dar.　　　　　What can be done?
Oh, I would give my fairyhood to save
The man thou lovest so—my dearly loved!
But stay, the counterpart of Lutin is
At once his henchman and his cunning leech;
Lutin has left our sphere, (*plucking rose from tree*) cast
　　this to earth, (*giving it*)
And summon mortal Lutin to his aid

He hath a charm to heal thy lover's wound.

Sel. Kind Heaven reward thee for thy ready wit,
My sister, thou hast saved both him and me!
My darling sister! (*Embracing her.*)

Dar. aside. Oh, thou hypocrite!

Sel. Fair rose, I name thee Lutin, go to earth,
And hither send the mortal counterpart
Of him whose name thou hast, and may the gods
Prosper thy mission! Kiss me, dear Darine, (*kissing her*)
For thou hast saved my Ethais for me! [*Exit* SELENE.

Dar. No, not for thee, good sister, for myself!
[*Exit* DARINE.

(*Hurried music. Enter* MORTAL LUTIN *over edge of
precipice, staggering on the stage as if violently
impelled from below.*)

Lut. What ho! help! help! Where am I? Not on earth
For I remember that a friendly cloud
Enveloped me, and whirled me through the air,
Just as my fair, but able-bodied, wife,
Began to lay my staff about my ears!

Enter NEODIE, LEILA, LOCRINE, *and others.*

Can this be death, and has she killed me? (*Sees them.*)
Well,
If I *be* dead, and if this *be* the place
In which I'm doomed to expiate my sins,
Taking my sins all round, I'm bound to say
It might have been considerably worse!

Loc. (*approaching him with great delight*). Why, this
is Lutin's mortal counterpart!

Neo. How quaint! How gloriously rugged?

Lei. Yes!
Such character and such expression!

All (*admiring him*). Yes!

Lut. By some mistake my soul has missed its way,
And slipped into Mahomet's Paradise!

Neo. No, this is fairyland. See, there's the earth
From which we summoned thee. These are the clouds.
Thou art not angry with us?

Lut. Angry? No!
I'm very well up here!

Loc. Then thou shalt stay!

Neo. Oh, tell me, are there many men on earth

As fair and pleasant to the eye as thou?

Lut. Not many, though I have met one or two
Who run me pretty close.

Neo. Tell us their names.

Lut. Well, let me see, Sir Phyllon has been thought
A personable man ; then Ethais
He's fairly well.

Neo. But these are *handsome* men—
We love thee for thy rugged homely face ;
Oh, we are sated with mere comeliness,
We have so much of that up here ! (*rises*) I love
A homely face !

Lut. I quite agree with you.
What do a dozen handsome men imply ?
A dozen faces cast in the same mould,
A dozen mouths all lip for lip the same,
A dozen noses all of equal length ?
But take twelve plain men, and the element
Of picturesque variety steps in,
You get at once unlooked-for hill and dale—
Odd curves and unexpected points of light,
Pleasant surprises—quaintly broken lines ;
All very pleasant, whether seen upon
The face of nature or the face of man.

Enter ZAYDA.

Loc. But stay—thou shouldst be faint, for lack of
food !

Neo. Nay, let me minister unto his wants !

Zay. Then go, beloved sisters, gather fruits,
And bring them here to him. Such frugal fare
Will have a daintier flavour than its own
When served by such fair hands ! (*Kissing them.*)

[*Exeunt* LOCRINE, NEODIE, *and others.*

Zay. (*suddenly*). We are alone !
One word of caution—shun my sisters all !

Lut. Are all those lovely girls your sisters ?

Zay. Yes ;
Rejoice that they are not thine own.

Lut. 1 do.
I very much prefer them as they are !
You're a fine family.

Zay. Fair to the eye ;

But take good heed—they are not what they seem !
Locrine, the fair, the beautiful Locrine,
Is the embodiment of avarice !
She seeks your gold.

    Lut.   I'm much obliged to her ;
I'll give her half she finds and thank her too !

    Zay. Darine is vain beyond comparison ;
Neodie is much older than she looks ;
Camilla hath defective intellect ;
Ena's a bitter shrew ; Colombe's a thief ;
And, last and worst of all—I blush to own,
Our queen Selene hath a tongue that stabs—
A traitor-tongue, that serves no better end
Than wag a woman's character away !

    Lut. I've stumbled into pretty company !
It seems you fairies have your faults !

    Zay.   Alas !
All but myself. *My* soul is in my face ;
I—only I—am what I seem to be ;
I—only I—am worthy to be loved.
(*Confidentially.*) If thou wilt love me I will dower thee
With wealth untold, long years and happy life,
Thou gallant churl—thou highly polished boor—
Thou pleasant knave—thou strange epitome
Of all that's rugged, quaint and picturesque !

    Lut. You don't take long in coming to the point.

    Zay. Forgive my clumsy and ill-chosen words ;
We gentle, simple fairies never loved
Until to-day.

    Lut.   And when you *do* begin,
You fairies make up for the time you've lost !
(*The Fairies enter with fruit. He sits up. They group
    about him.*)

    Neo. Hast thou a wife ?

    Lut.   Well, yes—that is—down there—
Up here I am a bachelor—as yet.

    Zay. (*offended*). As yet ! Be good enough to recollect
That we are good, and pure, and maidenly—
So prithee guard that errant tongue of thine.

    Loc. And does she love thee ?

    Lut.   Humph—we *do* fall out—
We did to-day.

    Neo.   And how came that about ? (*All anxious
    to know.*)

Lut. Why thus—to tell the truth—between ourselves—
There was a lady in the case.
Zay. (*apart, much shocked*). Hush—hush—
Confine thyself to matters that relate
To thine own sex.   Thy master, Ethais—
He fought with Phyllon—what was that about?
(*Crossing to* Lutin.)
Lut. Oh, it's the old, old story!
Loc.   Tell it.
Lut.   Well,
There was a lady in the case!
Zay.   Then, stop—
Go on to something else—Where wast thou born?
Lut. Why, in Bulgaria—some years ago—
(*whispering*) There was a lady in *that* case!
Zay. (*severely*).   It seems
There is a lady, sir, in every case.
Lut. In all those cases they *do* interfere!

Enter Darine *unobserved.*

Loc. And, Lutin, is thy wife as fair as thou?
Lut. I thought her pretty till I looked on thee.
Zay. Her hair?
Lut.   Is bright—but not as bright as thine.
Loc. Her figure?
Lut.   Neat and graceful of its kind,
But lacks thy pleasant plumpness.   Then, besides,
She has a long loud tongue, and uses it—
A stout and heavy hand—and uses that;
And large expressive eyes—and uses *them*!
Zay. And does she know that thou art here with us?
Lut. No—that's the joke!   No—that's the best of it!
The gods forbid she ever should know *that*!
She is so plaguey jealous!
Loc.   Is she so?
How is the lady called?
Lut.   Her name's Darine.
Dar. (*coming forward*). So I have found thee, Lutin.
Lut. (*aghast*).   Can it be
My wife!
Zay.   Thy wife?   This is Darine!
Lut.   I know!
(*They detain him*). Be quiet—don't—oblige me—let me
        go!

Do not suppose, my love, that these bold girls
Are friends of mine.
    Dar.   Come, I would speak with thee—
    Lut. Allow me to explain.
    Dar.   Attend to me.
Say, dost thou love thy master, Ethais ?
    Lut. My master ? Yes, most surely !
    Dar. (earnestly).   So do I !
Madly, unreasonably, recklessly. (LUTIN *much taken aback.*)
Love him with all the passion of a heart
That love has never kindled till to-day !
Thou, only thou, canst help me, noble sir.
The gods, the gods have sent thee to my aid !
    Lut. Have they ? In doing so the gods have not
Displayed their usual talent for intrigue.
O, thou abandoned woman !
    Dar.   Hear me, sir !
My Ethais is wounded in the arm.
Thou hast a remedy of wondrous power,
A charmèd remedy. Give it to me,
That I may work his cure.
    Lut.   Upon my soul,
Cure *him* for *thee !* This is a cool request !
    Dar. But why not heal thy master's wound ?
    Lut.   Because,
Under the circumstances, I prefer
My master wounded to my master well,
For when he's well, he's very well indeed !
(*Aside*) But stay—here is an essence that will drown
His soul in sleep till I awaken him (*taking bottle from
    pocket*).
Shall I ? I will ! He'll be much safer so !
(*Aloud.*) There, take the charm, and heal thy Ethais !
    Dar. A thousand thanks ! Now he indeed is mine !
    Lut. Oh ! this is inconceivable ! Come here (*Fairies
    advance*),
D' ye see these maidens, madam ? Hitherto
Thou hast been jealous, but without good cause ;
But now I'll give thee cause for jealousy ;
I'll pass my time with them—d'ye hear ? with them—
They're very pleasant, unaffected girls ;
I like them very much, and they like me—
I'll play the very devil with their hearts,
And let them play the very deuce with mine !

Dar. **Do so**; I'll not detain thee from thy loves—
See how impatiently they wait for thee;
Go—while the happy hours away with them.
    Lut. Is this thy jealousy, abandoned girl?
    Dar. (surprised). Jealous of thee? Good sir, I love
      thee not!
    Lut. You don't!
    Dar.   No, no—I love Sir Ethais;
And when I've healed his wound, sheer gratitude
Will wake *his* soul to love!
    Lut.   If he drinks that
Sheer gratitude won't wake him. After all (*looking at
    Fairies, who are endeavouring to persuade him to
    accompany them*)
Six pretty Zaydas to one Ethais—
He fast asleep, and they all wide awake,
Egad, I've six to one the best of that!
               [*Exeunt* LUTIN *and Fairies.*
    Dar. He comes! At last I shall behold my love!

        Enter ETHAIS *from bower.*

(*Tenderly.*) How fares Sir Ethais?
    Eth.   Why grievously.
I am no leech, and cannot dress my wound,
I'm sick and faint from pain and loss of blood.
    Dar. (aside). How shall I work my end? I have a
      plan!
Oh, powers of impudence, defend me now!
(*Aloud.*) Sir Ethais, if Phyllon's words be true,
Thy wound is but a scratch.
    Eth.   A scratch, forsooth!
The devil's nails could hardly scratch so deep.
    Dar. He says—I don't believe him—but he *says*
That thou hast magnified its character,
Because thou fearest to renew the fight.
He *says* thou art a coward!
    Eth. (furiously).   By my blood,
He shall atone for that! Did he say this
To thee?
    Dar. Ay, sir, to me—a minute since.
    Eth. Oh, Phyllon! Coward? Why, a dozen times
We two have fought our battles side by side;
And I'm to quail and blanch, forsooth, because

We two, at last, are fighting face to face?
Oh, curses on the wound! Were Lutin here,
My sword-arm soon would be in gear again.
   Dar. Lutin *is* here.
   Eth. (amazed).   Here? Lutin?
   Dar.   Yes. Behold! (*Shows flask.*)
I have obtained this precious charm from him.
Now, knight, to prove thy mettle!
   Eth. (furiously).   Give it me—
Give me the flask!
   Dar.   One moment, Ethais.
This flask is precious, and it hath a price.
   Eth. Name thou thy price, and I will give it thee.
Take money, jewels, armour, all I have,
So that thou leavest me one trusty sword!
   Dar. No, Ethais, I do not want thy wealth,
I want thy love—yes, Ethais, thy love;
That priceless love that thou hast lavished on
My worthless sister.
   Eth.   On Selene?
   Dar.   Yes,
Thou lovest her—and dost thou think that I
Will save thy life for her?
   Eth.   Selene? Bah!
True, she is fair. Well, thou art also fair.
What does it matter—her fair face or thine?
What matters either face—or hers or thine—
When weighed against this outrage on my fame?
   Dar. Give me this ring, and thou shalt have the charm.
   Eth. 'Tis thine. And now, Sir Phyllon, take good heed!

      Enter SELENE *from bower.*

   Sel. Darine! Thou here, alone with Ethais!
No, no. I will not doubt—
   Dar.   Doubt whom thou wilt!
Thou hypocrite! thou shameless hypocrite!
Thou wretched victim of thine own designs!
   Sel. Darine, what dost thou mean?

      Enter Fairies.

   Dar.   Doubt all of us,
For we are false to thee as thou to us.
I am as thou hast made me, hypocrite!

Sel. Thou art to me as thou hast ever been,
Most dearly loved of all these dearly loved.

Dar. Away! Thou art the source of all our ill;
For though we counselled thee to do the deed
That brought this blight upon our innocence,
'Twas but a test, and thou hast bent to it!

Zay. Oh, miserable woman, get thee hence!
Thou art no queen of ours!

Loc.   Away with her!
Down with the traitress queen! (SELENE *turns from one
    to another—all turn away from her.*)

Sel.   So let it be.
Yes, thou hast rightly said—I had a trust.
I have forsaken it. Through my default,
The taint of earth has fallen on our land.
Mine was the sin—be mine the punishment.
Well-loved Darine, take thou this diadem:
Wear it more worthily than I. (*Places her coronet on
    DARINE.*) Behold
How royally it rests upon her brow!
My gentle sisterhood, behold your queen! (*Fairies bow.*)
Let her fair face and form, untainted yet
By the iniquity of my default,
Recall the loved Darine of yesterday—
The gentle, loving, maidenly Darine—
Who would have been that loved Darine to-day,
But for my erring deed. Oh, shame on me!
Thou art as I have made thee. Who am I
That I should judge my sister? I am loved;
But had I lost that love, should I have borne
My loss more patiently than thou? Alas!
Thou, I, and all, are now as mortals are.

Dar. So may I fall if I forsake my trust.
Thy punishment is just. Thou wast a queen—
What art thou now?

Sel.   I have a kingdom yet!
I have a kingdom here—in Ethais' heart.
A kingdom? Nay, a world—my world—my world!
A world where all is pure, and good, and brave;
A world of noble thought and noble deed;
A world of brave and gentle chivalry;
A very goodly and right gallant world;—
This is my kingdom—for I am its queen!

Dar. Thou art no queen of his, for he is mine.

Aye, by the token that thou gavest him (*shows ring*),
Thou fond and foolish maiden!
   Sel. (*looking at it*).   No, no, no!
It is a counterfeit—no, no, Darine!
The punishments of Heaven are merciful.
     (*Takes* ETHAIS' *hand to kiss it; she sees that the
     ring is not there.*)
                                 Oh, Ethais!
Is that the ring with which I plighted thee?
   Eth. Aye, that's the bauble. I have naught to say.
   Sel. (*to* DAR.). It fell from him—where didst thou find
    it, speak?
   Eth. I sold it for a charm that I might have
An arm to flog a lying cur withal;
A traitor devil, whose false breath had blurred
My knightly honour, dearer to my heart
Than any love of woman—hers or thine!
I had no choice—my honour was at stake.
   Sel. Thine honour! Thou dost well to speak of that.
Can devils take the face and form of gods?
Are truth and treachery so near akin
That one can wear the other's countenance?
Are all men such as thou? Or art thou not
Of thine accursed race the most accursed?
Why, honourable sir, thou art a knight
That wars with womankind! Thy panoply
A goodly form, smooth tongue, and fair false face.
Thy shield a lie; thy weapon an embrace;
The emblem of thy skill a broken heart!
Thine is a gallant calling, Ethais—
Thou manly knight—thou soul of chivalry—
Thou most discreet and prudent warrior!
(*He approaches her.*) Away, and touch me not! **My**
    nature's gone.
May Heaven rain down her fury on thy soul!
May every fibre in that perjured heart
Quiver with love for one who loves thee not!
May thine untrammelled soul at last be caught,
And fixed and chained and riveted to one
Who, with the love of heaven upon her lips,
Carries the hate of hell within her heart!
Thou phantom of the truth—thou mimic god—
Thou traitor to thine own unhappy soul—
Thou base apostate to the lovely faith,

That thou hast preached with such false eloquence,
I am thine enemy! (*To her sisters.*) Look on your woi
My gentle sisters. (*They look in horror.*)   Are ye n
   content?
Behold! I am a devil, like yourselves!

ACT III.

Scene, *same as Acts I. and II.*

Lutin *discovered sitting, in deep dejection.* Zayda *is a*
   his feet trying to arouse him. Ethais *is lying in*
   sensible at entrance to bower, covered with a mantle.

Zay. Come, Lutin, speak to me—for hours in vain
I've sought to wean thee from thine inner self;
I've sung in vain to thee—thou wilt not sing—
   Lut. I cannot sing.
   Zay.   Or dance?
   Lut.   I do not dance.
   Zay. Then let us float on yonder silver stream (*they*
   rise),
Or plunge headlong into its mossy depths,
And wander, hand in hand, from grot to grot;
Or, if thou wilt, I'll whirl thee through the air,
And light with thee on yon tall pinnacle.
Come, Lutin—take my hand, and we'll away!
   Lut. Don't be ridiculous! I do not fly!
You're very good—you mean it well, I know—
But I've no taste for such alarming joys.
I can't help thinking of my lost Darine,
She was so much too good for me, and now
I am so much too good for her!
   Zay.   Alas!
Dost thou love *her?*
   Lut.   I can't help loving her.
   Zay. Dismiss the worthless creature from thy thoughts.
I know her well—she don't deserve thy love!
She always was a very wicked girl.
   Lut. Wicked? The best of women!
   Zay. (*maliciously*).   So she *seemed.*
   Lut. She had her faults, I know.

Zay.   She hath a soul
In which hypocrisy, intemperance,
Hate, envy, vanity, untruthfulness
Run riot at their will!
    Lut. (astonished).   You don't say so?
I'd no idea of this—   (*weeping*)
    Zay.   As for her crimes—
    Lut. Tell me the worst at once!
    Zay.   The worst?   No, that
Would be *too* cruel—but—bigamy's the best!
    Lut. What! Bigamy! Has she *two* husbands, then?
    Zay. Two? Half a dozen!
    Lut.   What!
    Zay.   Why even now
She seeks to add a seventh to her list!
Sir Ethais—
    Lut.   Ah, there I've thwarted her.

Enter Darine, *who goes to* Ethais. *She overhears what
follows.*

I have a potion that will heal his wounds;
She begged it of me, but I cheated her,
And put into her hands a sleeping draught.
By this time he's as helpless as the dead,
And she may shout until she wakes the dead,
Before she wakes him!

    (Darine *comes forward.* *Exit* Zayda, *in terror.*)

    Dar. (down). Why, thou envious churl—
Thou wanton trifler with the purest fire
That ever burnt in love-sick woman's breast,
Why hast thou done this thing?
    Lut.   She does not quail
Beneath her injured Lutin's outraged eye, (*she goes up to*
    Ethais)
But calmly asks him why he's done this thing!
    Dar. Say, is he dead? Come—answer quickly!
    Lut.   Well,
He's dead to all intents and purposes.
    Dar. How has he injured thee?
    Lut.   He hasn't as yet;
And I'll take care he don't!
    Dar.   Oh, misery!
In half an hour my brothers will be here;

In half an hour he must return to earth!
(*Referring to* ETHAIS.)

Awake, insensate knight—arouse thee, dolt!
I—I, Darine, am waiting here for thee.
Dost thou not hear me?   Ethais, awake!

   Lut. Oh—shout away!
   Dar.   Oh! I will be revenged!
(*To* LUTIN.) I know not why thou wagest bitter war
Against my unoffending happiness;
But I will thwart thy schemes.   Sir Phyllon comes!
[*Enter* PHYLLON.

Come hither, Phyllon—come to me, fair knight!
Say, dost thou love me still?

   Phy.   Indeed I do!
   Dar. (*to* LUTIN). Thou hearest him—he *loves* me!
      (*To* PHYLL.) Tenderly?
   Phy. Most tenderly!   (*Embracing her.*)
   Dar.   He loves *most* tenderly!
He is awake!

   Lut.   Yes, much too wide awake!
Disreputable woman, let him be!
Unhand this lady!

   Dar.   Why, thou selfish knave,
May I love nobody on earth but *thee?*

   Lut. Of course you may not!
   Dar.   Go, sir, get thee gone?
There are fair maids enough awaiting thee:
I do not interfere 'twixt thee and them.

   Lut. Well no, to do you justice, you do *not!*
I do not want them.   I'm a married man!
What married man cares twopence for intrigues
At which his wife connives?

   Phy.   Is this thy wife?
   Lut. I blush to say she is!
   Dar. (*amazed*).   I am thy wife!
Oh, monstrous!   Stay, there has been some mistake,
Some dreadful error!   See I've found a clue!
No doubt I am her fairy prototype,
In face resembling her, but that is all.

   Lut. Then thou art *not* my wife?
   Dar.   Not I, indeed!
(LUTIN *kisses her.*)

I am a fairy.   Be thou reassured;
Thy wife is on the earth (*kisses her again*)—Give me the
   charm

To cure my Ethais, and sit thee down (*he gives it to her*),
And I will send for Zayda and Locrine,
And thou shall talk of love to both of them.
    Lut. Well no—upon the whole—I'd rather not.
        (DARINE *administers the potion to* ETHAIS, *who gradu-
        ally revives.*)
I have reformed, Darine, and had I not,
I don't think I could talk to them of love
With all the eloquence the theme deserves,
In the distracting company of one,
Who, if she's not in point of fact my wife,
Is so uncomfortably like my wife,
That she may be my wife for aught I know ;
And more than that, I can't stand tamely by
And notice with uninterested gaze
A lady, who's so very like my wife,
Hanging on everybody's neck but mine.
Don't send for Zayda—I'm a married man !   [*Exit.*
    Dar. He wakes ! He lives—my own, own Ethais !
    Eth. (*awaking*). Why—where am I ? Have I then
      been asleep ?
    Dar. Indeed thou hast ! See, thou must soon return
To yonder earth—I've much to say to thee.
    Eth. But how came I to sleep ? I recollect !
Thou gavest me a potion, and I—(*sees* PHYLLON) Ha !
      (*Flies at his throat.*)
So I'm a cur, Sir Liar, and my wound
Is but a scratch which I have magnified
That I might shun the terrors of thy sword !
    Phy. Hands off, thou drunken madman ! Set me free.
I never said these things !
    Eth.   Thou craven cur,
Dost thou then fear to reap before my face
The crop that thou hast sown behind my back ?
Thy life shall pay for this !
    Phy. (*contemptuously*). I am not wont
To weigh the words I speak to such as thou.
No need to taint *thine* honour with a lie.
Why, Ethais, the truth is black enough ;
I know thee as a brawling tavern bully,
A hollow friend—a cruel unsparing foe—
A reckless perjurer—a reprobate—
The curse of woman and the scourge of man !
                (*Shaking him off.*)

Is not the *truth* enough, that I should grudge
The one brute-virtue of thy satyr-soul—
The instinct courage of a hungry dog!
 Eth. (*with suppressed fury*). I'll place these charges to
  the long account
That I've to settle when we go below!
(*To* Dar.) Didst thou not tell me he had said these things?
 Dar. I did, indeed!
 Phy.   And by what warrant, pray?
 Dar. It was an artifice to gain thy love. (*To* Ethais.)
Has man monopoly of lover's lies?
Forgive me, Phyllon—
 Phy.   Bah! Release my hand,
Thou shameless woman—I have done with thee.
             [*Exit* Phyl.
 Dar. Oh! Ethais, be not enraged with me—
Think of my love—
 Eth.   The devil take thy love—
I'll none of it! Begone! See, hither comes
The woman that thy bitter lie hath wronged.
Hast thou the heart to stand before her?
 Dar.   No! [*Exit.*

     Enter Selene *from bower.*

 Sel. Thou here? and with Darine!
 Eth.   Stay, hear me out!
It's true I've trifled with thy love, but then
Thy love is not as mortal woman's love.
I did not know that it would move thee thus?
 Sel. Thou didst not know!
Art thou so dull that thou canst understand
No pain that is not wreaked upon *thy* frame?
Hast thou no knowledge of the form of woe
That comes of cheated hopes and trampled hearts?
To find *thy* love a lie, *thy* kiss a jest,
The byewords of *thy* love a mockery?
Oh, there are words
For other agonies, but none for this!
 Eth. Nay, hear me! I have wronged thee bitterly—
I will atone for all!
 Sel.   Thou shalt atone;
I'll be the curse of thy remaining years!
Harkye, Sir Knight, I'll yield my fairyhood

That I may go to yonder earth, and join
The whispering sisterhood of hidden hate.
The busy band who bear within their lips
The deadliest weapon of earth's armoury :
A blighting tongue—a woman's blighting tongue !
I will so deftly wield this talisman
To twist and turn and torture good to ill,
That were it in thee to amend thy ways,
Turn anchorite, and yield to holy deeds
Of peace and prayer, goodwill and charity,
Thy holiness should seem an infamy,
Thy peace a war, thy charity a theft,
Thy calm a fury, and thy prayer a curse !
 Eth. Stay thine unholy tongue—go thou to earth,
And learn that that which thou hast undergone—
All women undergo.
 Sel.   Am I as they ?
I am immortal.   Can a few brief years
Of bitter shame and bitter sorrow weigh
Against an immortality of woe ?
A mortal's love is framed to last a life,
But my love to outlive eternity !
Blind mortal, as Eternity to Time—
So is my wrong to theirs !

Enter LOCRINE.

 Loc.   Selene, see,
Through the far distant air, with rapid flight,
Our absent brothers wing their way to us;
        [*Enter* ZAYDA *and* LUTIN.
These mortals must return to their own earth !
 Lut. Now, by my head, but this is welcome news !
 Zay. (*horrified*). Return to earth ? No, Lutin; no, not
  yet.
Life without Lutin ! what can that be worth ?
 Lut. I cannot tell you, for I never tried.
      [*Enter* DARINE *and* PHYLLON *struggling.*
Nay, seek not to detain me; I have had
Enough of fairy love—I seek my wife.
 Phy. Come, Ethais; to earth, to earth again !
 Dar. (*releasing him*). Aye, go, and take thy fellow man
  with thee. (LUTIN *and* PHYLLON *descend.*)
We want but this to crown our misery !
 (ETHAIS, *about to follow him, is detained by* SELENE.)

Sel. (*suddenly*). No! no! Thou shalt not go, thou shalt
    not go!
My hope—my shattered hope; but still my hope!
My love—my blighted love; but still my love!
My life—my ruined life; but still my life!
Forgive me, Ethais : thou hast withdrawn
The very core and substance of thy love.
No matter! give me but the empty husk,
And it will stay the famine of my heart.
I'll work and toil for thee—I'll be thy slave,
Thine humble, silent, and submissive slave;
I'll come but at thy beck—I will not speak
But at thy word—my Ethais! my love!
(*Furiously*) Nay, but I'll hold thee back! I have the
    strength
Of fifty women! See, thou canst not go! (*with passionate
    triumph.*)
Nay, but I'll *wrest* thy love away from thee,
And fetter it in bondage to my heart.
I will be one with thee; I'll cling to thee,
And thou *shalt* take me to that world of thine.
    Eth. Take *thee* to earth? I love the earth too well
To curse it with another termagant.
We have enough of them! Release me, fool!
Man hath no appetite for proffered love!
Away from me, I go to that good world
Where women are not devils till they die!
        [*Throws off* SELENE, *who falls senseless. He leaps
            through cloud, and descends. As* ETHAIS *dis-
            appears, the fairies, who have grouped themselves
            about the stage in attitudes of despair, gradually
            seem to wake as from a dream.*]
    Sel. Where am I? Zayda! Neodie! Darine!
Oh, sisters, I am waking from a dream—
A fearful dream—a dream of evil thoughts,
Of mortal passion and of mortal hate,
I thought that Ethais and Phyllon too
Had gone to mid-earth—
    Zay.   Nay, it was no dream,
A sad and sorrowful reality!
Yes, we have suffered much—but, Heaven be praised,
These mortal souls have gone to their own earth,
And taken with them the bad influence
That spread like an infection through our ranks.

See! we are as we were! *(Embracing her.)*
   Sel.   Darine! Darine!
My well-beloved sister—speak to me!
   Dar. I dare not speak to thee—I have no words—
I am ashamed.
   Sel.   Oh, sister, let that shame
Sit heavily on all—for all have sinned.
Oh, let us lay this lesson to our hearts;
Let us achieve our work with humbled souls,
Free from the folly of self-righteousness.
Behold, is there so wide a gulf between
The humbled wretch who, being tempted, falls,
And that good man who rears an honoured head
Because temptation hath not come to him?
Shall we, from our enforced security,
Deal mercilessly with poor mortal man,
Who struggles, single-handed, to defend
The demon-leaguered fortress of his soul?
Shall we not rather (seeing how we fell)
Give double honour to the champion, who
Throughout his mortal peril, holds his own,
E'en though
His walls be somewhat battered in the fight?
Oh let us lay this lesson to our hearts!

   Enter LUTIN, *followed by* ETHAIS *and* PHYLLON, *as
              fairies.*

   Lut. Your brothers have returned.
   Sel. (embracing ETHAIS).   My Ethais!
   Eth. Selene—sisters all—rejoice with us,
We bear the promise of a priceless gift,
A source of new and endless happiness! *(All eager to know.)*
Take every radiant blessing that adorns
Our happy land, and all will pale before
The lustre of this precious privilege.
It is—that we may love as mortals love!
   Sel. (eagerly). No, no—not that—no Ethais—not that!
It is a deadly snare—beware of it!
Such love is for mankind, and not for us;
It is the very essence of the earth,
A mortal emblem, bringing in its train
The direst passions of its antitype.
No, Ethais—we will not have this love;
Let us glide through our immortality

Upon the placid lake of sister-love,
Nor tempt the angry billows of a sea,
Which, though it carry us to unknown lands,
Is so beset with rocks and hidden shoals,
That we may perish ere our vessel reach
The unsafe haven of its distant shore.
No, Ethais—we will not have this love!

PYGMALION AND GALATEA.

AN ORIGINAL MYTHOLOGICAL COMEDY,

IN THREE ACTS.

DRAMATIS PERSONÆ.

PYGMALION, *an Athenian Sculptor* ... MR. KENDAL.

LEUCIPPUS, *a Soldier* ... ... MR. HOWE.

CHRYSOS, *an Art Patron* ... ... MR. BUCKSTONE.

AGESIMOS, *Chrysos's Slave* ... ... MR. BRAID.

MIMOS, *Pygmalion's Slave* ... ... MR. WEATHERSBY.

GALATEA, *an Animated Statue* ... ... MISS M. ROBERTSON.

CYNISCA, *Pygmalion's Wife* ... ... MISS CAROLINE HILL.

DAPHNE. *Chrysos's Wife* ... ... MRS. CHIPPENDALE.

MYRINE, *Pygmalion's Sister* ... ... MISS MERTON.

SCENE: PYGMALION'S STUDIO.

⁂ The action is comprised within the space of twenty-four hours.

PYGMALION AND GALATEA.

ACT I.

SCENE: *Pygmalion's Studio.*

Several classical statues are placed about the room; at the back a temple or cabinet containing a statue of GALATEA, *before which curtains are drawn concealing the statue from the audience.*

MIMOS, *a slave, is discovered at work on a half-finished statue To him enters* AGESIMOS.

Ages. (haughtily). Good day. Is this Pygmalion's studio?
Mim. (bowing). It is.
Ages. Are you Pygmalion?
Mim. Oh, no;
I am his slave.
Ages. And has Pygmalion slaves?
A stone-cutter with slaves to wait on him;
With slaves to fetch and carry—come and go—
And bend submissive uncomplaining backs
To whips and scourges, at a sculptor's whim!
What's the world coming to?
Mim. What is your will?
Ages. This: Chrysos will receive Pygmalion
At half-past three to-day: let him attend.
Mim. And are you Chrysos, sir?
Ages. (disconcerted). Well, no, I'm not.
That is, not altogether: I'm, in fact,
His slave.
Mim. (relieved). His slave!
Ages. (very proudly). My name's Agesimos!
Mim. And has Agesimos a master then,
To bid him fetch and carry—come and go—
And does he bend an uncomplaining back
To whips and scourges at that master's whim?

What's the world coming to?

Ages.   Poor purblind fool!
I'd sooner tie the sandals of my lord
Than own a dozen bondsmen such as you.
As for the scourge—to be by Chrysos flogged
Is honour in itself.   I'd rather far
Be flogged by Chrysos seven times a day,
Than whip you hence to the Acropolis;
What say you now?

Mim.   Why, that upon one point
Agesimos and I are quite agreed.
And who is Chrysos?

Ages.   Hear the slave, ye gods!
He knows not Chrysos!

Mim.   Verily, not I.

Ages. He is the chiefest man in Athens, sir;
The father of the arts—a nobleman
Of princely liberality and taste,
On whom five hundred starved **Pygmalions**
May batten if they will.

Enter PYGMALION.

Pyg.   Who is this man?

Ages. I'm Chrysos's slave—my name's Agesimos.
Chrysos has heard of you : he understands
That you have talent, and he condescends
To bid you call on him.   But take good care
How you offend him : he can make or mar.

Pyg. Your master's slave reflects his insolence!
Tell him from me that, though I'm poor enough,
I am an artist and a gentleman.
He should not reckon Art among his slaves :
She rules the world—so let him wait on her.

Ages. This is a sculptor!

Pyg. (*furiously*).   And an angry one!
Begone, and take my message to your lord.

                              [*Exit* AGESIMOS.

Insolent hound!

Enter CYNISCA.

Cyn.   Pygmalion, what's amiss?

Pyg. Chrysos has sent his slave to render me
The customary tribute paid by wealth

To mere intelligence.

Cyn.   Pygmalion!
Brooding upon the chartered insolence
Of a mere slave! Dismiss the thought at once.
Come, take thy chisel; thou hast work to do
Ere thy wife-model takes her leave to-day;
In half an hour I must be on the road
To Athens. Half an hour remains to thee—
Come—make the most of it—I'll pose myself;
Say—will that do?

Pyg.   I cannot work to-day.
My hand's uncertain—I must rest awhile.

Cyn. Then rest and gaze upon thy masterpiece,
'Twill reconcile thee to thyself—Behold !
   (*Draws curtain and discovers statue of* GALATEA.)

Pyg. Yes—for in gazing on my handiwork,
I gaze on heaven's handiwork—thyself!

Cyn. And yet, although it be thy masterpiece,
It has the fault thy patrons find with all
Thy many statues.

Pyg.   What then do they say?

Cyn. They say Pygmalion's statues have one head—
That head, Cynisca's.

Pyg.   So then it's a fault
To reproduce, maybe an hundred fold,
For the advantage of mankind at large,
The happiness the gods have given me!
Well, when I find a fairer head than thine
I'll give my patrons some variety.

Cyn. I would not have thee find another head
That seemed as fair to thee for all the world!
We'll have no stranger models if you please,
I'll be your model, sir, as heretofore,
So reproduce me at your will; and yet
It were sheer vanity in me to think
That this fair stone recalls Cynisca's face!

Pyg. Cynisca's face in every line!

Cyn.   No, no!
Those outlines softened, angles smoothed away,
The eyebrows arched, the head more truly poised,
The forehead ten years smoother than mine own
Tell rather of Cynisca as she was
When, in the silent groves of Artemis,
Pygmalion told his love ten years ago:

E

And then the placid brow, the sweet sad lips,
The gentle head down-bent resignedly,
Proclaim that this is not Pygmalion's wife,
Who laughs and frowns, but knows no meed between.
I am no longer as that statue is!   (*Closes curtain.*)
 Pyg. Why here's ingratitude, to slander Time,
Who in his hurried course has passed thee by!
Or is it that Cynisca won't allow
That Time *could* pass her by, and never pause
To print a kiss upon so fair a face?

Enter MYRINE.

 Myr. Pygmalion; I have news.
 Pyg.   My sister, speak.
 Myr. (*bashfully*). Send Mimos hence.
 Pyg. (*signs to* MIMOS).   Now we are quite alone.
 Myr. Leucippus—
 Cyn.   Well!
 Myr. (*to* PYG.)   He was thy schoolfellow,
And thou and he are brothers save in blood;
He loves my brother as a brother.
 Pyg.   Yes,
I'm sure of that; but is that all thy news?
There's more to come!
 Myr. (*bashfully*). He loves thy sister too.
 Pyg. Why this is news, Myrine—kiss me girl.
I'm more than happy at thy happiness,
There is no better fellow in the world!
 Cyn. But tell us all about it, dear. How came
The awkward, bashful, burly warrior,
To nerve himself to this confession?

LEUCIPPUS *appears at door.*

 Myr.   Why—
He's here—and he shall tell thee how it was.
 Leuc. In truth I hardly know! I'm new at it;
I'm but a soldier. Could I fight my way
Into a maiden's heart, why well and good;
I'd get there, somehow. But to talk and sigh,
And whisper pretty things—I can't do that!
I tried it, but I stammered, blushed, and failed.
Myrine laughed at me—but, bless her heart,

She knew my meaning, and she pulled me through!
Myr. I don't know how, Pygmalion, but I did.
He stammered, as he tells you, and I laughed;
And then I felt so sorry, when I saw
The great, big, brave Leucippus look so like
A beaten schoolboy—that I think I cried.
And then—I quite forget what happened next,
Till, by some means, we, who had always been
So cold and formal, distant and polite,
Found ourselves——
  Leuc.   Each upon the other's neck!
You are not angry? (*offering his hand.*)
 Pyg. (*taking it*).   Angry? overjoyed!
I wish I had been there, unseen, to see;
No sight could give me greater happiness!
 Leuc. What! say you so? Why then, Myrine, girl,
We'll reproduce it for his benefit. (*They embrace.*)
See here, Pygmalion, here's a group for thee!
Come, fetch thy clay, and set to work on it,
I'll promise thee thy models will not tire!
 Cyn. How now, Leucippus, where's the schoolboy blush
That used to coat thy face at sight of her?
 Leuc. The coating was but thin, we've rubbed it off!
       (*Kisses* MYRINE.)
 Pyg. Take care of him, Myrine; thou hast not
The safeguard that protects *her.* (*Indicating* CYNISCA.)
 Myr.   What is that?
 Cyn. It's a strange story. Many years ago
I was a holy nymph of Artemis,
Pledged to eternal maidenhood!
 Leuc.   Indeed!
 Myr. How terrible!
 Cyn.   It seemed not so to me;
For weeks and weeks I pondered steadfastly
Upon the nature of that serious step
Before I took it—lay awake at night,
Looking upon it from this point and that,
And I at length determined that the vow,
Which to Myrine seems so terrible,
Was one that I, at all events, could keep.
 Myr. How old wast thou, Cynisca?
 Cyn.   I was ten!
Well—in due course, I reached eleven, still
I saw no reason to regret the step;

Twelve—thirteen—fourteen saw me still unchanged;
At fifteen, it occurred to me one day
That marriage was a necessary ill,
Inflicted by the gods to punish us,
And to evade it were impiety;
At sixteen the idea became more fixed;
At seventeen I was convinced of it!

Pyg. In the mean time she'd seen Pygmalion.

Myr. And you confided all your doubts to him?

Cyn. I did, and he endorsed them—so we laid
The case before my mistress Artemis;
No need to tell the arguments we used,
Suffice it that they brought about our end.
And Artemis, her icy steadfastness
Thawed by the ardour of Cynisca's prayers,
Replied, " Go, girl, and wed Pygmalion;
" But mark my words, whichever one of you,
" Or he or she, shall falsify the vow
" Of perfect conjugal fidelity—
" The wronged one, he or she, shall have the power
" To call down *blindness* on the backslider,
" And sightless shall the truant mate remain
" Until expressly pardoned by the other."

Leuc. It's fortunate such powers as thine are not
In universal use; for if they were,
One-half the husbands and one-half the wives
Would be as blind as night; the other half,
Having their eyes, would use them—on each other!

(MIMOS *enters, and gives* PYGMALION *a scroll, which he reads.*)

Myr. But then, the power of calling down this doom
Remains with thee. Thou wouldst not burden him
With such a curse as utter sightlessness,
However grievously he might offend?

Cyn. I love Pygmalion for his faithfulness;
The act that robs him of that quality
Will rob him of the love that springs from it.

Myr. But sightlessness—it is so terrible!

Cyn. And faithlessness—it is so terrible!
I take my temper from Pygmalion;
While he is god-like—he's a god to me,
And should he turn to devil, I'll turn with him;
I know no half-moods, I am love or hate!

Myr. (to LEUC.*).* What do you say to that?

Leuc.   Why, on the whole

I'm glad *you're* not a nymph of Artemis!

[*Exeunt* MYRINE *and* LEUCIPPUS.

Pyg. I've brought him to his senses. Presently
My patron Chrysos will be here to earn
Some thousand drachmas.

Cyn.   How, my love, to earn?
He is a man of unexampled wealth,
And follows no profession.

Pyg.   Yes, he does;
He is a patron of the Arts, and makes
A handsome income by his patronage.

Cyn. How so?

Pyg.   He is an ignorant buffoon,
But purses hold a higher rank than brains,
And he is rich; wherever Chrysos buys,
The world of smaller fools comes following,
And men are glad to sell their work to him
At half its proper price, that they may say,
" Chrysos has purchased handiwork of ours."
He is a fashion, and he knows it well
In buying sculpture; he appraises it
As he'd appraise a master-mason's work—
So much for marble, and so much for time,
So much for working tools—but still he buys,
And so he is a Patron of the Arts!

Cyn. To think that heaven-born Art should be the slave
Of such as he!

Pyg.   Well, wealth is heaven-born too.
I work for wealth.

Cyn.   Thou workest, love, for fame.

Pyg. And fame brings wealth. The thought's con-
        temptible,
But I can do no more than work for wealth.

Cyn. Such words from one whose noble work it is
To call the senseless marble into life!

Pyg. Life! Dost thou call that life?

                    (*Indicating statue of* GALATEA.)

Cyn.   It all but breathes!

Pyg. (*bitterly*). It all but breathes—therefore it talks
        aloud!
It all but moves—therefore it walks and runs!
It all but lives, and therefore it is life!
No, no, my love, the thing is cold, dull stone,
Shaped to a certain form, but still dull stone,

The lifeless, senseless mockery of life.
The gods make life: I can make only death!
Why, my Cynisca, though I stand so well,
The merest cut-throat, when he plies his trade,
Makes better death than I, with all my skill!

Cyn. Hush, my Pygmalion! the gods are good,
And they have made thee nearer unto them
Than other men; this is ingratitude!

Pyg. Not so; has not a monarch's second son
More cause for anger that he lacks a throne
Than he whose lot is cast in slavery?

Cyn. Not much more cause, perhaps, but more excuse.
Now I must go.

Pyg.   So soon, and for so long!

Cyn. One day, 'twill quickly pass away!

Pyg.   With those
Who measure time by almanacks, no doubt,
But not with him who knows no days save those
Born of the sunlight of Cynisca's eyes;
It will be night with me till she returns.

Cyn. Then sleep it through, Pygmalion! But stay,
Thou shalt *not* pass the weary hours alone;
Now mark thou this—while I'm away from thee,
There stands my only representative. (*Indicating* GALATEA.)
She is my proxy, and I charge you, sir,
Be faithful unto her as unto me;
Intó her quietly attentive ear
Pour all thy treasures of hyperbole,
And give thy nimble tongue full license, lest
Disuse should rust its glib machinery;
If thoughts of love should haply crowd on thee,
There stands my other self; tell them to her;
She'll listen well. (*He makes a movement of impatience.*)
                    Nay, that's ungenerous,
For she is I, yet lovelier than I,
And hath no temper, sir, and hath no tongue!
Thou hast thy license, make good use of it.
Already I'm half jealous—(*draws curtains*)
                         There, it's gone.
The thing is but a statue after all,
And I am safe in leaving thee with her;
Farewell, Pygmalion, till I return.

                    (*Kisses him, and exit.*)

Pyg. "The thing is but a statue after all!"

Cynisca little thought that in those words
She touched the key-note of my discontent—
True, I have powers denied to other men ;
Give me a block of senseless marble—Well,
I'm a magician, and it rests with me
To say what kernel lies within its shell ;
It shall contain a man, a woman—child—
A dozen men and women if I will.
So far the gods and I run neck and neck ;
Nay, so far I can beat them at their trade !
I am no bungler—all the men *I* make
Are straight-limbed fellows, each magnificent
In the perfection of his manly grace :
I make no crook-backs—all my men are gods,
My women goddesses—in outward form.
But there's my tether ! I can go so far,
And go no farther ! At that point 1 stop,
To curse the bonds that hold me sternly back.
To curse the arrogance of those proud gods,
Who say, " Thou shall be greatest among men,
" And yet infinitesimally small ! "

    GALATEA. Pygmalion !
    Pyg.   Who called ?
    Gal.   Pygmalion !
    (PYG. *tears away curtain and discovers* GALATEA *alive.*)
    Pyg. Ye gods ! It lives !
    Gal.   Pygmalion !
    Pyg.   It speaks !
I have my prayer ! my Galatea breathes !
    Gal. Where am I ? Let me speak, Pygmalion ;
Give me thy hand—both hands—how soft and warm !
Whence came I ? (*Descends.*)
    Pyg.   Why, from yonder pedestal !
    Gal. That pedestal ? Ah, yes, I recollect,
There was a time when it was part of me.
    Pyg. That time has passed for ever, thou art now
A living, breathing woman, excellent
In every attribute of womankind.
    Gal. Where am I, then ?
    Pyg.   Why, born into the world
By miracle !
    Gal.   Is this the world ?
    Pyg.   It is.
    Gal. This room ?

Pyg.   This room is a portion of a house;
The house stands in a grove; the grove itself
Is one of many, many hundred groves
In Athens.
  Gal. And is Athens then the world?
  Pyg. To an Athenian—Yes—
  Gal.   And I am one?
  Pyg. By birth and parentage, not by descent.
  Gal. But how came I to be?
  Pyg.   Well—let me see.
Oh—you were quarried in Pentelicus;
I modelled you in clay—my artisans
Then roughed you out in marble—I, in turn,
Brought my artistic skill to bear on you,
And made you what you are—in all but life—
The gods completed what I had begun,
And gave the only gift I could not give!
  Gal. Then this is life?
  Pyg.   It is.
  Gal.   And not long since
I was a cold, dull stone! I recollect
That by some means I knew that I was stone:
That was the first dull gleam of consciousness;
I became conscious of a chilly self,
A cold immovable identity,
I knew that I was stone, and knew no more!
Then, by an imperceptible advance,
Came the dim evidence of outer things,
Seen—darkly and imperfectly—yet seen—
The walls surrounding me, and I, alone.
That pedestal—that curtain—then a voice
That called on Galatea! At that word,
Which seemed to shake my marble to the core,
That which was dim before, came evident.
Sounds, that had hummed around me, indistinct,
Vague, meaningless—seemed to resolve themselves
Into a language I could understand;
I felt my frame pervaded by a glow
That seemed to thaw my marble into flesh:
Its cold hard substance throbbed with active life,
My limbs grew supple, and I moved—I lived!
Lived in the ecstasy of new-born life!
Lived in the love of him that fashioned me!
Lived in a thousand tangled thoughts of hope,

Love, gratitude—thoughts that resolved themselves
Into one word, that word, Pygmalion! (*Kneels to him.*)
 Pyg. I have no words to tell thee of my joy,
O woman—perfect in thy loveliness!
 Gal. What is that word? Am I a woman?
 Pyg.   Yes.
 Gal. Art thou a woman?
 Pyg.   No, I am a man.
 Gal. What *is* a man?
 Pyg.   A being strongly framed,
To wait on woman, and protect her from
All ills that strength and courage can avert;
To work and toil for her, that she may rest;
To weep and mourn for her, that she may laugh;
To fight and die for her, that she may live!
 Gal. (*after a pause*). I'm glad I am a woman.
 Pyg.   So am I. (*They sit.*)
 Gal. That I escape the pains thou hast to bear?
 Pyg. That I may undergo those pains for thee.
 Gal. With whom then wouldst thou fight?
 Pyg.   With any man
Whose deed or word gave Galatea pain.
 Gal. Then there are other men in this strange world?
 Pyg. There are, indeed!
 Gal.   And other women?
 Pyg. (*taken aback*).   Yes;
Though for the moment I'd forgotten it!
Yes, other women.
 Gal.   And for all of these
Men work, and toil, and mourn, and weep, and fight?
 Pyg. It is man's duty, if he's called upon,
To fight for all—he works for those he loves.
 Gal. Then by thy work I know thou lovest me.
 Pyg. Indeed, I love thee! (*Embraces her.*)
 Gal.   With what kind of love?
 Pyg. I love thee (*recollecting himself and releasing her*)
 as a sculptor loves his work!
(*Aside*) There is a diplomacy in that reply.
 Gal. My love is different in kind to thine:
I am no sculptor, and I've done no work,
Yet I do love thee: say—what love is mine?
 Pyg. Tell me its symptoms, then I'll answer thee.
 Gal. Its symptoms? Let me call them as they come.
A sense that I am made *by* thee *for* thee;
That I've no will that is not wholly thine;

That I've no thought, no hope, no enterprise
That does not own *thee* as its sovereign ;
That I have life, that I may live for thee,
That I am thine—that thou and I are one!
  (*Embraces him passionately—then, frightened at her
   earnestness, she withdraws from him, still kneeling.*)
What kind of love is that ?
  Pyg.   A kind of love
That I shall run some risk in dealing with !
  Gal. And why, Pygmalion ?
  Pyg.   Such love as thine
A man may not receive, except indeed
From one who is, or is to be, his wife.
  Gal. Then *I* will be thy wife !
  Pyg.   That may not be ;
I have a wife—the gods allow but one.
  Gal. Why did the gods then send me here to thee ?
  Pyg. I cannot say—unless to punish me
For unreflecting and presumptuous prayer !
I prayed that thou shouldst live—I have my prayer,
And now I see the fearful consequence
That must attend it!
  Gal.   Yet thou lovest me ?
  Pyg. Who could look on that face and stifle love ?
  Gal. Then I am beautiful ?
  Pyg.   Indeed thou art.
  Gal I wish that I could look upon myself,
But that's impossible.
  Pyg.   Not so indeed.
This mirror will reflect thy face. Behold !
        (*Hands her a mirror.*)
  Gal. How beautiful ! I'm very glad to know
That both our tastes agree so perfectly ;
Why, my Pygmalion, I did not think
That aught could be more beautiful than **thou,**
Till I beheld myself. Believe me, love,
I could look in this mirror all day long.
So I'm a woman !
  Pyg.   There's no doubt of that !
  Gal. Oh happy maid to be so passing fair !
And happier still Pygmalion, who can gaze,
At will, upon so beautiful a face !
  Pyg. Hush ! Galatea—in thine innocence
Thou sayest words that never should be said.
  Gal. Indeed, Pygmalion ; then it is wrong

To think that one is exquisitely fair?

Pyg. Well, it's a confidential sentiment
That women cherish in their heart of hearts;
But, as a rule, they keep it to themselves.

Gal. And is thy wife as beautiful as I?

Pyg. No, Galatea, for in forming thee
I took her features—lovely in themselves—
And in the marble made them lovelier still.

Gal. (disappointed). Oh! then I'm not original?

Pyg. Well—no—
That is—thou hast indeed a prototype;
But though in stone thou dost resemble her,
In life the difference is manifest.

Gal. I'm very glad I'm lovelier than she.
And am I better?

Pyg. That I do not know.

Gal. Then she has faults?

Pyg. But very few indeed;
Mere trivial blemishes, that serve to show
That she and I are of one common kin.
I love her all the better for such faults!

Gal. (after a pause). Tell me some faults, and I'll commit them now.

Pyg. There is no hurry; they will come in time:
Though for that matter, it's a grievous sin
To sit as lovingly as we sit now.

Gal. Is sin so pleasant? If to sit and talk
As we are sitting, be indeed a sin,
Why I could sin all day! But tell me, love,
Is this great fault that I'm committing now,
The kind of fault that only serves to show
That thou and I are of one common kin?

Pyg. Indeed, I'm very much afraid it is.

Gal. And dost thou love me better for such fault?

Pyg. Where is the mortal that could answer "no"?

Gal. Why then I'm satisfied, Pygmalion;
Thy wife and I can start on equal terms.
She loves thee?

Pyg. Very much.

Gal. I'm glad of that.
I like thy wife.

Pyg. And why?

Gal. Our tastes agree;
We love Pygmalion well, and what is more,

Pygmalion loves us both.   I like thy wife;
I'm sure we shall agree.
 Pyg. (*aside*).   I doubt it much!
 Gal. Is she within?
 Pyg.   No, she is not within,
 Gal. But she'll come back?
 Pyg.   Oh, yes, she will come back.
 Gal. How pleased she'll be to know, when she returns,
That there was some one here to fill her place!
 Pyg. (*dryly*). Yes, I should say she'd be extremely
 pleased.
 Gal. Why, there is something in thy voice which says
That thou art jesting! Is it possible
To say one thing and mean another?
 Pyg.   Yes,
It's sometimes done.
 Gal.   How very wonderful;
So clever!
 Pyg. And so very useful.
 Gal.   Yes.
Teach me the art.
 Pyg.   The art will come in time.
My wife will *not* be pleased; there—that's the truth.
 Gal. I do not think that I *shall* like thy wife.
Tell me more of her.
 Pyg.   Well—
 Gal.   What did she say
When last she left thee?
 Pyg.   Humph! Well, let me see:
Oh! true, she gave thee to me as my wife,—
Her solitary representative;
She feared I should be lonely till she came,
And counselled me, if thoughts of love should come,
To speak those thoughts to thee, as I am wont
To speak to her.
 Gal. That's right.
 Pyg.   But when she spoke
Thou wast a stone, now thou art flesh and blood,
Which makes a difference!
 Gal.   It's a strange world!
A woman loves her husband very much,
And cannot brook that I should love him too;
She fears he will be lonely till she comes,
And will not let me cheer his loneliness;

She bids him breathe his love to senseless stone,
And when that stone is brought to life—be dumb!
It's a strange world—I cannot fathom it!

Pyg. (*aside*). Let me be brave, and put an end to this
(*aloud*). Come, Galatea—till my wife returns,
My sister shall provide thee with a home;
Her house is close at hand.

Gal. (*astonished and alarmed*). Send me not hence,
Pygmalion—let me stay.

Pyg.   It may not be.
Come, Galatea, we shall meet again.

Gal. (*resignedly*). Do with me as thou wilt, Pygmalion!
But we *shall* meet again?—and very soon?

Pyg. Yes, very soon.

Gal.   And when thy wife returns,
She'll let me stay with thee?

Pyg.   I do not know.
(*Aside*) Why should I hide the truth from her; (*aloud*) alas!
I may not see thee then.

Gal.   Pygmalion!
What fearful words are these?

Pyg.   The bitter truth.
I may not love thee—I must send thee hence.

Gal. Recall those words, Pygmalion, my love!
Was it for this that Heaven gave me life?
Pygmalion, have mercy on me; see,
I am thy work, thou hast created me;
The gods have sent me to thee.   I am thine,
Thine! only, and unalterably thine!
This is the thought with which my soul is charged.
Thou tellest me of one who claims thy love,
That thou hast love for her alone: Alas!
I do not know these things—I only know
That Heaven has sent me here to be with thee.
Thou tellest me of duty to thy wife,
Of vows that thou wilt love but her; Alas!
I do not know these things—I only know
That Heaven, who sent me here, has given me
One all-absorbing duty to discharge—
To love thee, and to make thee love again!

> [*During this speech* PYGMALION *has shown symptoms
> of irresolution; at its conclusion he takes her in
> his arms, and embraces her passionately.*]

ACT II.

SCENE, *same as Act I.*

PYGMALION *discovered at work on an unfinished statue.*

Pyg. To-morrow my Cynisca comes to me;
Would that she had never departed hence!
It took a miracle to make me false,
And even then I was but false in thought;
A less exacting wife might be appeased
By that reflection.   But Pygmalion
Must be immaculate in every thought,
Even though Heaven's armaments be ranged
Against the fortress of his constancy !

Enter MYRINE, *in great excitement.*

Myr. Pygmalion !
Pyg.   Myrine !
Myr.   Touch me not,
Thou hast deceived me, and deceived thy wife!
Who is the woman thou didst send to me
To share my roof last night ?
Pyg.   Be pacified :
Judge neither of us hastily ; in truth
She is as pure, as innocent as thou.
Myr. Oh, miserable man—confess the truth !
Disguise not that of which she boasts aloud !
Pyg. Of what then does she boast ?
Myr.   To all I say
She answers with one parrot-like reply,
" I love Pygmalion "—and when incensed
I tell her that thou hast a cheated wife,
She only says, " I love Pygmalion,
" I and my life are his, and his alone ! "
Who is this shameless woman, sir ?   Confess !
Pyg. Myrine, I will tell thee all.   The gods,
To punish my expressed impiety,
Have worked a miracle, and brought to life
My statue Galatea !
Myr. (incredulously). Marvellous,
If it be true !

Pyg. It's absolutely true.

(MYRINE *opens the curtains and sees the pedestal empty.*)

Myr. The statue's gone! (GALATEA *appears at door.*)

Pyg.   The statue's at the door!

Gal. At last we meet! Oh! my Pygmalion!
What strange, strange things have happened since we met.

Pyg. Why, what has happened to thee?

Gal.   Fearful things!

(*To* MYR.) I went with thee into thine house—

Myr.   Well, well.

Gal. And then I sat alone and wept—and wept
A long, long time for my Pygmalion.
Then by degrees, by tedious degrees,
The light—the glorious light!—the god-sent light!
I saw it sink—sink—sink—behind the world!
Then I grew cold—cold—as I used to be,
Before my loved Pygmalion gave me life.
Then came the fearful thought that, by degrees,
I was returning into stone again!
How bitterly I wept and prayed aloud
That it might not be so! "Spare me, ye gods!
"Spare me," I cried, "for my Pygmalion.
"A little longer for Pygmalion!
"Oh, take me not so early from my love;
"Oh, let me see him once—but once again!"
But no—they heard me not, for they are good,
And had they heard, must needs have pitied me;
They had not seen *thee,* and they did not know
The happiness that I must leave behind.
I fell upon thy couch (*to* MYRINE); my eyelids closed;
My senses faded from me one by one;
I knew no more until I found myself,
After a strange dark interval of time,
Once more upon my hated pedestal,
A statue—motionless—insensible;
And then I saw the glorious gods come down!
Down to this room! the air was filled with them!
They came and looked upon Pygmalion,
And, looking on him, kissed him one by one,
And said, in tones that spoke to me of life,
"We cannot take her from such happiness!
"Live, Galatea, for his love!" And then
The glorious light that I had lost came back—
There was Myrine's room, there was her couch,

There was the sun in heaven; and the birds
Sang once more in the great green waving trees,
As I had heard them sing—I lived once more
To look on him I love!

Myr.   'Twas but a dream!
Once every day this death occurs to us,
Till thou and I and all who dwell on earth
Shall sleep to wake no more?

Gal.   To wake no more?

Pyg. That time must come—may be not yet awhile—
Still it must come, and we shall all return
To the cold earth from which we quarried thee.

Gal. See how the promises of new-born life
Fade from the bright hope-picture, one by one!
Love for Pygmalion, a blighting sin;
His love a shame that he must hide away;
Sleep, stone-like senseless sleep, our natural state;
And life a passing vision born thereof!
How the bright promises fade one by one!

Myr. Why, there are many men whom thou mayst love;
But not Pygmalion—he has a wife.

Gal. Does no one love him?

Myr.   Certainly—*I* do.
He is my brother.

Gal.   Did he give thee life?

Myr. Why no; but then—

Gal.   He did not give thee life,
And yet thou lovest him! And why not I
Who owe my very being to his love?

Pyg. Well, thou mayst love me—as a father.

Myr.   Yes;
He *is* thy father, for he gave thee life.

Gal. Well, as thou wilt; it is enough to know
That I may love thee. Wilt thou love me too?

Pyg. Yes, as a daughter; there, that's understood.

Gal. Then I am satisfied.

Myr. (aside).   Indeed I hope
Cynisca also will be satisfied! [*Exit* MYRINE.

Gal. (*To* PYG.) Thou art not going from me?

Pyg.   For a while.

Gal. Oh, take me with thee; leave me not alone
With these cold emblems of my former self!

       (*Alluding to statues.*)

I dare not look on them!

Pyg.   Leucippus comes,
And he shall comfort thee till I return ;
I'll not be long !
Gal.   Leucippus ! Who is he ?
Pyg.   A man
Who's hired to kill his country's enemies.
Gal. (horrified). A paid assassin !
Pyg. (annoyed).   Well, that's rather strong.
There spoke the thoroughly untutored mind ;
So coarse a sentiment might fairly pass
With mere Arcadians—a cultured state
Holds soldiers at a higher estimate.
In Athens—which is highly civilized—
The soldier's social rank is in itself
Almost a patent of nobility.
Gal. He kills ! And he is paid to kill !
Pyg.   No doubt.
But then he kills to save his countrymen.
Gal. Whether his countrymen be right or wrong ?
Pyg. That's no affair of his—it's quite enough
That there are enemies for him to kill :
He goes and kills them when his orders come.
Gal. How terrible ! Why, my Pygmalion,
How many dreadful things thou teachest me !
Thou tellest me of death—that hideous doom
That all must fill ; and having told me this—
Here is a man, whose business is to kill :
To filch from other men the priceless boon
That thou hast given me—the boon of life—
And thou defendest him !
Pyg.   I have no time
To make these matters clear—but here he comes,
Talk to him—thou wilt find him kind and good,
Despite his terrible profession.
Gal. (in great terror).   No!
I'll not be left with him, Pygmalion. Stay!
He is a murderer !
Pyg.   Ridiculous !
Why, Galatea, he will harm thee not :
He is as good as brave. I'll not be long ;
I'll soon return. Farewell !   [*Exit.*
Gal.   I will obey,

F

Since thou desirest it ; but to be left
Alone with one whose mission is to kill !
Oh, it is terrible !

Enter LEUCIPPUS *with a Fawn that he has shot.*

Leuc.   A splendid shot,
And one that I shall never make again !
   Gal. Monster !   Approach me not !
                    (Shrinking into corner.)
   Leuc.   Why, who is this?
Nay, I'll not hurt thee, maiden !
   Gal.   Spare me, sir !
I have not done thy country any wrong !
I am no enemy !
   Leuc.   I'll swear to that !
Were Athens' enemies as fair as thou,
She'd never be at loss for warriors.
   Gal. Oh miserable man, repent ! repent !
Ere the stern marble claim you once again.
   Leuc. I don't quite understand—
   Gal.   Remember, sir,
The sculptor who designed you little thought
That when he prayed the gods to give you life,
He turned a monster loose upon the world !
See, there is blood upon those cruel hands !
Oh, touch me not !
   Leuc. (aside).   Poor crazy little girl !
Why—there's no cause for fear—I'll harm thee not—
As for the blood, this will account for it (*showing Fawn*).
   Gal. What's that ?
   Leuc.   A little fawn.
   Gal.   It does not move !
   Leuc. No, for I wounded her.
   Gal.   Oh, horrible !
   Leuc. Poor little thing !   'Twas almost accident :
I lay upon my back beneath a tree,
Whistling the lazy hours away—when, lo !
I saw her bounding through a distant glade ;
My bow was handy ; in sheer wantonness
I aimed an arrow at her, and let fly,
Believing that at near a hundred yards
So small a being would be safe enough,
But, strange to tell, I hit her.   Here she is ;
She moves—poor little lady !   Ah, she's dead !

Gal. Oh, horrible! oh, miserable man!
What have you done?—(*Takes Fawn into her arms*)—
                    Why, you have murdered her!
Poor little thing! I know not what thou art;
Thy form is strange to me; but thou hadst life,
And he has robbed thee of it! (*Gives it back to* Leuc.)
                    Get you hence!
Ere vengeance overtake you!
    Leuc.   Well, in truth,
I have some apprehension on that score.
It was Myrine's—though I knew it not!
'Twould pain her much to know that it is dead;
So keep the matter carefully from her
Until I can replace it.   [*Exit.* Leucippus *with Fawn.*
    Gal.   Get you hence;
I have no compact with a murderer!

Enter Myrine.

Myr. Why, Galatea, what has frightened thee?
Gal. Myrine, I have that to say to thee
That thou must nerve thyself to hear. That man—
The man thou lovest—is a murderer!
    Myr. Poor little maid! Pygmalion, ere he left,
Told me that by that name thou didst describe
The bravest soldier that our country owns!
He's no assassin, he's a warrior.
    Gal. Then what is an assassin?
    Myr.   One who wars
Only with weak, defenceless creatures. One
Whose calling is to murder unawares.
My brave Leucippus is no murderer.
    Gal. Thy brave Leucippus is no longer brave,
He is a mere assassin by thy showing.
I saw him with his victim in his arms,
His wicked hands dyed crimson with her blood!
There she lay, cold and stark—her gentle eyes
Glazed with the film of death. She moved but once,
She turned her head to him and tried to speak,
But ere she could articulate a word
Her head fell helplessly, and she was dead!
    Myr. Why, you are raving, girl! Who told you this?
    Gal. He owned it; and he gloried in the deed.
He told me how, in arrant wantonness,
He drew his bow, and smote her to the heart!

Myr. Leucippus did all this! Impossible!
You must be dreaming!
    Gal.   On my life, it's true.
See, here's a handkerchief which still is stained
With her life-blood—I staunched it with my hand.
    Myr. Who was his victim?
    Gal.   Nay—I cannot tell.
Her form was strange to me—but here he comes;
Oh, hide me from that wicked murderer!

               Enter LEUCIPPUS.

    Myr. Leucippus, can this dreadful tale be true?
    Leuc. (*to* GAL., *aside*). Thou should have kept my
        secret. See, poor girl,
How it distresses her. (*To* MYR.) It's true enough,
But Galatea should have kept it close,
I knew that it would pain thee grievously.
    Myr. Some devil must have turned Leucippus' brain!
You did all this?
    Leuc.   Undoubtedly I did.
I saw my victim dancing happily
Across my field of view—I took my bow,
And, at the distance of a hundred yards,
I sent an arrow right into her heart.
There are few soldiers who could do as much.
    Myr. Indeed I hope that there are very few.
Oh, miserable man!
    Leuc.   That's rather hard.
Congratulate me rather on my aim,
Of which I have some reason now to boast;
As for my victim—why, one more or less,
What does it matter? There are plenty left!
And then reflect—indeed, I never thought
That I should hit her at so long a range,
My aim was truer than I thought it was,
And the poor little lady's dead!
    Myr.   Alas!
This is the calmness of insanity.
What shall we do? Go, hide yourself away—
    Leuc. But—
    Myr.   Not a word—I will not hear thy voice,
I will not look upon thy face again;
Begone!

Gal. Go, sir, or I'll alarm the house!
Leuc. Well, this is sensibility, indeed!
Well, they are women—women judge these things
By some disjointed logic of their own,
That is not given to man to understand.
I'm off to Athens—when your reason comes
Send for me, if you will. Till then, farewell.

[*Exit angrily.*

Myr. Oh, this must be a dream, and I shall wake
To happiness once more!
Gal. A dream! no doubt!
We both are dreaming, and we dream the same!
But by what sign, Myrine, can we tell
Whether we dream or wake?
Myr. There are some things
Too terrible for truth, and this is one.

Enter PYGMALION, *with Fawn.*

Pyg. Why, what's the matter with Leucippus, girl?
I saw him leave the house, and mount his horse
With every show of anger.
Myr. He is mad,
And he hath done a deed I dare not name.
Did he say ought to thee before he left?
Pyg. Yes; when I asked him what had angered him,
He threw me this (*showing Fawn*).
Gal. (*in extreme of horror*). His victim! take it hence!
I cannot look at it!
Myr. Why, what is this?
Gal. The being he destroyed in wantonness;
He robbed it of the life the gods had given.
Oh! take it hence; I dare not look on death!
Myr. Why, was this *all* he killed?
Gal. (*astonished*). All!!! And enough!
Myr. Why, girl—thou must be mad! Pygmalion—
She told me he had murdered somebody,
But knew not whom!
Pyg. The girl will drive us mad!
Bid them prepare my horse—I'll bring him back.

[*Exit* MYRINE

Gal. Have I done wrong? Indeed, I did not know:
Thou art not angry with me?
Pyg. Yes, I am;

I'm more than angry with thee—not content
With publishing thine unmasked love for me,
Thou hast estranged Leucippus from *his* love
Through thine unwarrantable foolishness.

Enter MIMOS.

Mim. Sir, Chrysos and his lady are without.
Pyg. I cannot see them now.   Stay—show them in.
                              [*Exit* MIMOS.
(*To* GAL.) Go, wait in there.   I'll join thee very soon.
                            [*Exit* GALATEA.

Enter DAPHNE.

Daph. Where is Pygmalion?
Pyg.   Pygmalion's here.
Daph. We called upon you many months ago,
But you were not at home—so being here,
We looked around us and we saw the stone
You keep so carefully behind that veil.
Pyg. That was a most outrageous liberty.
Daph. Sir! Do you know me?
Pyg.   You are Chrysos' wife.
Has Chrysos come with you?
Daph.   He waits without.
I am his herald to prepare you for
The honour he confers.   Be civil, sir,
And he may buy that statue ; if he does
Your fortune's made !
Pyg. (*to* MIMOS). You'd better send him in.
                            [*Exit* MIMOS.

Enter CHRYSOS.

Chry. Well—is the young man's mind prepared ?
Daph.   It is ;
He seems quite calm.   Give money for the stone,
I've heard that it is far beyond all price,
But run it down ; abuse it ere you buy.
Chry. (*to* PYG.). Where is the statue that I saw last year ?
Pyg. Sir—it's unfinished—it's a clumsy thing.
I am ashamed of it.
Chry.   It isn't good.
There's want of tone ; it's much too hard and thin ;

Then the half distances are very crude—
Oh—very crude indeed—then it lacks air,
And wind and motion, massive light and shade;
It's very roughly scumbled; on my soul
The scumbling's damnable!
 Daph. (aside to him). Bethink yourself!
That's said of painting—this is sculpture!
 Chry.   Eh?
It's the same thing, the principle's the same;
Now for its price. Let's see—what will it weigh?
 Daph. A ton, or thereabouts.
 Chry.   Suppose we say
A thousand drachmas?
 Pyg.   No, no, no, my lord!
The work is very crude and thin, and then
Remember, sir, the scumbling—
 Chry.   Damnable!
But never mind, although the thing is poor,
'Twill serve to hold a candle in my hall.
 Pyg. Excuse me, sir; poor though that statue be,
I value it beyond all price.
 Chry.   Pooh, pooh!
I give a thousand drachmas for a stone
Which in the rough would not fetch half that sum!
 Daph. Why, bless my soul, young man, are you aware
We gave but fifteen hundred not long since
For an Apollo twice as big as that?
 Pyg. But pardon me, a sculptor does not test
The beauty of a figure by its bulk.
 Chry. Ah! then *she* does.
 Daph.   Young man, you'd best take care,
You are offending Chrysos!   [*Exit.*
 Chry.   And his wife. (*going.*)
 Pyg. That's a calamity I must endure.
Sir, once for all, the statue's not for sale. [*Exit.*
 Chry. Sir, once for all, I will not be denied;
Confound it—if a patron of the arts
Is thus to be dictated to *by* art,
What comes of that art patron's patronage?
He must be taught a lesson—where's the stone?
     (*Goes to pedestal and opens curtains.*)
It's gone! (*Enter* GALATEA, *he stares at her in astonish-*
 ment.) Hallo! What's this?
 Gal.   Are you unwell?

Chry. Oh, no—I fancied just at first—pooh, pooh!
Ridiculous. (*Aside.*) And yet it's very like!
(*Aloud.*) I know your face, haven't I seen you in—
In—in (*puzzling himself*).

Gal. In marble? Very probably.

Chry. Oh, now I understand. Why this must be
Pygmalion's model! Yes, of course it is.
A very bold-faced woman, I'll be bound.
These models always are. Her race is fair,
Her figure, too, is shapely and compact ;
Come hither, maiden.

Gal. (*who has been examining him in great wonder*).
Tell, me, what *are* you?

Chry. What am I?

Gal. Yes, I mean, are you a man?

Chry. Well, yes : I'm told so.

Gal. Then believe them not
They've been deceiving you.

Chry. The deuce they have !

Gal. A man is very tall, and straight, and strong,
With big brave eyes, fair face, and tender voice.
I've seen one.

Chry. *Have* you?

Gal. Yes, you are no man.

Chry. Does the young person take me for a woman ?

Gal. A woman? No; a woman's soft and weak,
And fair, and exquisitely beautiful.
I am a woman ; you are not like me.

Chry. The gods forbid that I should be like you,
And farm my features at so much an hour!

Gal. And yet I like you, for you make me laugh ;
You are so round and red, your eyes so small,
Your mouth so large, your face so seared with lines,
And then you are so little and so fat !

Chry. (*aside*). This is a most extraordinary girl.

Gal. Oh, stay—I understand—Pygmalion's skill
Is the result of long experience.
The individual who modelled you
Was a beginner very probably ?

Chry. (*puzzled*). No. I have seven elder brothers.
Strange
That one so young should be so very bold.

Gal. This is not boldness, it is innocence ;
Pygmalion says so, and he ought to know.

Chry. No doubt, but I was not born yesterday. (*Sits.*)

Gal. Indeed !—*I was.* (*He beckons her to sit beside him.*)
     How awkwardly you sit.
Chry. I'm not aware that there is anything
Extraordinary in my sitting down.
The nature of the seated attitude
Does not leave scope for much variety.
Gal. I never saw Pygmalion sit like that.
Chry. Don't he sit down like other men ?
Gal.   Of course !
He always puts his arm around my waist.
Chry. The deuce he does ! Artistic reprobate !
Gal. But you do not. Perhaps you don't know how ?
Chry. Oh yes ; I *do* know how !
Gal.   Well, do it then !
Chry. It's a strange whim, but I will humour her.
You're sure it's innocence ?   (*Does so.*)
Gal.   Of course it is.
I tell you I was born but yesterday.
Chry. Who is your mother ?
Gal.   Mother ! what is that ?
I never had one. I'm Pygmalion's child ;
Have people usually mothers?
Chry.   Well,
That is the rule.
Gal.   But then Pygmalion
Is cleverer than most men.
Chry.   Yes, I've heard
That he has powers denied to other men,
And I'm beginning to believe it !

Enter DAPHNE.

Daph.   Why!
What's this? (CHRYSOS *quickly moves away from* GAL.)
Chry.   My wife !
Daph.   Can I believe my eyes ? (GAL. *rises.*)
Chry. No!
Daph. Who's this woman ? Why, how very like—
Chry. Like what ?
Daph.   That statue that we wished to buy,
The self-same face, the self-same drapery,
In every detail it's identical.
Why, one would almost think Pygmalion,
By some strange means, had brought the thing to life,

So marvellous her likeness to that stone!

Chry. (*aside*). A very good idea, and one that :
May well improve upon. It's rather rash,
But desperate ills need desperate remedies.
Perceptive Daphne, you have guessed the truth.
You say she's like the statue—so she is,
And well she may be, for the gods have worked
A miracle, and brought the stone to life!

  Daph. Bah! Do you think me mad?

  Gal.   His tale is true
I was a cold unfeeling block of stone,
Inanimate—insensible—until
Pygmalion, by the ardour of his prayers,
Kindled the spark of life within my frame
And made me what I am!

  Chry. (*aside to* GAL.). That's very good;
Go on and keep it up.

  Daph.   You brazen girl,
I am his wife!

  Gal. His wife? (*To* CHRYSOS.) Then get you hence.
I may not love you when your wife is here.

  Daph. Why, what unknown audacity is this?

  Chry. It's the audacity of innocence ;
Don't judge her by the rules that govern you,
She was born yesterday, and you were *not!*

      Enter MIMOS.

  Mim. My lord, Pygmalion's here.

  Chry. (*aside*).   He'll ruin all.

  Daph. (*to* MIMOS). Who is this woman?

  Chry.   Why, I've told you, she——

  Daph. Stop, not a word! I'll have it from *his* lips!

  Gal. Why ask him when I tell you—?

  Daph.   Hold *your* tongue!
(*To* MIMOS.) Who is this woman? If you tell a lie
I'll have you whipped.

  Mim.   Oh, I shall tell no lie!
That is a statue that has come to life.

  Chry. (*aside to* MIMOS). I'm very much obliged to you!
        (*Gives him money.*)

Enter MYRINE.

Myr. What's this?
Is anything the matter?
Daph. Certainly.
This woman——
Myr. Is a statue come to life.
Chry. I'm very much obliged to *you!*

Enter PYGMALION.

Pyg. How now,
Chrysos?
Chry. The statue!——
Daph. Stop!
Chry. Let me explain.
The statue that I purchased——
Daph. Let me speak.
Chrysos—this girl, Myrine, and your slave,
Have all agreed to tell me she is·——
Pyg. The statue, Galatea, come to life?
Undoubtedly she is!
Chry. It seems to me,
I'm very much obliged to every one!

Enter CYNISCA.

Cyn. Pygmalion, my love!
Pyg. Cynisca here!
Cyn. And even earlier than hoped to be.
(*Aside.*) Why, who are these? (*Aloud.*) I beg your
pardon, sir,
I thought my husband was alone.
Daph. (*maliciously*). No doubt.
I also thought *my* husband was alone:
We wives are too confiding.
Cyn. (*aside to* PYGMALION). Who are these?
Pyg. Why, this is Chrysos, this is Daphne. They
Have come—
Daph. On very different errands, sir.
Chrysos has come to see this brazen girl;
I have come after Chrysos—
Chry. As you keep
So strictly to the sequence of events,

Add this—Pygmalion came after *you* !

   Cyn. Who is this lady (*alluding to* GALATEA)? Wh
      impossible!

   Daph. Oh, not at all!

   Cyn. (*turning to pedestal*). And yet the statue's gone !

   Pyg. Cynisca, miracles have taken place ;
'The gods have given Galatea life!

   Cyn. Oh, marvellous! Is this indeed the form
That my Pygmalion fashioned with his hands ?

   Pyg. Indeed it is.

   Cyn.   Why, let me look at her !
Yes, it's the same fair face—the same fair form ;
Clad in the same fair folds of drapery !

   Gal. And dost thou know me then ?

   Cyn. Hear her ! she speaks !
Our Galatea speaks aloud ! Know thee ?
Why I have sat for hours, and watched thee grow ;
Sat—motionless as thou—wrapped in his work,
Save only that in very ecstasy
I hurried ever and anon to kiss
The glorious hands that made thee all thou art !
Come—let me kiss thee with a sister's love. (*Kisses her.*)
See, she *can* kiss !

   Daph.   Yes, I'll be bound she can !

   Cyn. Why, my Pygmalion, where is the joy
That ought to animate that face of thine,
Now that the gods have crowned thy wondrous skill ?

   Chry. (*aside to* PYG.) Stick to our story ; bold-faced
      though she be,
She's very young, and may perhaps repent ;
It's terrible to have to tell a lie,
But if it must be told—why, tell it well !

   Cyn. I see it all. I have returned too soon.

   Daph. No, I'm afraid you have returned too late ;
Cynisca, never leave that man again,
Or leave him altogether !

   Cyn. (*astonished*).   Why, what's this ?

   Gal. Oh, madam, bear with him, and blame him not ;
Judge him not hastily ; in every word,
In every thought he has obeyed thy wish.
Thou badst him speak to me as unto thee ;
And he and I have sat as lovingly
As if thou hadst been present to behold
How faithfully thy wishes were obeyed !

Cyn. Pygmalion! What is this?
Pyg. (*to* Gal.). Go, get thee hence;
Thou shouldst not see the fearful consequence
That must attend those heedless words of thine!
Gal. Judge him not hastily, he's not like this
When he and I are sitting here alone.
He has two voices, and two faces, madam,
One for the world, and one for him and me!
Cyn. Thy wife against thine eyes! those are the stakes!
Well, thou hast played thy game, and thou hast lost!
Pyg. Cynisca, hear me! In a cursed hour
I prayed for power to give that statue life.
My impious prayer aroused the outraged gods,
They are my judges, leave me in their hands;
I have been false to them, but not to thee!
Spare me!
Cyn. Oh, pitiful adventurer!
He dares to lose, but does not dare to pay!
Come, be a man! See, *I* am brave enough,
And I have more to bear than thou! Behold!
I am alone, thou hast thy statue bride!
Oh, Artemis, my mistress, hear me now,
Ere I remember how I love that man,
And in that memory forget my shame!
If he in deed or thought hath been untrue,
Be just and let him pay the penalty!
> (Pygmalion, *with an exclamation, covers his eyes with
> his hands.*)
Gal. Cynisca, pity him!
Cyn. I know no pity, woman; for the act
That thawed thee into flesh has hardened me
Into the cursed stone from which thou cam'st.
We have changed places; from this moment forth
Be *thou* the wife and I the senseless stone!
> (*Thrusts* Galatea *from her.* Galatea *falls senseless
> at* Cynisca's *feet.*)

ACT III.

SCENE: SAME AS ACTS I. AND II.

Enter DAPHNE.

Daph. It seems Pygmalion *has* the fearful gift
Of bringing stone to life. I'll question him
And ascertain how far that power extends.

Enter MYRINE, *weeping.*

Myrine—and in tears! Why, what's amiss?
  Myr. Oh, we were all so happy yesterday,
And now, within twelve miserable hours,
A blight has fallen upon all of us.
Pygmalion is blind as death itself,
Cynisca leaves his home this very day,
And my Leucippus hath deserted me!
I shall go mad with all this weight of grief!
  Daph. All this is Galatea's work?
  Myr.   Yes, all.
  Daph. But can't you stop her? Shut the creature up,
Dispose of her, or break her? Won't she chip?
  Myr. No, I'm afraid not.
  Daph.   Ah, were I his wife,
I'd spoil her beauty! There'd be little chance
Of finding him and her alone again!
  Myr. There's little need to take precautions now,
For he, alas! is blind.
  Daph.   Blind! What of that?
Man has five senses; if he loses one
The vital energy on which it fed
Goes to intensify the other four.
He had five arrows in his quiver; well,
He has shot one away, and four remain.
My dear, an enemy is not disarmed
Because he's lost one arrow out of five!
  Myr. The punishment he undergoes might well
Content his wife!
  Daph.   A happy woman, that!
  Myr. Cynisca happy?

Daph.   To be sure she is;
She has the power to punish faithlessness,
And she has used it on her faithless spouse.
Had I Cynisca's privilege, I swear
I'd never let my Chrysos rest in peace,
Until he warranted my using it!
Pygmalion's wronged her, and she's punished him.
What more could woman want?

Enter CYNISCA.

Cyn.   What more?   Why, this!
The power to tame my tongue to speak the words
That would restore him to his former self!
The power to quell the fierce, unruly soul
That battles with my miserable heart!
The power to say, " Oh, my Pygmalion,
" My love is thine to hold or cast away,
" Do with it as thou wilt; it cannot die! "
I'd barter half my miserable life
For power to say these few true words to him!
    Myr. Why, then there's hope for him?
    Cyn.   There's none indeed!
This day I'll leave his home and hide away
Where I can brood upon my shame.   I'll fan
The smouldering fire of jealousy until
It bursts into an all-devouring flame,
And pray that I may perish in its glow!
    Daph. That's bravely said, Cynisca!   Never fear;
Pygmalion will give thee wherewithal
To nurture it.
    Cyn. (*passionately*). I need not wherewithal!
I carry wherewithal within my heart!
Oh, I can conjure up the scene at will
When he and she sit lovingly alone.
I know too well the devilish art he works,
And how his guilty passion shapes itself.
I follow him through every twist and turn
By which he wormed himself into *my* heart;
I hear him breathing to the guilty girl
The fond familiar nothings of *our* love;
I hear him whispering into *her* ear
The tenderness that he rehearsed on me.
I follow him through all his well-known moods—

Now fierce and passionate, now fanciful;
And ever tuning his accursed tongue
To chime in with the passion at her heart:
Oh, never fear that I shall starve the flame!
When jealousy takes shelter in *my* heart,
It does not die for lack of sustenance!

Daph. Come to my home, and thou shalt feed it there:
We'll play at widows, and we'll pass our time
Railing against the perfidy of man.

Cyn. But Chrysos?—

Daph.   Chrysos? Oh, you won't see him.

Cyn. How so?

Daph.   How so? I've turned him out of doors!
Why, does the girl consider jealousy
Her unassailable prerogative?
Thou hast thy vengeance on Pygmalion—
He can no longer feast upon *thy* face.
Well, Chrysos can no longer feast on mine!
I can't *put out* his eyes (I wish I could!)
But I can *shut* them out, and that I've done.

Cyn. I thank you, madam, and I'll go with you.

Myr. No, no; thou shalt not leave Pygmalion;
He will not live if thou desertest him.
Add nothing to his pain—this second blow
Might well complete the work thou hast begun!

Cyn. Nay, let me go—I must not see his face;
For if I look on him I may relent.
Detain me not, Myrine—fare thee well!

                [*Exit* CYNISCA, MYRINE *follows her.*

Daph. Well, there'll be pretty scenes in Athens now
That statues may be vivified at will.

                (CHRYSOS *enters unobserved.*)
Why, I have daughters—all of them of age—
What chance is there for plain young women, now
That every man may take a block of stone
And carve a family to suit his tastes?

Chry. If every woman were a Daphne, man
Would never care to look on sculptured stone!
Oh, Daphne!

Daph.   Monster—get you hence away!
I'll hold no converse with you, get you gone.
(*Aside.*) If I'd Cynisca's tongue I'd wither him!
(*Imitating* CYNISCA.) "Oh, I can conjure up the scene at
        will

" Where you and she sit lovingly alone!
" Oh, never fear that I will starve the flame :
" When jealousy takes shelter in *my* heart,
" It does not die for lack of sustenance ! "
    Chry. I'm sure of that ! your hospitality
Is world-renowned. Extend it, love, to me !
Oh, take me home again !
    Daph.   Home? no, not I !
Why I've a gallery of goddesses,
Fifty at least—half-dressed bacchantes, too—
Dryads and water-nymphs of every kind ;
Suppose I find, when I go home to-day,
That they've all taken it into *their* heads
To come to life—what would become of them,
Or me, with Chrysos in the house ? No—no,
They're bad enough in marble—but in flesh ! ! !
I'll sell the bold-faced hussies one and all,
But till I've sold them, Chrysos stops outside !
    Chry. What *have* I done ?
    Daph.   What have you *not* done, sir ?
    Chry. I cannot tell you—it would take too long !
    Daph. I saw you sitting with that marble minx,
Your arm pressed lovingly around her waist.
Explain *that*, Chrysos.
    Chry.   It explains itself:
I am a zealous patron of the arts,
And I am very fond of statuary.
    Daph. Bah—I've artistic tastes as well as you.
But still, you never saw *me* sitting with
My arms around a stone Apollo's waist !
As for this " statue "—could I see her now,
I'd test your taste for fragments !
    Chry.   Spare the girl,
She's very young and very innocent;
She claims your pity.
    Daph.   *Does* she ?
    Chry.   Yes, she does.
If I saw Daphne sitting with her arm
Round an Apollo, I should pity *him*.
    Daph. (*relenting*). *Would* you ?
    Chry.   I should, upon my word, I should.
    Daph. Well, Chrysos, thou art pardoned. After all
The circumstances were exceptional.
    Chry. (*aside*). Unhappily, they were!

                                    G

Daph.   Come home, but mind
I'll sell my gallery of goddesses ;
No good can come of animating stone.
  Chry. Oh, pardon me—why every soul on earth
Sprang from the stones Deucalion threw behind.
  Daph. But then Deucalion only *threw* the stones,
He left it to the gods to fashion them.
  Chry. (*aside—looking at her*). And we who've seen the
      work the gods turn out,
Would rather leave it to Pygmalion!
  Daph. (*taking* CHRYSOS' *arm, who is looking at a statue
      of Venus.*)
Come along, do!   [*Exeunt.*

            Enter MYRINE, *in great distress.*

  Myr. Pygmalion's heard that he must lose his wife,
And swears, by all the gods that reign above,
He will not live if she deserts him now !
What—what is to be done ?

            Enter GALATEA.

  Gal.   Myrine here !
Where is Pygmalion ?
  Myr.   Oh, wretched girl !
Art thou not satisfied with all the ill
Thy heedlessness has worked, that thou art come
To gaze upon thy victim's misery ?
Well, thou hast come in time !
  Gal.   What dost thou mean ?
  Myr. Why this is what I mean—he will not live
Now that Cynisca has deserted him.
Oh, girl, his blood will be upon thy head !
  Gal. Pygmalion will not live ! Pygmalion die !
And I, alas, the miserable cause !
Oh, what is to be done ?
  Myr.   I do not know.
And yet there is one chance, but one alone;
I'll see Cynisca, and prevail on her
To meet Pygmalion but once again.
  Gal. (*wildly*). But should she come too late ? He may
      not live
Till she returns.

Myr.   I'll send him now to thee,
And tell him that his wife awaits him here.
He'll take thee for Cynisca; when he speaks
Answer thou him as if thou wast his wife.
Gal. Yes, yes, I understand.
Myr.   Then I'll begone;
The gods assist thee in this artifice!   [*Exit* MYRINE.
Gal. The gods will help me, for the gods are good.
Oh, Heaven, in this great grief I turn to thee.
Teach me to speak to him, as, ere I lived,
Cynisca spake to him. Oh, let my voice
Be to Pygmalion as Cynisca's voice,
And he will live—for her and not for me—
Yet he will live. I am the fountain head.

Enter PYGMALION, *unobserved, led by* MYRINE.

Of all the horrors that surround him now,
And it is fit that I should suffer this;
Grant this, my first appeal—I do not ask
Pygmalion's love; I ask Pygmalion's life!
    (PYGMALION *utters an exclamation of joy.   She rushes to
        him and seizes his hand.*)
Pygmalion!
Pyg.   I have no words in which
To tell the joy with which I heard that prayer.
Oh, take me to thine arms, my dearly loved!
And teach me once again how much I risked
In risking such a heaven-sent love as thine.
    Gal. (*believing that he refers to her*). Pygmalion! my
        love! Pygmalion!
Once more those words! again! say them again!
Tell me that thou forgivest me the ill
That I unwittingly have worked on thee!
    Pyg. Forgive *thee?* Why, my wife, I did not dare
To ask *thy* pardon, and thou askest mine.
The compact with thy mistress Artemis
Gave thee a heaven-sent right to punish me,
I've learnt to take whate'er the gods may send.
    (GALATEA, *at first delighted, learns in the course of this
        speech that* PYGMALION *takes her for* CYNISCA, *and
        expresses extreme anguish.*)
    Gal. (*with an effort*). But then, this woman, Galatea—
    Pyg.   Well°

Gal. Thy love for her is dead ?

Pyg.   I had no love.

Gal. Thou hadst no love ?

Pyg.   No love.   At first, in truth,
In mad amazement at the miracle
That crowned my handiwork, and brought to life
The fair creation of my sculptor's skill,
I yielded to her god-sent influence,
For I had worshipped her before she lived,
Because she called Cynisca's face to me ;
But when she lived—that love died, word by word.

    Gal. That is well said : thou dost not love her then ?
She is no more to thee than senseless stone ?

    Pyg. Speak not of her, Cynisca, for I swear

Enter CYNISCA, *unobserved.*

The unhewn marble of Pentelicus
Hath charms for me, which she, in all her glow
Of womanly perfection, could not match.

    Gal. I'm very glad to hear that this is so.
Thou art forgiven ! (*Kisses his forehead.*)

    Pyg.   Thou hast pardoned me,
And though the law of Artemis declared
Thy pardon should restore to me the light
Thine anger took away, I would be blind,
I would not have mine eyes lest they should rest
On her who caused me all this bitterness!

    Gal. Indeed, Pygmalion—'twere better thus—
If thou couldst look on Galatea now,
Thy love for her, perchance, might come again !

    Pyg. No, no.

    Gal.   They say that she endureth pains
That mock the power of words !

    Pyg.   It should be so !

    Gal. Hast thou *no* pity for her ?

    Pyg.   No, not I.
The ill that she hath worked on thee—on me—
And on Myrine—surely were enough
To make us curse the hour that gave her life.
She is not fit to live upon this world !

    Gal. (*bitterly*). Upon this worthy world, thou sayest
    well,
The woman shall be seen of thee no more.

(Takes CYNISCA's *hand and leads her to* PYG.)
What wouldst thou with her now ?   *Thou hast thy wife !*
(She substitutes CYNISCA, *and retires, weeping.* CYNISCA
*takes him to her arms and kisses him. He recovers
his sight.)*
Pyg. Cynisca ! see ! the light of day is mine !
Once more I look upon thy well-loved face !

Enter MYRINE *and* LEUCIPPUS.

Leuc. Pygmalion ! Thou hast thine eyes again
Come—this is happiness indeed !
 Pyg.   And thou !
Myrine has recalled thee ?
 Leuc.   No, I came,
But more in sorrow than in penitence ;
For I've a hardened and a blood-stained heart !
I thought she would denounce me to the law,
But time, I found, had worked a wondrous change
The very girl, who half a day ago
Had cursed me for a ruthless murderer,
Not only pardoned me my infamy,
But absolutely hugged me with delight,
When she, with hungry and unpitying eyes,
Beheld my victim—at the kitchen fire !
The little cannibal !

Enter GALATEA.

 Pyg.   Away from me,
Woman or statue ! Thou the only blight
That ever fell upon my love—begone,
For thou hast been the curse of all who fell
Within the compass of thy waywardness !
 Cyn. No, no—recall those words, Pygmalion,
Thou knowest not all.
 Gal.   Nay—let me go from him
That curse—*his* curse—still ringing in mine ears,
For life is bitterer to me than death.
               (She mounts the steps of pedestal.)
Farewell, Pygmalion ! Farewell ! Farewell !
               (The curtains conceal her.)
 Cyn. Thou art unjust to her as I to thee !
Hers was the voice that pardoned thee—not mine.

I knew no pity till she taught it me.
I heard the words she spoke, and little thought
That they would find an echo in my heart;
But so it was.   I took them for mine own,
And asking for thy pardon, pardoned thee!

 Pyg. (amazed). Cynisca! Is this so?

 Cyn.   In truth it is!

 Gal. (behind curtain). Farewell, Pygmalion! Farewell!
  Farewell!

 (PYGMALION *rushes to the veil and tears it away,
  discovering* GALATEA *as a statue on the pedestal,
  as in Act I.*)

CHARITY.

A PLAY,

IN FOUR ACTS.

DRAMATIS PERSONÆ.

Dr. Athelney, *a Colonial Bishop-Elect* ... Mr. Chippendale.
Ted Athelney, *his son, aged 38* ... ... Mr. Teesdale.
Mr. Smailey, *a Country Gentleman, aged* 60 Mr. Howe.
Fred Smailey, *his son, aged 22* ... ... Mr. Kendal.
Mr. Fitz-Partington, *a Private Inquiry*
Officer ... ... Mr. Buckstone.
Butler ... ... Mr. Clark.
Footman ... ... Mr. James.
Mrs. Van Brugh, *a widow, aged 35* ... ... Miss M. Robertson.
(Mrs. Kendal.)
Eve, *her daughter, aged 17* ... ... Miss Amy Roselle.
Ruth Tredgett, *a tramp, aged 37* ... ... Miss Woolgar.
(Mrs A. Mellon.)

ACTS I. AND II.
BOUDOIR IN MRS. VAN BRUGH'S COUNTRY HOUSE.

ACT III.
ROOM IN MR. SMAILEY'S HOUSE.

ACT IV.
LIBRARY AT DR. ATHELNEY'S.

[A few days' interval between each Act.]

CHARITY.

ACT I.

Scene: *A pretty boudoir in* Mrs. Van Brugh's *country-house.*

Eve *discovered with* Frederick ; Frederick *on chair,* Eve *on footstool.*

Fred. (*dictating to* Eve, *who writes in a memorandum book at his feet*). Let me see. Three hundred oranges, six hundred buns, thirty gallons of tea, twelve large plum cakes. So much for the school-children's bodies. As for their minds—

Eve. Oh, we've taken great care of their minds. In the first place, the amateur minstrels from Locroft are coming, with some lovely part songs.

Fred. Part songs. Come, that's well. Dr. Watts?

Eve. Oh dear, no. Doctors Moore and Burgess!—Much jollier. (*He shakes his head gravely.*) Then we have a magic lantern. Here are the views. (*Handing them.*)

Fred. (*examining them*). A person on horseback, galloping at full speed. Here he is again. Probably the flight of Xerxes.

Eve. No—the flight of John Gilpin.

Fred. Very trivial, Eve dear ; very trivial.

Eve. Oh, but it will amuse them much more than the flight of Xerxes.

Fred. (*gravely*). My dear Eve, is this giddiness quite consistent with the nature of the good work before us?

Eve. Mayn't one be good and jolly too?

Fred. Scarcely. Grave work should be undertaken gravely, and with a sense of responsibility.

Eve. But I don't call a school feast grave work.

Fred. All work is grave when one has regard to the issues that may come of it. This school feast, trivial as it may seem to you—this matter of buns and big plum cakes—may be productive, for instance, of much—of much—

Eve. Indigestion? That's grave indeed! (*He seems annoyed.*) There, I'm very sorry I teased you, dear old boy; but you look at everything from such a serious point of view.

Fred. Am I too serious? Perhaps I am. And yet in my quiet undemonstrative way I am very happy.

Eve. If *you* are not happy dear, who *should* be?

Fred. Yes, Eve, who indeed! (*Kisses her.*)

Eve. I did not mean that. There is very little in me to make such a man as you happy, unless it be the prospect of making me as good and earnest as yourself—a poor prospect, I'm afraid, for I'm a very silly little girl.

Fred. At least I will try.

Eve. Begin now; tell me of my faults.

Fred. No, no; that would be a very ungrateful task.

Eve. Oh, if you neglect all tasks that are not pleasant you are too like me to allow of my hoping to learn anything of you.

Fred. Very aptly put, Eve. Well, then, you are too giddy, and too apt to laugh when you should sigh.

Eve. Oh, but I am naturally rather—jolly. Mamma has taught me to be so. Mamma's views are so entirely opposed to yours.

Fred. Yes; I am deeply sorry for it. If it were not so, perhaps Mrs. Van Brugh would like me better.

Eve. Mamma does like you, dear. She thinks you are very grave and precise and methodical, but I am sure she likes you—or why did she consent to our engagement?

Fred. Because she loves you so well that she has the heart to thwart you in nothing. She is an admirable woman—good, kind—charitable beyond measure—beloved, honoured, and courted by all—

Eve. The best woman in the world!

Fred. But she does not understand me. Well, time will work a change, and I must be content to wait.

Enter SERVANT.

Servant. Mr. Edward Athelney, miss, is in the drawing room.

Eve. Dear me, how tiresome.

Fred. (*calmly*). Miss Van Brugh is not at home.

Eve (*astonished*). Oh, Frederick, I am!

[*Exit* SERVANT.

Fred. Well, yes, of course in one sense, you certainly are. But being engaged upon a good work, with which an interruption would seriously interfere, you may be said—metaphorically, of course, and for the purposes of this particular case—to be, to a certain extent, out.

Eve (puzzled). I am quite sure I am at home, dear, in every possible sense of the word. You don't dislike Edward, do you ?

Fred. You know very well that I dislike no one.

Eve. I'm sure of that. You love all men.

Fred. No doubt, Eve, I love all men. But you will understand that I love some men less than others; and, although I love Edward Athelney very much indeed, I love him, perhaps, less than anybody else in the world.

Eve. But this is quite astonishing! Has Ted Athelney a fault ? What is it ? Come, sir, name one fault if you can. And mind, he's my big brother, or as good, so be careful.

Fred. "Frater nascitur non fit."

Eve. Oh!

Fred. I don't believe in your amateur brother. With every desire to confine himself to the duties of the character he undertakes, he is nevertheless apt to overlook the exact point where the brother ends and the lover begins.

Eve (puzzled). The lover!

Fred. The brother by birth keeps well within bounds, but the amateur treads so often on the border line that in time it becomes obliterated and the functions merge.

Eve. Ted Athelney a lover of mine! Oh, that's too absurd. Ted Athelney—that great, clumsy, middle-aged, awkward, good-natured, apple-faced man, a lover of anybody's, and, least of all, of mine! Why he's forty! Oh, it's shocking—it's horrible! I won't hear anything so dreadful of any one I love so much.

Fred. You admit that you love him ?

Eve. Oh, yes, I *love* him—but I don't LOVE him. (*Nestling against* FRED.) Don't *you* understand the difference ?

Fred. I don't like his calling you Eve.

Eve. Why you wouldn't have him—oh, you never *could* want Ted Athelney to call me Miss Van Brugh ?

Fred. Then he kisses you.

Eve. Of course he does, dear. Kisses me ? So does mamma!

Fred. No doubt, but there's some difference.

Eve. A difference! What difference ?

Fred. This, if no other : that I object to the one and don't object to the other. (*Turns away.*)

Eve (*disappointed*). Then I'm not to kiss Ted Athelney any more.

Enter TED ATHELNEY.

. *Ted.* Well, Eve, old lady, here I am, back again—well and hearty.

Eve. Ted, stand back ; I'm not to kiss you.

Ted. Eh ? Why not ?

Eve. It's wrong. Isn't it ? (*To* FRED.)

Fred. I'm sorry you think it necessary to ask the question.

Eve. There, Ted. Only think of the wrong we've been doing for years and years, and never knew it !

Ted. But who told you it was wrong. Not conscience, I'll be sworn.

Eve. No ; that's the worst of it. There's something wrong with my conscience ; it doesn't seem to be up to its work. From some motive—mistaken politeness, perhaps—it declines to assert itself. Awful, isn't it ?

Ted. Come, something's happened during my absence in town ; tell me what it is.

Eve. Something of a tremendous nature *has* happened ! Ted Athelney, I mustn't call you Ted Athelney any longer !

Ted. What ?

Eve. And I mustn't let you kiss me, because I'm going to be married.

Ted. Married ! (*Starting.*)

Eve. Yes.

Ted. To—? (*Indicating* FREDERICK.)

Eve. Yes. (*He is much agitated.*) Won't you tell me that you are glad to hear it ?

Ted (*after a pause*). Yes, Eve, I'm glad of anything that makes you happy. It has come upon me very suddenly. I never thought of your getting married. I was a great ass, for it must have come about some time or other, and why not now ? and it must have been to some fellow, and why not Fred Smailey ? God bless you, Eve. I must get it well into my mind before I can talk about it, and mine is a mind that takes a good deal of getting at. I hope and believe that you will be happy. (*She retires.*) Fred, old man—

   (*Goes to* FRED ; *takes his hand and tries to speak, but in vain.*)

Enter MRS. VAN BRUGH.

Mrs. V. B. Well, I've done for myself now : go away from me; I'm a pariah, an outcast; don't, for goodness' sake, be seen talking with me.

Eve. Why, mamma dear, what on earth have you been doing?

Mrs. V. B. Doing? Listen and shudder! I've put a dissenter into my almshouses! (*Sits at table.*)

Fred. (*rising.*) A Dissenter?

Mrs. V. B. A real live Dissenter. Isn't it awful!

Fred. No, awful is too strong a term; but I think it was a very, very sad mistake.

Mrs. V. B. A thousand thanks for your toleration—I shall never forget it. The village is outraged—they have stood my eccentricities long enough. It was bad enough when I put a Roman Catholic in, but in consideration of the almshouses being my own they were good enough to swallow the Roman Catholic. Then came a Jew—well, the village was merciful, and with a few wry faces they swallowed even the Jew. But a Dissenter! The line *must* be drawn somewhere, and high and low church are agreed that it must be drawn at dissenters. The churchwardens look the other way when I pass. The clerk's religious zeal causes him to turn into the "Red Cow," rather than touch his hat to me, and even the dirty little boys run after me shouting "No Popery" at the top of their voices, though I'm sure I don't see how it applies.

Fred. But, my dear Mrs. Van Brugh, you mean well I'm sure—but a Jew, a Catholic, and a Dissenter!—is there no such thing as a starving Churchman to be found?

Mrs. V. B. There are but too many starving men of all denominations, but while I'm hunting out the Churchman, the Jew, the Catholic, and the Dissenter will perish, and that would never do, would it?

Fred. That is the Christianity of Impulse. I would feed him that belonged to my own church, and if he did not belong to it, I would not feed him at all.

Mrs. V. B. That is the Christianity of Religious Politics. As to these poor people, they will shake down and agree very well in time. Nothing is so conducive to toleration as the knowledge that one's bread depends upon it. It applies to all conditions of life, from almshouses to Happy Families. Where are you going?

Eve. We are going down to the school to see the cakes and oranges and decorations—

Fred. (seriously). And to impress upon the children the danger of introducing inharmonious elements upon *their* little almshouses.

Mrs. V. B. Well, I hope you'll be more successful with them than with me. Their case is much more critical than mine, I assure you. (*Exeunt* Eve *and* Fred. Mrs. Van Brugh *sees* Edward, *who is sitting at back, with his head between his hands.*) Why, who's this? Edward Athelney, returned at last to his disconsolate village? Go away, sir—don't come near me—you're a reprobate—you've been in London ten days and nobody to look after you. Give an account of yourself. It's awful to think of the villainy a thoroughly badly disposed young man can get through in ten days in London, if I'm not there to look after him—come, sir, all your crimes, please, in alphabetical order—now then, A—Arson. Any arson? No? Quite sure? Come now, that's something—Then we go to Burglary? Bigamy? No Bigamy? Come, it's not as bad as I thought.—Why (*seeing that he looks very wretched*), what on earth is the matter—why, my poor Ted—what is distressing you? I never saw you look so wretched in my life!

Ted. Oh! Mrs. Van Brugh, I'm awfully unhappy!

Mrs. V. B. My poor old friend—tell me all about it.

Ted. It's soon told—Mrs. Van Brugh, you have a daughter, who's the best and loveliest girl I ever saw in my life.

Mrs. V. B. (pause). My poor Edward!

Ted. Did—did you know that I—that I was like this?

Mrs. V. B. No! no! no!

Ted. Nor I, it came on me like a thunderclap—my love for that little girl has grown as imperceptibly as my age has grown —I've taken no note of either till now—when I rub my eyes and find that I love her dearly, and that I'm eight and thirty!

Mrs. V. B. But, surely you know—you must have heard—

Ted. Yes, yes, I've just heard—Fred Smailey's a lucky fellow, and he deserves his luck.

Mrs. V. B. Perhaps. I don't know. I don't like Fred Smailey.

Ted (amazed). You don't like Smailey?

Mrs. V. B. No, I don't, and I'm afraid I show it. My dear old friend, it would have made me very happy to have seen you married to Eve, but he was first in the field, and she loves him. At first I wouldn't hear of it—but she fell ill—might have died—well, I'm her mother, and I love her, and I gave in. I know nothing against him.

Ted. Oh, Fred Smailey's a good fellow, a thorough good fellow. You do him an injustice, indeed you do; I never knew a man with such a sense of gratitude—it's perfectly astonishing. Remember how he gave me that splendid collie, when I pulled him out of the ice, last February, and how in return for my lending him money to pay his college debts, he got his father to let me shoot over Rushout—no—no—if Fred Smailey has a fault, he's too good for this world.

Mrs. V. B. Is he?—at all events he's too solemn.

Ted. Here's the dad coming—he mustn't see me like this. Good-bye, Mrs. Van Brugh. You won't speak of this to any one, I know—not that I've reason to be ashamed of it, but it'll pain Eve and Fred too. I'll bear up, never fear, and Eve shall never know—after all her happiness is the great end, and, so that it's brought about, what matter whether Fred or I do it, so that it's done. It's Fred's job, not mine—better luck for him, worse luck for me.   [*Exit.*

Mrs. V. B. Poor fellow! There goes a heart of gold with a head of cotton-wool! Oh, Eve, Eve, my dear, I'm very sad for you! Is it head or heart that makes the best husband? Better that baby-hearted simpleton than the sharpest Smailey that ever stepped! I'm very unjust. Heaven knows that I, of all women in this world, should be slow to judge. But my dislike to that man, to his family, to everything that relates to him, is intuitive. However, the mischief, if mischief there be, is done; I'll make the best of it.

Enter Dr. Athelney, *very hurriedly.*

Dr. A. My dear Mrs. Van Brugh, I come, without a moment's loss of time, to thank you in my late curate Twemlow's name for your great kindness in presenting him to the Crabthorpe living. He has a wife and four children, and is nearly mad with joy and gratitude. I've brought you his letter.

Mrs. V. B. I won't read it, doctor. I can't bear gratitude; it makes my eyes red. Take it away. I am only too glad to have helped a struggling and deserving man. Now, I'm very glad you've come, because I want to consult you on a business matter of some importance.

Dr. A. My dear Mrs. Van Brugh, I have been the intellectual head of this village for fifty-three years, and nobody ever yet paid me the compliment of consulting me on a matter of business.

Mrs. V. B. Then I've no doubt I'm going to hit upon a neglected mine of commercial sagacity!

Dr. A. It's very possible. I was second wrangler of my year.

Mrs. V. B. I told you last night of Eve's engagement. Well, old Mr. Smailey has sent me a note to say that he will call on me to-morrow week to talk over the settlement I propose to make on the occasion of my darling's marriage with his son. Now, doctor, look as wise as you can, and tell me what I ought to do.

Dr. A. Well, in such a case I should be very worldly. I think, my dear, I should prepare a nice little luncheon, with a bottle of that Amontillado, and then, having got him quietly and cozily *tête-à-tête*, I should ask him what *he* proposes to do.

Mrs. V. B. Very good indeed, doctor. Upon my word, for a colonial bishop-elect, that's not bad. But, unfortunately, I've already ascertained that he proposes to do nothing. All his money is tied up.

Dr. A. Oh, is it indeed? Bless me! Tied up, is it? And may I ask, what do you understand by that expression?

Mrs. V. B. Well, in round terms, it's his, but he mustn't spend it. Do you understand?

Dr. A. Oh, yes. When I was a boy my uncle gave me a guinea on those terms.

Mrs. V. B. Now come, doctor dear, the young people look to me, and, when one is looked to, one should be equal to the emergency. What would you advise me to do?

Dr. A. *Your* property is not, I suppose, tied up?

Mrs. V. B. No; it is quite unfettered, and consists principally of long leaseholds and funded property, left me by my god-father, and a small sum of money acquired by Captain Van Brugh on his first marriage.

Dr. A. His first marriage! Bless me, I never knew he had been married before.

Mrs. V. B. Yes (*much agitated*), a most unhappy match. She—left him under discreditable circumstances—went to Australia—resumed her maiden name, and, under that name, died in Melbourne.

Dr. A. And when did this unhappy lady die?

Mrs. V. B. (*still agitated*). Oh! years ago—It's a terrible story. I don't like to think of it—I can't bear to talk of it.

Dr. A. (*aside*). What a blundering old savage I am! If there is a pitfall open, ten to one I tumble into it! (*Aloud.*)

I have always understood that where marriage settlements of any consideration are concerned, it is customary to employ a solicitor. I can't quote my authority, but I feel sure that I am right.

Mrs. V. B. Old Mr. Smailey is an executor under Captain Van Brugh's will, and *his* solicitor has always acted for me.

Dr. A. His solicitor! what, that queer little red-faced fellow who accompanies him everywhere?

Mrs. V. B. No. Ha! ha! ha! I suppose Mr. Fitz-Partington is a junior partner, or head clerk, or something of the kind—at all events, his name doesn't appear in the firm.

Dr. A. Well, leave it to me, Mrs. Van Brugh, and I'll write to my brother, the Vice-Chancellor, who will tell us what to do. Now I'm off. (*Noise without.*) Why—what's this? Bless me, Mrs. Van Brugh, what is the cause of this commotion?

(*Noise heard without, as of people struggling with a woman, who rudely expostulates with them.*)

Mrs. V. B. Why, what in the world is the matter?

Enter three or four Servant-men *with* Ruth Tredgett *in custody. She is wild-looking and dishevelled, as if she had been struggling violently.*

Groom. We've got her, ma'am. Don't be afraid. (*To* Ruth.) Stand quiet, you jade, will yer? Woa, there! We've got her, sir, but we've had a desperate hard job to do it.

Dr. A. What has been done?

Groom. She's knocked two teeth clean out of my head, sir, and give notice to quit to a dozen more.

Dr. A. We will hear your grievance presently. What has this woman done that she is brought here?

All. Done, sir, why——

But. (*with dignity to the others*). If you please! (*To* Mrs. Van Brugh.) Ma'am, Edwards found this 'ere woman creepin' out of my pantry, ma'am, on all fours.

Dr. A. On what?

But. On her hands and knees, like a quadruped, **sir.**

Dr. A. Have you searched her?

But. (*shocked*). No, sir, I have *not* searched her.

Dr. A. Well, well, I mean has she been searched?

But. (*with dignity*). I put my hand in her pocket, sir, and I looked under her shawl.

Dr. A. Well, you didn't search her, but you put your hand

H

in her pocket, and you looked under her shawl. What did you find there?

But. A decanter of sherry, sir. (*Producing it.*)

Dr. A. (*to* Mrs. V. B.). Your sherry, Mrs. Van Brugh?

But. *Our* sherry, Dr. Athelney.

Dr. A. Well, you hear what this man says; did you take this wine?

Ruth. Ay, I took it, sure enough.

Dr. A. Why did you take it?

Ruth. Why, to drink, of course. Why *should* I take it?

Dr. A. You *shouldn't* take it.

Ruth. Don't you never take wine?

Dr. A. Not other people's wine—except, of course, with their permission.

Ruth. Maybe you've got a cellar of your own.

Dr. A. Maybe I have.

Ruth. Well, maybe *I* haven't. That's my answer.

Dr. A. Now, what are we to do with her?

Mrs. V. B. Leave her to me. Dr. Athelney, please remain here with me. Every one else, except the woman, leave the room.

But. She's a desperate character, ma'am; it took six of us, including me, to bring her here.

Mrs. V. B. Never mind. Dr. Athelney and I will see her alone. Take your hands from her and go.

But. Hadn't we better keep within hearing? If help was wanted——

Mrs. V. B. No help will be wanted. I am in earnest. Go. Shut the door. (*The* SERVANTS *reluctantly depart.*)

Ruth. You're a cool hand, missis; ain't you afeard on me?

Mrs. V. B. Not at all. Why should I be afraid of you? I mean you no harm.

Ruth. Who's he?

Mrs. V. B. Dr. Athelney, a clergyman and a magistrate.

Ruth. Beak, is he? Well, let him make out the committal. Where's it to be? Sessions?

Mrs. V. B. We have no wish to prosecute you. We wish to help you to arrive at a sense of right and wrong.

Ruth. Can't it be done without a parson? I dunno much good o' parsons. I'd rather it was done without a parson.

Dr. A. (*kindly*). Don't think of me as a clergyman, if that calling is distasteful to you. Perhaps some day we may succeed in overcoming your prejudice. In the mean time, think of me only as a harmless old gentleman, who is willing and able to help you to earn your living respectably, if you desire to do so.

Ruth. Ah, I've come across the likes o' you afore now. Three weeks agone comes a parson, as it might be you. " I've come to help you, poor fallen creetur," says he ; " I've come to tell you blessed truths, poor miserable outcast," says he. " Read that, wretched lost sheep," says he. " I'll call again in a month and see how you feel," says he. A month! Heugh! When I was bad with fever the doctor come every day. *He* never come no more. There's ladies come odd times. I call to mind one—come in a carriage *she* did. Same story—poor, miserable, ·st one—wretched, abandoned fellow-creetur, and that. She ·alled me a brand from the burnin', and wanted to stretch out a hand to save me, *she* did. Well, she stretched it out, and I thought she meant it (for I was green then), and, fool-like, I took it, and kissed it. She screeched as tho' I'd bit her !

Mrs. V. B. Will you take *my* hand?

Ruth (*astonished*). Do you know what I am ?

Mrs. V. B. Yes ; I know well what you are. You are a woman who wants help, and I a woman who will help you. (*Taking her hand.*)

Ruth (*much moved*). Thankee, missis! you've spoke fair to me. I've had no one speak like that to me for many a long year. Thankee, missis. (*Struggling with tears.*) Don't mind me. (*Throws her apron over her face and sobs.*) They *will* come odd times !

Mrs. V. B. Will you tell me your name ?

Ruth. Ruth Tredgett. I come from Cambridge.

Dr. A. Born there ?

Ruth. I dunno as I was born there, but I come from there.

Dr. A. What are you ?

Ruth. I s'pose I'm a thief. I s'pose I'm what gentlefolks thinks is wus than a thief. God help me ! I s'pose I'm as bad as I can be. (*Weeping.*)

Mrs. V. B. Are your parents alive?

Ruth. No, I never had no father—my mother was such as me. See here, lady. Wot's to become of a gal whose mother was such as me ? Mother ! Why, I could swear afore I could walk !

Dr. A. But were you not brought up to any calling ?

Ruth. Yes, sir, I were ; I were brought up to be a thief. Every soul as I knowed was a thief, and the best thief was the best thought on. Maybe a kid not long born ought to have knowed better. I dunno, I must ha' been born bad, for it seemed right enough to me. Well, it was *in* prison and *out o'* prison—three months here and six months there—till I was sixteen. I sometimes thinks as if they'd bin half as ready to show me how to go right as they was to punish me for goin' wrong, I might have took the right turnin' and stuck to it afore this. At sixteen I got seven year for shop-liftin', and was sent out to Port Philip. I soon got a ticket and tried service and needlework, but no one wouldn't have me ; and I got sick and tired of it all, and began to think o' putting a end to it, when I met a smooth-spoken chap—a gentleman, if you please—as wanted to save me from the danger afore me. Well, wot odds? He was a psalm-singing villain, and he soon left me. No need to tell the rest—to such as you it can't be told. I'm 'most as bad as I can be—as bad as I can be !

Mrs. V. B. I think not; I think not. What do you say, Doctor?

Dr. A. (*struggling with his tears*). Say, ma'am? I say that you, Ruth Tredgett, have been a most discreditable person, and you ought to be heartily ashamed of yourself, Ruth Tredgett; and as a clergyman of the Church of England I feel bound to tell you that—that your life has been—has been what God knows it couldn't well have helped being under the circumstances.

Mrs. V. B. Ruth Tredgett, I am very, very sorry for you. If you are willing to leave this unhappy course of life I will provide you with the means of earning your living honestly.

Ruth. Honestly ! Why, lady, I'm too fur gone for that !

Mrs. V. B. I hope not. I have assisted many, very many such women as yourself, and I have seldom found my efforts wasted.

Ruth. But you—a lady, high-born, high-bred, beautiful, rich, good—— (*In amazement.*)

Mrs. V. B. Hush. (*Rises.*) No matter what I am. (*With emotion.*) Who shall say what the very best of us might not have been but for the accident of education and good example? Tell me, Ruth Tredgett, will you accept my offer?

Ruth (*kneels at her feet and looks up into her face*). I will!

ACT II.

SCENE: *same as in* ACT I.

Enter MR. SMAILEY *and* Servant.

Mr. S. (very gently). Will you have the goodness to tell Mrs. Van Brugh that Mr. Smailey is here to see her, by appointment?

Serv. Mr. Smailey, sir? Yes, sir. (*Going.*)

Enter MR. FITZ-PARTINGTON.

Fitz. (stopping SERVANT). *And* his solicitor.

Mr. S. (with mild sternness). You have followed me again, sir?

Fitz. Followed you again, sir; according to contract.

Mr. S. There is no contract between us that entitles you to dog my footsteps as though you were hunting down a thief.

Fitz. Hunting down a thief? Oh yes. To enable me to assist you in blighting the character of the best and loveliest woman that ever shed a light upon a private detective's thorny path, I am to have the free run of your house and papers; I am to accompany you wherever you go, and you are to introduce me everywhere as your solicitor.

Mr. S. Sir, you are not the least like a solicitor. You are a ridiculously dressed person. You are like nothing in the world but what you are—a private detective. I desire to press hardly on no fellow-creature, but you are a spy! that base and utterably abject thing—a spy!

Fitz. Mr. Smailey, when you complain that you find my society irksome, you have my profoundest sympathy; I find it so myself. When you revile my profession, my sentiments are entirely in accord, for I have the very poorest opinion of it. But when you imply that I don't look the character I undertake to represent, why, *then*, sir, you touch the private detective on the most sensitive part of his moral anatomy. I'm not a blameless character, but if I undertook to personate the Archbishop of Canterbury I believe I should look the part, and my conversation would be found to be in keeping with the character.

Mr. S. Pray, silence; oh, pray, pray, silence. You shock me inexpressibly. It is most painful to me to have to resort to your assistance. My son, my dear son, has engaged himself to marry Mrs. Van Brugh's daughter. I have lately had reason to believe that there is something discreditable in Mrs. Van Brugh's marriage relations, though I do not know its precise nature. You tell me that you have a certain clue to this flaw, though you decline to tell me what it is until your proofs are matured. Well, sir, the Smaileys are a very old and very famous family. Caius Smaileius came over with Julius Cæsar: his descendants have borne an untarnished scutcheon for eighteen hundred years. In its interest I am bound to employ you, and upon your own most exacting terms, though I cannot think of your contemptible calling without a feeling of the most profound abhorrence.

Fitz. Sir, I am heartily ashamed of it.

Mr. S. You are a professional impostor; a hired lie.

Fitz. It is too true. I not only lie myself, but I am the cause of lying in others.

Mr. S. For the lies that have to be told in accounting for you I hold you entirely responsible. I wish that to be understood. I wash my hands of them altogether; and, when I think of the deep, deliberate, and utterly indefensible falsehoods that I have had to utter on your behalf, I tremble for your future—I tremble for your future.

Fitz. Unselfish man.

Mr. S. As for the preposterous terms you have dictated——

Fitz. Terms! I have ensured to myself the unbroken enjoyment of your desirable society for six weeks; and believe me, when I say that if I had been acquainted with the inexpressible charms of the most fascinating woman that ever shed a light upon the private detective's thorny path, I wouldn't have undertaken the job, no, not even for a lifetime of your society!

Enter Mrs. Van Brugh.

Mrs. V. B. Good morning, Mr. Smailey. I am sorry to have kept you waiting. (*Aside.*) That absurd little man with him again. (*Aloud.*) Good morning, Mr. ——

Fitz. Fitz-Partington.

Mrs. V. B. Fitz-Partington, of course.

Fitz. (*aside*). She might remember *my* name. I can't conceive any circumstances under which I could forget *hers!*

Mr. S. Mr. Fitz-Partington is entirely in my confidence. I brought him, because I believed that his familiarity with legal forms might assist us in our interview. You can speak without reserve before Mr. Fitz-Partington. (*Aside to* FITZ.) A lie, sir! Another lie, from first to last!

Mrs. V. B. I suppose the facts will come before Mr. Fitz-Partington when they are decided on. The steps by which they are arrived at will only bore him. I'm sure Mr. Fitz-Partington won't be angry with me, when I ask him to amuse himself in the next room until preliminaries are arranged.

Fitz. Mrs. Van Brugh, I have made it a part of my moral code to step without hesitation into any apartment you may think fit to indicate. [*Exit.*

Mrs. V. B. Now, Mr. Smailey, about these settlements. I will tell you at once what I propose to do. My income is, as you know, a very large one—much larger than any one would suppose who judges from the quietness of my mode of life. I am an odd woman, and I spend my money in my own way. I have very many claims upon it, and, although I wish to deal handsomely with my darling Eve, I must not disappoint those who have counted upon me for some years past. To come to the point, I propose to settle my Buckinghamshire farm upon her, on the usual terms of a marriage settlement. I don't know the technical expression—but on the usual terms.

Mr. S. The Buckinghamshire farm, yes. Thank you. I forget whether that is the leasehold or the freehold farm, for you have two.

Mrs. V. B. You mustn't ask me. Your solicitor knows. It's worth £500 a year, and that, I suppose, is the main point.

Mr. S. Not altogether; the difference in value may be prodigious. Have you a copy of the will?

Mrs. V. B. No. I never saw the will.

Mr. S. Never saw the will? I think I have a copy of it at home—with your permission I will go and fetch it, and the matter can be decided at once.

Mrs. V. B. Do, by all means. I only know that my property is all my own, and that I can do what I like with it; and I assure you, Mr. Smailey, I avail myself of the privilege.

Mr. S. You do indeed. And that reminds me, Mrs. Van Brugh, that I am anxious to speak to you on another topic—a topic of a singularly painful character. I will endeavour, Mrs. Van Brugh, to approach it as delicately as possible.

Mrs. V. B. Indeed! (*Alarmed.*) You rouse my curiosity, Mr. Smailey. Does it—does it refer in any way to myself?

Mr. S. Directly to yourself.

Mrs. V. B. (much alarmed). May I ask in what way?

Mr. S. As I said before, it is a most difficult subject to approach, and I would willingly spare you. Give me a moment to think how I can best put it to you.

Mrs. V. B. Pray have no hesitation in telling me what it is. (*With half-disguised emotion.*) Does it—does it refer in any way to my—to my past life, for instance? (*With affected cheerfulness.*)

Mr. S. It does refer to incidents in your past life. To many incidents in general, and to one incident in particular.

Mrs. V. B. For Heaven's sake, sir, be explicit. Speak out, I implore you. (*With suppressed agitation.*)

Mr. S. You seem strangely agitated, Mrs. Van Brugh.

Mrs. V. B. No, no; I am ill and nervous to-day. Your manner is rather alarming. (*With affected cheerfulness.*) You know I'm a very bad hand at guessing riddles, Mr. Smailey. Come, what is it? I give it up. (*He hesitates.*) Why have you any hesitation in telling me?

Mr. S. Because it involves a particularly delicate moral point. (*She is much agitated.*) God bless me, you seem very much alarmed.

Mrs. V. B. (with determination). Mr. Smailey, once and for all, I insist upon knowing what it is.

Mr. S. Well, then, to be quite plain with you, it is currently reported in the village that you have taken a miserable woman from the streets and established her in the character of a respectable workwoman within a hundred yards of this spot. (MRS. VAN BRUGH, *whose agitation and alarm have been intense, is greatly relieved.*) Moreover, I have been informed that you have, for some years past, been in the habit of searching out women of bad character who profess penitence, with the view of enabling them to earn their living in the society of blameless Christians.

Mrs. V. B. I have.

Mr. S. I tell you at once that I am loth to believe this thing.

Mrs. V. B. (with indignant surprise). Why are you loth to believe this thing?

Mr. S. Why? (*Rises.*) Because its audacity, its want of principle, and, above all, its unspeakable indelicacy, shock me beyond power of expression.

Mrs. V. B. Mr. Smailey, is it possible that you are speaking deliberately? Think of any blameless woman whom you love and honour, and who is loved and honoured of all. Think of the shivering outcast whose presence is contamination, whose touch is horror unspeakable, whose very existence is an unholy stain on God's earth. Woman—loved, honoured, courted by all. Woman—shunned, loathed, and unutterably despised, but still—Woman. I do not plead for those whose advantages of example and education render their fall ten thousand times more culpable. Let others speak for such as they. (*With a broken voice.*)—It may be that something is to be said, even for them. I plead for those who have had the world against them from the first—who with blunted weapons and untutored hands have fought society single-handed, and fallen in the unequal fight. God help them!

Mr. S. Mrs. Van Brugh, I have no desire to press hardly on any fellow-creature; but society, the grand arbiter in these matters, has decided that a woman who has once forfeited her moral position shall never regain it.

Mrs. V. B. Even though her repentance be sincere and beyond doubt?

Mr. S. Even so.

Mrs. V. B. Even though she fell unprotected, unadvised, perishing with want and chilled with despair?

Mr. S. Even so. For such a woman there is no excuse—for such a woman there is no pardon.

Mrs. V. B. You mean no pardon on earth?

Mr. S. Of course I mean no pardon on earth. What can I have to do with pardon elsewhere?

Mrs. V. B. Nothing. Mr. Smailey, when you have procured the will, I shall be ready to see you; but before you go let me tell you that I am inexpressibly shocked and pained at the terrible theory you have advanced. (*He endeavours to speak.*) Oh, understand me, I do not charge you with exceptional heartlessness. You represent the opinions of society, and society is fortunate in its mouthpiece. Heaven teaches that there is a pardon for every penitent. Earth teaches that there is one sin for which there is no pardon—when the sinner is a woman!

(RUTH *has entered. She is quietly and decently dressed, and carries a parcel of needlework in her hand.*)

Mr. S. (*aside*). Mrs. Van Brugh, pray be quiet; we are observed.

Mrs. V. B. By the subject of our conversation.

[*Exit* MRS. VAN BRUGH.

Ruth. I beg pardon—I thought the lady was alone. (*Going.*)

Mr. S. Stop, woman. (*She turns and advances.*) Don't—don't approach me—we have nothing in common. Listen at a distance. Mrs. Van Brugh has thought proper to place you on a pedestal that levels you, socially, with respectable Christians.

In so doing, I consider that she has insulted respectable Christians. She thinks proper to suffer you to enter *my* presence. In so doing I consider that she has insulted *me*. I desire you to understand that when a woman of your stamp enters the presence of a Christian gentleman, she——

Ruth (who has been looking at him in wonder during this speech). Smailey! That's never *you*! (*Mr. S. falls back in his chair.*)

Ruth. Ay, Smailey, it's Ruth Tredgett.

Mr. S. (very confused). I did not know whom I was speaking to.

Ruth. But you knowed *what* you was speakin' to, Jonas Smailey. Go on. I'm kinder curous to hear what *you've* got to say about a woman o' my stamp. I kinder curous to hear wot Jonas Smailey's got to say about his own work.

Mr. S. We meet in a strange way after so many years.

Ruth. Yes; we do meet in a strange way. Seems to me it's suthin' of a topsy-turvy way. But it's a topsy-turvy world, ain't it?

Mr. S. (recovering himself, with bland dignity). I have no desire to press hardly on any fellow-creature——

Ruth (quietly). Come, that's kind, anyhow.

Mr. S. Perhaps, after all, you were not entirely to blame.

Ruth. Well, p'raps not.

Mr. S. Perhaps I myself was not altogether without reproach in the matter. But in my case allowance should, in common charity, be made for follies that arise from extreme youth and—and inexperience. I was barely forty then.

Ruth. And I was just sixteen. Well, I forgive you, along o' your youth, as I hope to be forgiven along o' my childhood.

Mr. S. (rises). The tone you adopt is in the worst possible taste. The misguided lady who has taken upon herself, most wickedly, to foist you upon society, has committed a fraud, which——

Ruth. Stop *there*, Smailey! You're getting on dangerous ground. Best leave that lady alone. She's a bit chipped off heaven—she's good right through. She's—she's—I'm slow at findin' words that mean goodness. My words run mostly the other way, wus luck. If I had to tell o' *you*, Smailey, they'd come handy and strong. I can't find words that mean *her*!

Mr. S. I have no wish to be hard on you, but it *is* a fraud, and——

Ruth. Fraud? Fraud's a bad word to come from *you*, Smailey. I'd ha' thought you'd ha' fought shy o' that word, for the rest o' your days.

Mr. S. (taken aback). 1 don't know what you refer to.

Ruth. I'm referring to Martha Vane of Melbourne. What, yer recklect Martha Vane, do yer?

Mr. S. Martha Vane! Yes, I remember Vane. Pooh! There is nothing to connect me with that matter.

Ruth. Nothing? I've writin' of yours which is fourteen year, if it's a day.

Mr. S. And do you mean to say that you would be guilty of such inhumanity—such devilish inhumanity (I use the word "devilish" in its religious sense) as to bring up an act of youthful folly—guilt if you will—against me now that I have achieved wealth, reputation, and social position?

Ruth. No, you're safe, Smailey. Bring it up agin yer now? Why, you may have repented—who knows? You was a bad lot, sure enough; but that's twenty years agone, and you may ha' repented.

Mr. S. I have; I'm an altered person—I—I—will make it well worth your while to give me up that writing you refer to. I will pay you very handsomely for it.

Ruth. Pay! no; I ain't on that lay. I'm square now. I'm a 'spectable woman. I only takes money wot I earns. It comes slow, but it comes comfortable.

Mr. S. Your sentiments do you credit. I confess I did not look for such delicacy of feeling in you; it exalts one's idea of human nature. I am thankful for anything that exalts one's idea of human nature. Thank you, Tredgett. Give me these papers.

Ruth. No; I'm 'spectable, but I ain't a fool. I'll keep 'em, case I want 'em.

Mr. S. As you please. Remember, Tredgett, I am a person of influence here, and a county magistrate——

Ruth. What, d'you sit at quarter sessions?

Mr. S. Certainly.

Ruth. And sentence poor prigs?

Mr. S. Yes. Why do you ask?

Ruth. Nothing; go on—it's all topsy-turvy!

Mr. S. I shall be happy if I can serve you in any way. I shall always be glad to hear that you are doing well, and I feel certain that the admirable lady who has so kindly taken you in hand will have no reason to regret her charity. It is easy to fall, and hard to rise again—Heaven bless those who extend a helping hand. I am very glad indeed that we have met. I've no wish to press hardly on any fellow-creature. [*Exit.*

Ruth. Jonas Smailey! Smailey here! Things come about

queerly. I seed him last at t'other end o' the world, and to meet him here! Who's that? (FITZ-PARTINGTON *has entered unobserved on tiptoe, and tapped her on the shoulder.*)

Fitz. Come here. (*Taking out note-book.*) Your name's Ruth Tredgett?

Ruth (*surprised*). Ay.

Fitz. What are you?

Ruth. A 'spectable woman. Wot are *you?*

Fitz. A detective.

Ruth (*falling back horrified*). Wot's it for?

Fitz. Nothing. *You* ain't wanted, but your address is.

Ruth. I'm living at Barker's in the village.

Fitz. Present occupation?

Ruth. Needlewoman.

Fitz. Late occupation?

Ruth. Tramp. There's nothin' agin me?

Fitz. Nothing against you, everything for you, even this half-crown.

Ruth. I don't like p'leece money. I never took none yet, I ain't agoin' to begin now. I wish yer good day. I don't like p'leece money.   [*Exit.*

Fitz. I'm not a policeman, I'm a private detective; but we won't split hairs. (*Pockets coin.*) I thought Smailey was my man, now I'm sure of it. Ha! ha! Now, Smailey has a game. The question is, what is it? He says it's his scutcheon, but that is Walker, because his father was a wig-maker. However, it's quite clear that, whatever his game may be, it is my duty to put that inestimable woman on her guard.

Enter MRS. VAN BRUGH.

Mrs. V. B. Has not Mr. Smailey returned?

Fitz. No, ma'am, he has not. (*He shows traces of emotion.*)

Mrs. V. B. Mr. Fitz-Partington, is anything the matter?

Fitz. Ma'am, you have come upon me in a moment of professional conscientiousness. Avail yourself of it, for such moments are rare and fleeting. Beware of Smailey.

Mrs. V. B. What in the world do you mean?

Fitz. I mean that he is endeavouring to prove that—that you were not legally married to Captain Van Brugh.

Mrs. V. B. (*intensely agitated*). Mr. Fitz-Partington, you cannot be aware of the full import of your words. What can be Mr. Smailey's motive for making these preposterous inquiries?

Fitz. That's just what I want to get at. In a general way it's sure to be something dirty. Perhaps he thinks that the property you inherit from Captain Van Brugh isn't legally yours, and, therefore, can't be settled by you on your daughter.

Mrs. V. B. But I inherited very little indeed from Captain Van Brugh. The bulk of my property was left me by my godfather.

Fitz. Then I'm wrong. But does Smailey know this?

Mrs. V. B. Know it! Why, of course he knows it. He's my godfather's nephew, and next-of-kin.

Fitz. What! His next-of-kin? Next-of-kin is a fruitful expression. I see a whole plantation of motives cropping out of "next-of-kin." Have you a copy of the will?

Mrs. V. B. No. But Mr. Smailey has—indeed, he has gone to fetch it.

Fitz. Can you tell me the terms of the legacy?

Mrs. V. B. No, not precisely. I have never seen the will. My solicitor has told me its purport in general terms.

Fitz. Are you referred to in that will by your married or maiden name?

Mrs. V. B. Oh, by my maiden name.

Fitz. You are sure of that?

Mrs. V. B. Quite sure. At least, I *feel* quite sure. I can't be absolutely certain, but—oh yes; I am sure of it.

Fitz. What was the date of the will?

Mrs. V. B. 1856.

Fitz. What was the year of your marriage?

Mrs. V. B. (*after a pause*). 1856.

Fitz. My dear Mrs. Van Brugh, this is most important. The news of your marriage might or might not have reached the testator in Australia. If there is any flaw in your marriage, and if you are described in that will as Captain Van Brugh's wife, every penny you possess will revert to Smailey. Now, Smailey is a scoundrel.

Mrs. V. B. Mr. Fitz-Partington, pray explain yourself.

Fitz. In the full conviction that what I am going to say will be treated as confidential, I *will* explain myself. I'm after Smailey. Smailey will soon be wanted.

Mrs. V. B. This is scarcely an explanation.

Fitz. Scarcely an explanation. Twenty years ago, when in Australia, Smailey forged a burial-certificate to get some trust-funds into his possession. The job was given to our house to investigate, only six weeks ago. Two days after, who should come to us for a detective to inquire into your affairs but

Smailey; so we put the two jobs together, and I'm doing 'em both.

Mrs. V. B. But how is it that a gentleman in your profession——

Fitz. A gentleman! Mrs. Van Brugh, for reasons that will go down with me to the tomb, I am humbly and hopelessly anxious to stand high in your good opinion. Appreciate my disinterestedness, when I voluntarily tell you that which will blight me in your estimation for ever. You think I'm an eminent solicitor. I ain't; I'm the insignificant minion of a Private Inquiry Office.

Mrs. V. B. But you were introduced to me as a solicitor.

Fitz. It is a tantalizing feature of my contemptible calling, that I am continually being introduced as somebody I should particularly like to be. In the course of the last twelve months I've been a Spanish Hidalgo, a Colonel of Hussars, an Ashantee Nobleman, and a Bishop of the Greek Church. What was the date of your marriage?

Mrs. V. B. Some time in February, '56 (*with hesitation.*)

Fitz. Day?

Mrs. V. B. The—the 30th.

Fitz. The 30th? Try again. Never more than twenty-nine days in February—seldom that.

Mrs. V. B. I forget the exact date.

Fitz. Where were you married, and by whom?

Mrs. V. B. By—by (*after some hesitation*)—Sir, by your own admission you are a mere spy. How am I to know that you are not asking these questions with a view to using them against me?

Fitz. (*much hurt*). Ma'am, may you never know the depth of the wound you have inflicted. It will canker, ma'am; but don't be alarmed, it shall not inconvenience you, for I will remove it from your sight. When we meet again, you will find me in the assumed character of a person who has not had his best feelings harrowed up for a considerable time. It will be a difficult assumption, ma'am, but I will do my best to sustain the fiction. [*Exit.*

Mrs. V. B. At last! at last my punishment is at hand. And Eve—great heavens, what will become of *her!* Eve—who loves and honours me—Eve, my child! I mustn't think of that. It will madden me. I shall want all my head for what is to come! If news of this—marriage of mine (*with a bitter laugh*) had reached my godfather, he would have described me in his will as Captain Van Brugh's wife, and then

I am lost, and Eve is lost. Oh, why don't that man come ? This suspense is terrible. At last ! He's here !

Enter EVE *and* FRED *with* DR. ATHELNEY.

Eve. Mr. Smailey has returned with the will. Frederick has been explaining to me the difference between freehold and leasehold, and you don't know how anxious I am to know which it is.

Fred. Eve, Eve, this is very mercenary.

Enter SMAILEY.

Mr. S. Mrs. Van Brugh, I am most happy to tell you that it is everything that could be wished. My dear Mrs. Van Brugh, the Buckinghamshire farm is freehold. Here is the clause which refers to it : (*Reads very deliberately.*) After giving you Westland Park, the Blackfriars estate, and the two reversions, the testator goes on to say, "And I further will and bequeath all that messuage known as Goldacre Farm, together with all out-houses, ways, watercourses, trees, commonable rights, easements and appurtenances, and all the estate and rights of the said Richard Goldacre in and to the same, unto and to the use of the said Catherine Ellen, wife of Richard Van Brugh, Esq., a captain in the Royal Navy, her heirs and assigns for ever."

(MRS. VAN BRUGH *falls senseless into a chair, her daughter bending over her.*)

ACT III.

SCENE : *Morning room in* SMAILEY'S *house. Door at back, giving on to a pretty garden.*

FREDERICK *discovered sealing a letter.*

Fred. "Your eternally attached Frederick." If there was any flaw in Mrs. Van Brugh's marriage, as my father seems to suspect—and his suspicions are corroborated by her astonishing behaviour on his reading her godfather's will—then Mrs. Van

Brugh is penniless—and Eve is penniless too. Poor little lady! I'm afraid I shall have to cry off. I'm sorry for the poor child, because I'm sure she is fond of me. I'm sorry for myself, because I'm sure I'm fond of her. But when a man proposes to marry, he must not allow himself to be misled by his affections. As far as Eve is concerned, I see no difficulty. She is a tender-hearted and sensitive little thing, Heaven bless her, and can be easily shaken off. But my poor old father; how indignant he will be if I dare to suggest what he would consider a dishonourable course! Why, if he thought me capable of breaking a solemn engagement for a mercenary motive, he'd disown me! No, I must rest my excuse on a surer ground. I must touch his sense of family pride. I must remind him of the blight that would fall on our race, if I intermarried with a tainted family. A really good man does a deal of harm in the world. One has to stoop to so much dirty dissimulation before one can meet him on equal terms.

Enter Mr. Smailey.

Mr. S.) Frederick, I want to speak seriously——
Fred. ∫ Father, I want to speak seriously——
Mr. S. Eh ?
Fred. I beg your pardon.
Mr. S. I was about to say that I want to speak to you on a most serious and important matter.
Fred. Dear me, that's very odd! Do you know I was about to say the very same thing! I am most anxious to speak to *you* on a *most* serious and *most* important matter. Excuse me for one moment, while I give this note to Robins.
Mr. S. Whom are you writing to ?
Fred. To my darling, of course. 　　　　　　　　[*Exit.*
Mr. S. To his darling! Poor lad! He's a noble fellow! No mercenary thought in connection with the girl has ever entered his head! But he must never marry her. Everything points to the fact that Mrs. Van Brugh's marriage was illegal, and, if so, her daughter is portionless. Thank Heaven! his sense of moral rectitude is so high that when he knows that her mother's conduct is open to suspicion he may feel bound to dissociate himself from her. Ah, it is a pleasant and a goodly thing when a parent finds that the strict principles he has instilled into his offspring are bearing golden fruit on which they both may feed!

Enter FREDERICK.

Mr. S. (aside).⎱ How shall I break it to him?
Fred. (aside). ⎰ How shall I begin?
Fred. Now I'm at your disposal.

Mr. S. Frederick, my dear lad, this life of ours is made up of hopes frustrated, and cherished schemes brought to nothing.

Fred. Very true. A man who places himself under the sweet dominion of his conscience, must not count on the fulfilment of even his most innocent intentions.

Mr. S. Unforeseen circumstances occasionally arise that render it almost criminal to carry out an otherwise laudable purpose.

Fred. For instance: a discovery that a contemplated act would, if carried out, bring dishonour on a long line of ancestors.

Mr. S. Or give an implied sanction to a discreditable, if not an immoral, relationship. Events might occur which would justify him in breaking the most solemn pledge.

Fred. Justify him! I can conceive a state of things under which he would be morally bound to cast his most sacred obligations to the wind.

Mr. S. My dear boy!
Fred. My dear father! (*They shake hands.*)

Mr. S. Now, Fred, this is what I was coming to, my boy. We are the last descendants of a very noble family.

Fred. So I have often heard you say. And that reminds me to mention a matter, upon which I have long desired to talk to you——

Mr. S. (interrupting). I am free to admit that I am proud of my ancestry.

Fred. My dear father, the safe keeping of their honour is my dearest aim. And, talking of my ancestors' honour, reminds me——

Mr. S. (interrupting). If Caius Smaileius heard that one of his race was about to marry, for instance, into a tainted family, I believe the doughty old Roman would turn in his tumulus!

Fred. What you say about a tainted family is so true, that I venture——

Mr. S. My dear Fred, it's no use beating about the bush. The girl you are engaged to—as good a girl as ever lived—is (there is no use in disguising it) a member of a tainted family. (FRED *turns from* SMAILEY.) It is therefore my duty to urge upon you, as the last of our line, the propriety, the necessity, of

I

releasing Eve from her engagement. (FREDERICK *appears hurt and indignant.*) I know I am asking much, very much, of you. I know how tenderly you love the girl; but a flaw, my dear Fred, and you a Smailey! My boy, it is impossible.

Fred. (*in affected indignation*). Am I to understand that you require me to surrender my darling Eve? Never! With all possible respect for your authority—Never!

Mr. S. But, Fred, remember, my boy, remember, her mother has committed a *faux pas* of some kind.

Fred. It would certainly seem so; but I have given my word, and it is my duty to keep it.

Mr. S. What is duty to the living compared with duty to the dead? Think what your ancestors have done for you. And are we to neglect our duty to them, because they can do no more for us? Oh! shame, shame!

Fred. (*with apparent reluctance*). There is much truth in what you say, still——

Mr. S. To marry into such a family as hers, now that we know the truth, would be, as it were, to countenance her guilt.

Fred. I cannot deny it Nevertheless, I——

Mr. S. Would it be just—would it be *moral* to do this?

Fred. No, no; I see it now.

Mr. S. Show yourself to be a man of moral courage. As for what the world will say, do the right thing, my boy, and let them say what they please.

Fred. (*after a pause*). Father, you are right. As a moral man I have no alternative but to comply with your wish. At any cost it must be done—at any cost it *shall* be done!

Mr. S. That's right, my dear, dear boy; and you shall find that you have lost little by your determination. And now that that's settled, let us enter into *your* affairs. What was it that you wanted to speak to me so seriously about just now?

Fred. I? Oh dear, no.

Mr. S. But surely, you said——

Fred. Oh, to be sure! I—oh, it's not of the least consequence.

Mr. S. Something about poor little Eve, wasn't it?

Fred. Yes; about poor little Eve. How little do we know what five minutes may bring forth! I was actually going to consult you about fixing a day for our wedding. (*Wiping his eyes.*)

Mr. S. My poor boy, you have behaved nobly. You are a true Smailey.

Fred. (*taking his hand*). I hope it is not presumptuous in me, but I sometimes think I am.

Mr. S. I have wounded you deeply. Let me compensate you by telling you a more pleasant piece of news. I have discovered Fitz-Partington's clue.

Fred. Indeed! I am rejoiced to hear it.

Mr. S. Yes. Mrs. Van Brugh told me on Tuesday that she had never actually seen her godfather's will. So I felt it to be my duty to make an excuse for reading aloud that part of the will in which she is particularly described. I did so, and she fainted. Now, my dear Fred, what does this point to?

Fred. I should say bigamy.

Mr. S. You would say bigamy, and so should I. I suggested this to Fitz-Partington, and he seemed amazed at my penetration. We laid our heads together, and, at his suggestion, I drew up this advertisement. (*Hands MS. advertisement, which he has taken from table-drawer.*)

Fred. (*reads*). *£50 Reward. This sum will be paid for a true copy of the burial certificate of the first wife of the late Captain Van Brugh, R.N. She is known to have died at Melbourne within the last eight years.* Are you sure Fitz-Partington is acting straightforwardly with you?

Mr. S. Why should he do otherwise?

Fred. £50 is a large sum.

Mr. S. A large sum? If I can only establish the fact that the first Mrs. Van Brugh died within the last eight years, every penny of this so-called Mrs. Van Brugh's income—£8000 a year at least—reverts to me.

Fred. Then, dear me——

Mr. S. Eh?

Fred. Poor Eve will lose her settlement!

Mr. S. True; quite true. Dear me, I never thought of that. Poor Eve!

Fred. Poor, poor Eve!

Enter RUTH.

Ruth. I've brought this note from my lady.

Mr. S. Oh! There may be an answer. Stay.

Ruth (*quietly*). Yes; I'll stay.

Mr. S. (*reads note*). Oh! Mrs. Van Brugh writes to say that she wishes to see me this afternoon—alone.

(*Sits down to write.*)

Fred. Alone! Oh, then—then perhaps I'd better withdraw. (*With affected emotion.*)

Ruth. Aye, perhaps you better had.

(*She follows him with her eyes as he goes to the door. He seems uneasy. Then exit.*)

Mr. S. There is the answer. (*Finishing note.*)

Ruth. Smailey; wot's wrong about my lady?

Mr. S. Wrong?

Ruth. Aye, there's ruin comin' to her, and she knows it. She's been queer-like these two days. I've come upon her cryin' odd times, and she's as white as death. Wot is it, Smailey?

Mr. S. Probably a headache. I'm not a doctor.

Ruth. I am. It's no headache—it's heartache. It's ruin.

Mr. S. It *is* ruin; to her wealth, and her good name.

Ruth. Her good name? Why, *you're* never goin' to meddle wi' *that.*

Mr. S. You are deceived in your mistress. (*Rises.*) I will tell you what she has been——

Ruth. Stop! I won't hear it, Smailey—I won't hear it. Let bygones go by: no odds what she *has* been; think wot she is: think wot *you've* been. As I've dealt fair wi' you, deal you fair wi' her. Take wot's yourn, but don't take no more.

Mr. S. My rights and her good name are bound up together; I cannot claim the one without destroying the other. I only want what the law will give me, if I commence proceedings.

Ruth (*changing her tone*). If you commence proceedings, wot the law will give you is fourteen year, take my word for it. I've spoke fair, and no good's come of it, so I'll speak foul. Look here, Smailey, you've put a plot afoot to ruin my lady. Now, my lady's got a dog, Smailey, and that dog won't stand no plots. Do you hear that, Smailey? Stir hand or foot to harm that pure and spotless creature, and sure as my lady's dog has a set of fangs she'll fix them in your throat.

Mr. S. This is hard. This is very hard. Even Mrs. Van Brugh would herself at once admit the justice of my claim.

Ruth. Well, wait till she does.

Mr. S. (*after a pause*) There is a good deal of sound common sense in what you say, 'rredgett. Still, if—*if* Mrs. Van Brugh should at any time make a statement of *her own free will,* you will surely allow me to profit by it?

Ruth. Wotever my lady does of her own free will is angels' doin', and is right accordin'.

Mr. S. (*aside*). Then I think I see my way. (*Aloud.*) Well, Ruth, on that understanding you have my promise.

Ruth. Promise? *Your* promise? Smailey, don't you meddle with things you don't understand. Promises are ticklish goods in *your* hands. They're temptin' things to break, and you was always easy tempted. No, no; don't *you* promise. *I'll* promise this time, Smailey. *I'll* promise. [*Exit* RUTH.

Mr. S. A sin, an early sin—a sin committed twenty years ago—brought up against me now that I am an honest man, and a regular church-goer! I am absolutely bound hand and foot by it—and to what end? For the protection of a woman who has committed Heaven knows what offence against morality. If this crime were to be proved against me, what on earth would become of me? For years I have endeavoured to atone for my sin against society by treating wrong-doers brought before me with the strictest and most unflinching severity. Would Society be grateful for this—would it even take heed of it? No; my atonement would go for nothing—absolutely nothing. Ah! this is a merciless world, and one in which penitence is taken no account of. But have a care, Mrs. Van Brugh; I'll bide my time. You shall yet see that a sin against morality is not to be wiped out by a few years of sentimental self-denial!

Enter EVE *and* FRED.

Fred. Father, I met Mrs. Van Brugh and my darling on their way here, so I turned back with them.
Mr. S. My dear Eve. (*Kisses her.*)

Enter MRS. VAN BRUGH.

Mrs. Van Brugh, I am very pleased to see you. Pray sit down. You look pale; I am afraid you are tired.
Mrs. V. B. No, I have not been very well lately.
Eve. Mamma wished to come alone, as she wants to speak to you on business, but I wouldn't hear of that, as she is really very far from well, so I've brought her to you, Mr. Smailey; and now I'm going to take a turn in the garden with Fred. Dr. Athelney is waiting for us in the arbour.
Fred. If the arbour were a consecrated arbour, and I had a licence in my pocket, we might take a turn—in the garden—that would surprise our dear friends.
Eve. What, without a wedding-dress and bridesmaids, and bouquets and presents, and a breakfast? My dear Fred, it wouldn't be legal! [*Exeunt* EVE *and* FRED *into the garden.*
Mrs. V. B. (*after a pause*). Mr. Smailey, I come to you in great distress. On Tuesday last. a circumstance occurred, no matter what it was, that induced me to believe that there was

a flaw—a vital flaw—in my title to all I possess. Mr. Smailey, I haven't a shilling in the world.

Mr. S. A shilling! My very dear lady, you haven't a penny.

Mrs. V. B. What! Do you know this?

Mr. S. Mrs. Van Brugh, I will be candid with you. The Smaileys are a very, very old and very famous family. No suspicion of a bar sinister has ever shadowed their escutcheon. My son is betrothed to your daughter, and I have reason to believe that you are not entitled to the name you bear. Therefore, in his interests, and in those of his slumbering ancestors, I have taken steps to ascertain the truth.

Mrs. V. B. (*much agitated*). What do you hope to prove?

Mr. S. That when you went through the form of marriage with the late Captain Van Brugh you knew that his first wife was still alive.

Mrs. V. B. (*wildly*). No, no, no! Mr. Smailey, it is bad enough, but not so bad as that. Oh, Mr. Smailey, dismiss that fearful thought from your mind. and I will tell you the truth I came here to tell. It's a bitter, bitter truth, but not so bad as you would make it out to be.

Mr. S. What is the truth? (*Sternly.*)

Mrs. V. B. I—I—when I met Captain Van Brugh—I was very young, and my mother was dead—and——

(*Bursts into tears and sobs wildly, laying her head on the table.*)

Mr. S. What is the truth?

Mrs. V. B. Oh, man, man, can't you read it in these tears? Is there not shame enough in my face, that you want it in shameful words? Read what you see before you, and as you are a man with a heart, keep my secret; oh, keep my unhappy secret!

Mr. S. What! am I to understand that you never even went through the *form* of marriage with Captain Van Brugh?

Mrs. V. B. (*under her breath*). Never!

Mr. S. (*after a pause*). I decline to believe you. I had hoped that it was barely possible you were the unconscious dupe of a reckless scamp. I now believe that you were well aware of the crime you were committing, and you take this step to avoid its legal consequences.

Mrs. V. B. (*with forced calmness*). Mr. Smailey, I have, perhaps, no right to be indignant at this insult; but you are mistaken—utterly mistaken. Have you no pity, no sympathy? See, everything I possess is legally yours; I leave your presence penniless. Commence an action against me, and I will quietly yield up everything before the case comes into court; but, if you love your son, spare me the shame, the intolerable shame, of a public exposure!

Mr. S. I will spare you nothing; neither will I take the step you suggest, nor any other step to dispossess you. In this matter I am passive; I leave you to act as conscience may prompt you. But understand that I will be a party to no concealment, no subterfuge. On these terms, and on no other, will I consent to take this property.

Mrs. V. B. (wildly). What am I to do? I cannot keep it, and I have no one to advise me!

Mr. S. I will advise you. You have sinned, and must make atonement. There are witnesses at hand; let them hear the truth: whatever the truth may be, let them hear it.

Mrs. V. B. What witnesses?

Mr. S. Dr. Athelney, my dear son, Ruth Tredgett, and your daughter.

Mrs. V. B. (wildly). No, no; not before Eve. You cannot mean that I am to say this before Eve. Think, Mr. Smailey, what you are asking me to do. I am her mother!

Mr. S. I desire to press hardly on no fellow-creature, but it is meet that she should know the truth. Indeed, as a principle, truth cannot be too widely known.

Mrs. V. B. But she knows nothing of this miserable matter. She believes, as others believe, that I was married abroad and that my husband died soon after.

Mr. S. A mother seeking to deceive her own child!

Mrs. V. B. Take every penny I possess, but for Eve's sake spare me this intolerable shame. I will sign any deed you please that will convey my property to you, but leave me the love and honour of my darling child.

Mr. S. I decline to place myself in the invidious position of one who takes steps to dispossess a helpless lady; I also decline to be a party to any deception. If you refuse to make the public admission I require, you may *keep* your ill-gotten wealth.

Mrs. V. B. Keep it! Why, I am here, of my own free will, to surrender into your hands my wealth, and with it my good name!

Mr. S. I feel it to be my duty to remind you that you have as little right to the one as to the other.

Mrs. V. B. What shall I do—what shall I do? If I refuse to publish my sin, this man will make it known to the whole world.

Mr. S. No; there you wrong me. That would be an un-manly act indeed, Miss Brandreth.

Mrs. V. B. Miss Brandreth!

Mr. S. That, I presume, is your name. Pardon me, but now that I know the truth, I could not conscientiously call you Mrs. Van Brugh. It would be a lie. For the future I shall call you Miss Brandreth, but—I shall systematically withhold my reasons for so doing.

Mrs. V. B. Mr. Smailey, think what you are compelling me to do. I have sinned, and for many years I have unceasingly endeavoured to atone for that sin. Blessed with an ample fortune, I have devoted four-fifths of it to the rescue of the unhappiest among unhappy women. In my search for them I have waded, year after year, through the foulest depths of misery and disgrace, with ears and eyes outraged at every turn. In the face of galling rebuke and insult unspeakable, in the face of cold ridicule and insolent misconstruction, I have held on to the task I set myself, and through the mercy of Heaven— the infinite mercy of Heaven—I have succeeded. I have no desire to speak of these things, and to no other man will I utter them. But you talk to me of atonement; and have I not atoned? Oh! have I not atoned?

Mr. S. See how the deeds and words of these last years show in the fierce light you have just thrown upon them. You have lost no opportunity of rebuking my hardness of heart because I cannot pardon an act of immorality. See from what a foul and muddy source your own forgiveness springs. You have taunted me with my severity towards wrong-doers. See from what an interested motive your own leniency arises. You have publicly assailed my want of charity. Had I the control of another man's income my charities might perhaps outvie your own. In one word, if you retain your social position, you are morally an impostor. If you retain my property, you are morally——

Mrs. V. B. (*interrupting him*). Enough! You have spoken, and I know you now. I can see through those cold hard eyes down into the cold hard heart from which they take their tone. I read there the stony creed, " A woman who has once fallen shall never rise again." So let it be. You are strong—for you have the world on your side. I am weak—for I am alone. If I am to die this moral death, it shall be by my own hand. They *shall* hear the truth. (EVE *and* FREDERICK *have ap-peared at the door; she turns and sees them; they are followed by* DR. ATHELNEY *and* EDWARD.) Come here, Eve; come here,

Dr. Athelney; all of you come here. (EVE *comes forward and kneels at her mother's feet.*) Eve, my darling, my pet—Eve dear, kiss me. Kiss me again and again—my child, my child! Kiss me now, for you may never kiss me again. Dr. Athelney, you love me, I know. Edward, my dear old friend, listen while I tell you what manner of woman you have loved——

Ruth (rushing forward). No, no, mistress, you mustn't say it; don't, don't speak it; for the love of mercy don't speak it. As I'm a sinful woman, it'll be worse than death to me.

Mrs. V. B. I must go on to the end. Do you know on what kind of thing you have lavished the treasure of your love? You have lavished it on a fallen woman—an unhappy creature, who has committed that one sin for which on earth there is no atonement—no forgiveness. You think of me as Captain Van Brugh's widow; God forgive me, I never was his wife!

(RUTH *recoils from her with an exclamation of horror.* EVE *falls senseless into* EDWARD'S *arms.* SMAILEY *and* FREDERICK *watch the group from a corner of the stage.*)

ACT IV.

SCENE : *Library at* Dr. ATHELNEY'S.

MRS. VAN BRUGH *discovered seated, reading letters.*

Mrs. V. B. " The Rev. Mr. Twemlow presents his compliments to Mrs. Van Brugh, and begs to return her annual subscription of fifty guineas to the Fund for providing Shelter for the Homeless Poor. He does not feel justified, under the circumstances, in accepting any aid from Mrs. Van Brugh on their behalf. With respect to the living to which Mrs. Van Brugh has recently presented Mr. Twemlow, he desires that she may understand that, if he consents to retain it, it is because he feels that it affords him a more extended sphere of spiritual usefulness than the curacy he has hitherto held." (*Opens another letter.*) " We, the aged occupants of the Locroft Almshouses, are humbly pained and respectfully shocked at the disclosures that have recently been made with reference to Miss Brandreth's relations with the late Captain Van Brugh. We trust that it is unnecessary for us to add that, if it were not that the Almhouses pass at once from Miss Brandreth's hands into those of an upright and stainless Christian, whom it is an honour respectfully to know and a satisfaction humbly to profit by, we would not have consented to occupy them for another day ; we would rather have worked for our living. Signed." (*Opens another letter.*)

"HONOURED MADAM,
  "We shall feel greatly flattered and obliged if you will kindly afford us a sitting for your photograph at your earliest convenience.
              "We are, Honoured Madam,
                "With much esteem,
                  "Most respectfully yours,
                            "SCUMLEY & RIPP."

When these people address me, I am degraded indeed! My name a word of reproach in every household in the country ; my story a thing to be whispered and hinted at, but not to be openly discussed, by reason of its very shame. My years of atonement held to be mere evidence of skilfully sustained hypocrisy. Myself a confessed counterfeit, a base and worthless imposition, a living fraud on the immaculate beings with whom I dared to surround myself. And Ruth—Ruth, to whom my heart opened—even Ruth has left me. Poor blind, wayward woman, you are of the world, worldly ; your idol is shattered, and there is the end. So let it be ; it is meet that such as I should be alone !

Enter EVE, *who has overheard the last few lines. She approaches her mother quietly, and places her arms round her neck.*

Eve. Mamma, you have many kind friends left to you ; Dr. Athelney, who has given you a home ; Edward and myself.
  Mrs. V. B. A daughter's love comes of honour. Can that love live without the honour that gives it sustenance?
  Eve. Mamma, I am very young, and I know little of the world and its ways. Will you forgive me if I speak foolishly? Dear mamma, I think my love for you began with my life. It was born with me, and came of no other cause than that you are my mother. As I brought it with me into the world, so I believe I shall take it with me out of the world. Do you understand me? I mean, that if I had no other reason for loving you than that you are my mother, I should still love you, for I am your child.

Mrs. V. B. A child to whom I have given a life that is worse than death; a life that brings with it a curse that will be flung in your teeth by all who know you, and first of all, and above all, by him who was to have married you.

Eve. No, no; your bitter sorrow has made you unjust. Remember, he loves me. I do not know why he loves me, but whatever he saw in me to love is there still. *I* am not changed, and why should *he* change? I trust his heart as I trust my own.

Mrs. V. B. Eve, I know the world too well. That man will visit my fault upon you. He will renounce you now, my poor child, and the world will say that he is right.

Eve. I will believe this when I hear it from his own lips.

Mrs. V. B. You will hear it to-day. It is part of the punishment of women who sin as I have sinned, that those who are dearest to them shall suffer with them. See how I am punished. I have placed a mark of shame on you whom I love beyond all on earth. I have inflicted a lasting injury on you whom I would have died to serve. I have cursed you whom I would have blessed. I have degraded you whom I would have exalted. Eve, my darling—out of my sin has come your love for me. I have no claim to that love. I have cheated you into honouring me; for that honour comes of my sin. I do not ask for love—I do not ask for honour. Humbled, unworthy, and spirit-broken, I plead to you for pardon—only for pardon. (*Kneels to* EVE.)

Eve. Pardon! My mother — my gentle-hearted mother. There is no thought in my mind but of the perfect woman of the past eighteen years. The lustre of those years fills my world. I can see nothing else; I will see nothing else. As you have always been to me, so shall you always be—the type of gentle charity, tender helpfulness, brave, large-hearted womanly sympathy. When the bright light of those bygone years pales in my eyes, then let me suffer ten times the sorrow of to-day, for indeed I shall have deserved it. (*She rises and they embrace.*)

Enter FITZ-PARTINGTON *cautiously,* L.

Mrs. V. B. Mr. Fitz-Partington?

Fitz. Yes, but don't be alarmed. If it is open to a person in my debased position to be regarded as a friend, regard me as one.

Mrs. V. B. Mr. Fitz-Partington, I did you an injustice when

I saw you last—I doubted you. Will you forgive me? (*Holding out her hand.*)

Fitz. (*much affected, takes it*). Ma'am, this is the most unprofessional moment of my career. No one ever apologized to me before. It is very unmanning. It is like having a tooth out. I hope no one will ever apologize to me again.

Eve. Have you brought us any news, Mr. Fitz-Partington? I am sure you are here for some kind purpose.

Fitz. It is my fate to appear continually before you in the character of the Mysterious Warner of penny romance. Mrs. Van Brugh, once more, beware of Smailey. That abject man is going at you again.

Mrs. V. B. Has he not done with me yet? Can I be poorer than I am—or more unhappy—or more despised?

Fitz. He proposes to make you so, but he will be sold.

Eve. But with what motive does he do this?

Fitz. Revenge. To adapt the words of the poet to Smailey's frame of mind, " Revenge is sweet, especially on women."

Mrs. V. B. Revenge on *me!* Through him, whom I have never injured, I have lost my home, my fortune, and my good name, and *he* seeks revenge on *me !*

Fitz. Mrs. Van Brugh, if it is a source of pain to you to know that your friends have cut *you,* it may console you to know, that in their strict impartiality they have also cut *him.* He is hooted in the streets. His windows are a public cockshy. Nobody is at home to him, and though he is at home to everybody, it is to no purpose. The very tradesmen refuse to supply him. He is a desolate, and a hungry being, and nobody calls on him except the taxes.

Eve. I fear, Mr. Fitz-Partington, that you may yourself have suffered from your association with this man.

Fitz. (*to* Eve). I? I believe you! Why, I go about in fear of my life. Not only am I deprived of the necessaries of existence, but I have become the very focus of public execration. I couldn't be more unpopular if I had come down to stand for the borough.

Eve. But, Mr. Fitz-Partington, how in Heaven's name does he propose to injure my mother? What can he do to her, that he has not already done?

Fitz. He is advertising for the present Mrs. Van Brugh's marriage certificate, and the late Mrs. Van Brugh's burial certificate, with a view to a prosecution for bigamy.

Eve. Mamma, mamma, do you hear this? (*Crosses to her.*)

Mrs. V. B. Yes, I hear it. I knew that he had conceived

this monstrous idea, but I have already assured him there is no ground for his suspicion. I have told him (*after a pause, and with much shame*) the truth.

Fitz. Yes, but he don't believe you. Read that. (*Hands newspaper to* Eve, *who gives it to* Mrs. Van Brugh, *pointing out advertisement.*) Such is the snake-like and foxy character of that unparalleled old Pharisee, that he don't believe you. Why, I am a professional sceptic at two guineas a day, and even I believe you.

Mrs. V. B. (*who has been reading the advertisement*). This is most shameful. This is monstrous beyond expression. I have borne my terrible punishment to this point patiently, and without undue murmur, but I will bear no more. Let that man know this. He has roused me at last, and I will meet him face to face. Let him know that, helpless and friendless as he believes me to; crushed as I am under the weight of the fearful revelation he has extorted from me; shunned as I am, and despised even by those whom all despise but I, I am yet strong in this, that I have nothing more to lose. He has made desperate, and let him beware. There are men in these days as hot in the defence of an insulted woman as in the days gone by, and he shall have a legion of them about his ears. I have been punished enough. I will be punished no further.

Eve. But who could have put this monstrous scheme into his head? What demon could have suggested it to him?

Fitz. I suggested it to him, but I ain't a demon.

Eve and Mrs. V. B. You!

Fitz. I—I drew up the advertisement, put it in, and paid for it. It's a dodge; I've put him on a wrong scent.

Mrs. V. B. How am I to understand this?

Fitz. That's just it; you are *not* to understand—at present. You are to do me justice to believe that, when you *do* understand it, you will like it very much. I've put him on a wrong scent, and if I'm not very much mistaken, it will have the effect of taking him in his own toils. For the present it is enough to tell you that his advertisement has been answered, and that the person who answered it is to meet him here this afternoon.

Mrs. V. B. Here? Why does he come to *me?*

Fitz. Because he conceives, with some reason, that you are not likely to go to him. But don't be alarmed. *I* shall accompany him, as per usual. [*Exit* Fitz-Partington.

Mrs. V. B. (*covering her face*). Oh, the shame of it! Oh, the shame of it! To know that my terrible story is the common gossip of every plough-boy in the village; to feel that there is not a flighty servant-girl who does not gather her skirts about her as she passes me; to be certain when women cross the road it is to escape the contamination of my presence; and when they meet me face to face, it is that they may toss their head and tell each other that they knew it from the first! Oh, the shame of it! Oh, the shame of it!

Eve. But Mr. Smailey can do nothing. His wicked schemes must recoil upon himself. We will leave Locroft; we will leave this fearful place. Dr. Athelney sails in a fortnight, and he has made arrangements that we may accompany him. There, in a new world, with new friends and new duties, we shall forget all that is bitter in the past, and gather new stores of happiness from the future that is before us. (*They embrace.*)

Enter Dr. ATHELNEY, L.D. *Crosses to* EVE.

Dr. A. Mrs. Van Brugh; Eve, my dear, prepare yourself for a surprise. This morning, Mrs. Van Brugh and I were discussing Frederick Smailey's probable course of action. That very good or very bad young man is at this moment crossing the lawn with my son, Ted. He is coming with the view, no doubt, of setting all future discussion on that point at rest. Let us suspend judgment on that admirable or detestable lad until he has explained himself.

Eve. I knew he would come; I was sure of it. Mamma dear, I told you he loved me; I told you he would come.

Enter FRED *and* TED ATHELNEY, *arm-in-arm.*

Fred. Eve!

Eve (*running to him*). Fred, my dear Fred! (*He embraces her.*)

Ted. Here he is; I was sure of him; Eve and I were both sure of him. We knew him, Eve, didn't we?

Fred. Edward came to me, Mrs. Van Brugh, and told me that—that you doubted me. (*Much affected.*)

Ted. Yes, I told him that. Don't be angry with me, but when Fred Smailey's honour is at stake, Ted Athelney doesn't beat about the bush. I went straight to him and told him at once how the land lay. " Fred," said I, " Eve knows you, and I know you, but the others don't. Come over with me, and show them what you really are. Show them that you are the brave, straight-hearted, thorough-going fellow I know you to be." He didn't give me time to say it twice.

Fred. Mrs. **Van** Brugh, will you take my hand ? (*Shakes her hand. Crosses to* Dr. A., *then shakes his hand.*) Dr. Athelney, my very dear friend, this is very, very kind of you. You are too noble-hearted a man to confound the son with the father.

Dr. A. I hope and trust, sir, that I have done you an injustice. (*Goes up.*)

Fred. Mrs. Van Brugh, I know not how to express my opinion of my father's behaviour in terms that would be consistent with my duty as a son. I am most painfully situated. Permit me to content myself with offering you my deepest and most respectful sympathy

Mrs. V. B. Mr. Smailey, you speak very kindly.

Ted. And he means kindly, mind that. I'll stake my life he means kindly.

Fred. Thank you, Edward; thank you very heartily. My father, Mrs. Van Brugh, is, I have learnt, a very hard man ; a good man, a truly good man, but a very hard one. He is unaccountably incensed against you; I have pleaded for you, but, alas! in vain. I have implored him to allow you, at least, to continue to occupy the cottage which is endeared to me by so many happy recollections, dear Eve, but in vain. (*He takes* Eve's *hand.*) He—he answered me harshly for the first time in his life. (*Much moved.*)

Ted. My very dear fellow, Heaven bless you for that.

Fred. Under these circumstances I said to myself, How can I lighten this intolerable burden to them ? If not to Mrs. Van Brugh, at least to Eve. I lay awake all last night, thinking it over, and at last—at last I saw my way.

Ted (*to* Dr. A.). Trust Fred Smailey to find the right thing to do.

Fred. I said to myself, Here is an amiable and blameless young lady placed, through no fault of her own, in the painful position of being engaged to a member of a family which has done her and her mother a fearful and irreparable injury. Association with such a family must be, to her, a source of inconceivable distress. To a sensitive and high-minded girl, such as I know my darling to be, an alliance with such a family must be simply insupportable. Deeply as I love her, and because I love her deeply, I will fight with the great love that is within me; I will act as becomes a man of honour ; I will at once, and of my own free will, release her from this engagement. Eve, my dear Eve, you are free. (Eve *faints in* Mrs. Van Brugh's *arms.*)

Mrs. V. B. My darling! My poor, poor darling!

Dr. A. (c.) Sir, I have been a clergyman of the Church of England for five and forty years, and, until to-day, I have never regretted the restrictions that my calling has imposed upon me. My hands, sir, are tied. Ted, my boy, these remarks do not apply to you.

Ted (crosses to Fred Smailey). You infernal villain! You unutterably mean and sneaking villain! (*Seizing him.*)

Mrs. V. B. Edward! Edward!

Ted. Don't stop me, or I shall kill him. Look there, you miserable hound (*pointing to* Eve), look there! Do you see the work that your infernal heart has done? Why, you miserable cur, she loved you! You trembling hypocrite, she loved you! Eve loved you—loved *you!* Look at her, man, and if your devil's heart don't beat the harder for the sight, it hasn't a beat left in it!

Mrs. V. B. Dr. Athelney, pray, pray stop him.

Dr. A. Stop him? No, certainly not. I'm too fond of plain truth, and I hear it too seldom to stop it when I do hear it. Go on with your remarks, my boy, if you've anything else to say.

Enter Smailey, *followed by* Fitz-Partington, l.

Mr. S. When your son has quite finished shaking my son, perhaps you will kindly devote a little attention to me.

Fred. Edward, I sincerely hope you may live to apologize for this. (*Offers to shake hands ;* Ted *refuses.*)

Dr. A. Mr. Smailey, I must tell you that your presence here is an act of audacity for which I was not prepared.

Mr. S. I fear that the surprise of my appearance here is but the first of a series of surprises in store for you.

Fitz. And I am convinced of it.

Dr. A. Leave my house, Sir! (*To* Smailey.)

Mr. S. Nay, nay. I am here in the discharge of a high public duty, and I propose to remain. Come, Dr. Athelney, is this quite considerate? Is this quite as it should be? You are a minister of the Church, about to be invested with the very highest Colonial functions. In affording shelter to this unhappy person, have you not allowed your sympathy for her misfortunes to blind you to the fact that you are a clergyman?

Dr. A. Sir, I never had my duty as a clergyman so strongly before my eyes as when I placed my home at the disposal of this admirable lady. And, believe me, sir, I never felt so strongly disposed to forget my duty as a clergyman as I do at this moment. My hands are tied. Ted, my boy, these remarks do not apply to you.

Ted. Mr. Smailey, if you'll come with me, I'll see you out.

Fitz. (*to* TED). See him out? Nonsense. Hear him out. He's worth listening to, I can tell you.

Mr. S. Miss Brandreth (*to* Mrs. VAN BRUGH), when you denied having ever gone through the form of marriage with Captain Van Brugh, I considered it my duty, as a magistrate accustomed to deal with evidence, to disbelieve you. At the suggestion of my solicitor (*Aside, to* FITZ.) A lie, sir, for you are no solicitor; Heaven forgive you! (*Aloud.*) At his suggestion I advertised for the burial certificate of the late Mrs. Van Brugh. That advertisement has been answered.

Fitz. That advertisement has been answered.

Mr. S. The person who answered it is at this moment waiting without.

Fitz. Waiting without.

Mr. S. And, with or without your permission, shall be introduced.

Fitz. Shall be introduced.

Mr. S. Mr. Fitz-Partington shall introduce him.

Fitz. It ain't a *him*, it's a *her*. (*Opens door, and discovers* RUTH.)

Mrs. V. B. Ruth Tredgett!

Ruth. Ay, missis, 'tain't no other.

Mr. S. What does this mean? Is this a hoax? (*Indignantly, to* FITZ-PARTINGTON.)

Fitz. Is this a hoax? (*Appealing to the others.*)

Mr. S. What does this woman want here?

Fitz. Woman, what do you want here?

Ruth. Want to help you agin *her*. (*Indicating* Mrs. VAN BRUGH.)

Mrs. V. B. Oh, Ruth, Ruth!

Mr. S. Do you mean this, Tredgett? (*Crosses to* RUTH.)

Ruth. Ay, I mean it, Smailey. It's justice; and justice must be done. It was done agin me, years ago, and why not agin her now?

Mr. S. Dr. Athelney, this poor woman is an example to you. she has learned her mistress's true character.

Ruth. Ay, I have. I have learned my missis's true character.

Mrs. V. B. Ruth, how have I injured you, that even you turn against me? I loved you, Ruth!

Ruth (*with some emotion*). You ha'n't injured me, but I'm a

K

'spectable woman. You've made me 'spectable, and you must bide the consequence. (*To* Mr. SMAILEY.) You want the burial-ticket of Captain Van Brugh's dead wife?

Mr. S. Yes; I have offered £50 for it.

Ruth. Gi' us the money.

Mr. S. Why?

Ruth. I've got the paper.

Mr. S. How? How did you get it?

Ruth. No odds how. I've got it.

Mr. S. Give it to me, and you shall be paid.

Ruth. Nay, I must ha' the brass first.

Mr. S. As soon as I've verified it you shall be paid.

Ruth. Maybe you'll take some time over it. I must ha' the brass.

Mr. S. (*giving her a banknote.*) There is the money, but mind, if you are deceiving me, there is a constable outside.

Ruth. No fear. (*Tears up the note.*)

Mr. S. You fool, what have you done! Give me the paper.

Ruth. I'll give it to him. (*Indicating* FITZ-PARTINGTON, *who has come between them.*)

Fitz. (*takes paper and reads*). "St. Andrew's Church, Port Philip, 17 July, 1858."

Mr. S. '58! Why, she died in '69—I know she died in '69. This is some forgery. We shall want the constable yet.

Fitz. This is some forgery. We shall want the constable yet. (*Reads.*) "This is to certify that on the above date I read the burial service over the remains of Martha Vane, of Port Philip." (SMAILEY *sinks into a chair.*)

Dr. A. Martha Vane!

Mrs. V. B. That was her maiden name, the name under which she passed when she left her husband.

Mr. S. (*much confused*). This is not what I advertised for.

Fitz. No, but it's what *I* advertised for.

Mr. S. You? What have you to do with this?

Fitz. I was engaged to trace this forgery to you at the time when you engaged me to undermine the character of this inestimable lady. In strict compliance with the terms of our contract, you have allowed me the free run of all your books, papers, and memoranda, and I am much obliged to you.

Fred. (*who has heard this with the greatest concern*). Father! Tell them that it's a lie.

Fitz. It ain't a lie. The case is only too clear. Tredgett and he were both in it, but she turns Queen's evidence. Mr. Smailey, I desire to press hardly on no fellow-creature, but your own policeman is without, and he will be happy to walk off with you whenever you find it convenient to be arrested. (*About to touch* SMAILEY *on shoulder.*)

Fred. Father, tell them that it's a lie. (*To* FITZ.) Keep your hands off him—stand back—it's a lie, I tell you. Stand back, or I shall do you a mischief. Father, whatever others believe of you, *I* believe you to be the best and truest man on earth. For my sake, for the sake of my belief, tell them that it's a lie. For the love of God, tell them it's a lie.

Mr. S. I have nothing to say, my boy; I have lied enough.

Fred. But they will take you away! Great Heaven, think what will follow!

Mr. S. I care not what may follow. Whatever punishment may be in store for me, will be as nothing compared to the bitter shame of my degradation in the eyes of my poor boy, whom I have loved. He will desert me now! And what matters the rest—what matters the rest?

Fred. Father, I swear that where you are, there will I be to the end.

Mr. S. Heaven bless you for that.

Fred. Whatever you may have been—whatever *I* may have been—I am your son, and I love you; and I will be with you —to the end!

Mr. S. And the end is at hand.

Fitz. And the end is at hand.

[*Exeunt* FREDERICK SMAILEY, *followed by* FITZ-PAR-TINGTON. EVE *stretches out her arms towards* FREDERICK *as he goes, but he does not see her.*

Ruth (*who, during the preceding dialogue, has been kneeling at* Mrs. VAN BORGH's *feet*). Mistress, my good and kind mistress, I had that paper in safe keeping miles away. I walked day and night to fetch it. It was hard to have to leave you in your sorrow, but none other could have got it. My mistress, my pure and perfect mistress, my angel from heaven, we will never part again.

Mrs. V. B. We will never part again, Ruth. Under the guidance of our loving friend, we will sail to the new land, where, humbly as becomes penitents, cheerfully as becomes those who have hope, earnestly as becomes those who speak out of the fulness of their experience, we will teach lessons of loving-kindness, patience, faith, forbearance, hope, and charity.

Dr. A. " And the greatest of these is CHARITY."

THE PRINCESS.

A WHIMSICAL ALLEGORY.

(Being a Respectful Perversion of Mr. Tennyson's Poem.)

DRAMATIS PERSONÆ.

KING HILDEBRAND	MR. DAVID FISHER.	
PRINCE HILARION, *his Son*	MISS MARIA SIMPSON (MRS. W. H. LISTON).	
CYRIL, } *his friends, Noblemen of King*	MISS AUGUSTA THOMSON.	
FLORIAN, } *Hildebrand's Court*	MISS MONTGOMERY.	
KING GAMA	MR. ELLIOTT.	
PRINCE ARAC	MISS JESSIE EARLE.	
PRINCE GURON } *his Sons*	MISS HARRINGTON.	
PRINCE SCYNTHIUS }	MISS EWELL.	
ATHO, *King Hildebrand's Chamberlain* ...	MR. FRANKS.	
FIRST OFFICER	MR. ARTHUR BROWN.	
SECOND OFFICER	MR. DAVIS.	
GOBBO ... ... *a Porter* ...	MR. ST. MAUR.	
PRINCESS IDA { *Daughter of King Gama, and Principal of the Ladies' University.*	MISS MATTIE REINHARDT.	
LADY PSYCHE { *Professor of Experimental Science.*	MISS FANNY ADDISON.	
LADY BLANCHE { *Professor of Abstract Philosophy.*	MRS. POYNTER.	
MELISSA, *her daughter*	MISS PATTI JOSEPHE.	
BERTHA	MISS JOY.	
ADA	MISS CLYFOARD.	
CHLOE	MISS MOORE.	
SACHARISSA } *Undergraduates*	MISS ALMA.	
SYLVIA	MISS EVERARD.	
PHŒBE	MISS FITZJAMES.	
PHYLLIS	MISS CORINNE.	
AMARANTHE	MISS GRAHAM.	
LAURA	MISS CLARA.	

Undergraduates, Soldiers, Courtiers, Pages, etc.

THE PRINCESS.

SCENE FIRST.—*Court in King Hildebrand's Palace.*

KING HILDEBRAND, *discovered seated, in gloomy mood—* FLORIAN *and other* COURTIERS *discovered looking off through telescopes—*CYRIL *standing by the* KING.

Hilde. See you no sign of Gama?
Flori.   None, my liege.
Hilde. It's very odd indeed!   If Gama fails
To put in an appearance at our court,
Before the sun has set in yonder west,
And fails to bring the Princess Ida here—
To whom our son Hilarion was betrothed
At the extremely early age of one—
There's war between King Gama and ourself.
(*Aside to* CYRIL.) Oh, Cyril, how I dread this interview!
It's twenty years since he and I have met.
He was a twisted monster—all awry,
As though Dame Nature, angry with her work,
Had crumbled it in fitful petulance!
   Cyril. But, sir, a twisted and ungainly trunk
Often bears goodly fruit—perhaps he was
A kind, well-spoken gentleman?
   Hilde.   Oh no—
For, adder-like, his sting lay in his tongue!
His bitter insolence still rankles here,
Although a score of years have come and gone!
His outer man, gnarled, knotted as it was,
Seemed to his cruel and cynical within,
Hyperion to a Saturday Review!
   Cyril. Oh, bear with him—he is an old, old man.
Old men are fretful—peevish, as we know.
A worm will sometimes turn—so will the milk
Of human kindness, if it's kept too long.
   Flori. (*looking through glass*). But stay, my liege; o'er
         yonder mountain's brow
Comes a small body bearing Gama's arms;

And, now I look more closely at it, sir,
I see attached to it King Gama's legs;
From which I gather this corollary—
That that small body must be Gama's own!
    Hilde. Ha! Is the Princess with him?
    Flori.   Well, my liege,
Unless her ladyship is six feet high,
And wears moustachios, too, and smokes cigars,
And rides *en cavalier*, in coat of mail,
I do not think she is.
    Hilde. (excited).   Come, bustle there!
For Gama, place the richest robes we have!
For Gama, place the coarsest prison dress!
For Gama, let our best spare bed be aired!
For Gama, let our deepest dungeon yawn!
For Gama, lay the costliest banquet out!
For Gama, place cold water and dry bread!
For as King Gama brings the Princess here,
Or brings her not, so shall King Gama have—
Much more than everything—much less than nothing!

Enter PRINCE HILARION.

    Hilar. Well, father, is there news for me, at last?
    Hilde. My son, King Gama's host is now in sight:
Prepare to meet the fascinating bride
To whom you were betrothed so long ago.
Why, how you sigh!
    Hilar.   My liege, I'm much afraid
The Princess Ida has not come with him.
    Hilde. And why?
    Hilar.   I've heard she has forsworn the world.
And, with a band of women, shut herself
Within a lonely country house, and there
Devotes herself to stern philosophies.
    Hilde. Then, I should say, the loss of such a wife
Is one to which a reasonable man
Would easily be reconciled.
    Hilar.   Oh no—
Or I am not a reasonable man.
She *is* my wife: has been for twenty years.
    Hilde. That's true—you were a baby in long clothes
When you gained Ida's heart and she gained yours.
    Hilar. Yes—I remember—each of us was won!

I think I see her now!   (*Looking through telescope.*)
   Hilde.   Ha! let me look!
   Hilar. In my mind's eye, I mean—a blushing bride—
All bib and tucker—frill and furbelow!
How exquisite she looked as she was borne
Recumbent in the monthly nurse's arms!
How the bride wept!—nor would be comforted
Until the hireling mother-for-the-nonce
Administered refreshment in the vestry.
And I remember feeling much annoyed
That she should weep at marrying with me;
"But then," I thought, "these brides are all alike!
Cry on, young lady—brides are bound to cry.
You cry at marrying me?   How much more cause
You'd have to cry if it were broken off!"
These were my thoughts—I kept them to myself,
For, at that age, I had not learnt to speak.
   Hilde. Your memory is singularly good.
   Hilar. Do you remember, too, the wedding feast—
Rolls steeped in milk, and other softened food,
Fit for our undeveloped little gums?
And talk of drink, I never shall forget,
How merrily we passed that nursing-bottle!
A curly-headed patriarch of three—
The Princess Ida's uncle—then proposed
The happy couple's health—the bridesmaids then,
Fifteen in number, each six weeks of age,
Began to weep—the fifteen groomsmen, too
(The eldest of them eighteen months or so),
Wept also—then, remembering they were men,
Dashed from their eyes the unaccustomed brine!
We parted then—and since, for twenty years,
We have not met.   It seems quite strange that she
Should have become a woman in the while!
She speaks a hundred languages, I'm told.
   Hilde. Your late mamma had mastered only one,
Yet she was never at a loss for words!
   Hilar. But think how useful is a wife who can
Express her fancies in a hundred tongues.
   Hilde. You will find one, of average length, enough.
   Hilar. I've heard she hopes to make all women swear
That they'll abjure, for aye, the tyrant Man!
She's far before the age in which she lives!
   Hilde. At all events she's singular in that,

Most grown-up ladies of our court give out
That they are several years behind their age!
Hilar. A woman thus endowed should have been born
A century hence, at least!
Hilde.   The day will come
When you will most devoutly wish she had.

Enter CYRIL.

Cyril. My liege, King Gama's train is at the gate
And prays admission.
Hilde.   Cyril, show him in.
Though Princess Ida wore a Gorgon's head,
He shall not tamper with King Hildebrand!

Flourish—Procession.   Enter CYRIL, FLORIAN *and* COURT,
ushering KING GAMA, *and one* ATTENDANT.

Gama. So this is Castle Hildebrand?—well, well—
Dame Rumour whispered that the place was grand;
She told me that your taste was exquisite—
Superb—unparalleled——
Hilde.   Oh, really, king——
Gama. But she's a liar! Why, how old you've grown!
Is this Hilarion?—why, you've changed, too!
You were a singularly handsome child!
(*To* CYRIL.) Are you a courtier? Come, then, ply your
        trade!
Tell me some lies: how do you like your king?
Vile Rumour says he's all but imbecile—
Now that's not true!
Cyril.   My lord, we love our king:
His wise remarks are valued by his court
As precious stones.
Gama.   And for the self-same cause!
Like precious stones the wit of Hildebrand
Derives its value from its scarcity!
Come now, be honest, tell the truth for once,
Tell it of me! Come, come, I'll harm you not!
This leg is crooked—this foot is ill-designed—
This shoulder wears a hump—come, out with it!
Look, here's my face—now am I not the worst
Of Nature's blunders?
Hilar.   Nature never errs;

To those who know the workings of your mind,
Your face and figure, sir, suggest a book
Appropriately bound.
 Gama.   Why, harkye, sir!
How dare you bandy words with me?
 Hilar.   No need
To bandy aught that appertains to you.
 Gama (to HILDEBRAND). Do you permit this, king?
 Hilde.   We are in doubt
Whether to treat you as an honoured guest,
Or as a traitor knave who plights his word
And breaks it!
 Gama.   If the casting vote's with me
I give it for the former.
 Hilde.   We shall see:
By the terms of our contract, signed and sealed,
You're bound to-day to bring the Princess here
To join her spouse. Why is she not with you?
 Gama. Why? Come, I'll tell you, if you'll answer
  this:
What think you of a wealthy purse-proud man
Who, when he calls upon a starving friend,
Pulls out his gold, and flourishes his notes,
And flashes diamonds in the pauper's eyes—
What name have you for such an one?
 Hilde.   A snob!
 Gama. Just so: King Hildebrand, I am no snob.
The girl has beauty, virtue, learning, wit,
Grace, humour, wisdom, charity, and pluck.
Would it be kindly, think you, to parade
These brilliant qualities before *your* eyes?
Oh no, King Hildebrand, I am no snob!
 Hilde. But hang it, man, the contract that we signed
Some twenty years ago——
 Gama.   Why, here's good news!
(*To Court.*) At last your king is going to redeem
His lengthy list of broken promises—
And very properly, as wise men should,
Begin at the beginning!
 Hilde.   Stop that tongue,
Or you shall lose the monkey head that holds it!
Oh, I'll be even with you, yet, for this.
 Gama. Bravo! Your king deprives me of my head,
That he and I may meet on equal terms!

Hilde. Of this anon—we'll try the force of arms—
Where is she now?
Gama.   In Castle Adamant—
One of my many country houses.   There
She rules a woman's University,
With full five hundred girls who learn of her.
  Cyril. Five hundred girls!   Five hundred ecstasies!
  Gama. But no mere girls, my good young gentleman!
With all the college learning that you boast,
The youngest there will prove a match for you!
  Cyril. With all my heart, if she's the prettiest!
Fancy—five hundred matches—all alight!
That's if I strike them, as I hope to do.
  Gama. Despair your hope—their hearts are dead to
        man.
He who desires to gain their favour must
Be qualified to strike their teeming brains,
And not their hearts!   They're safety-matches, sir,
And they light only on the knowledge box,
So *you've* no chance!
  Hilar.   We'll try, at all events.
I'll take no soldiers, father, in my train—
Cyril and Florian here will go with me,
And we will storm them ere the week is out.
  Gama. That's brave!   They're only women—storm
        away!
  Hilar. Oh, don't mistake us, sir; we mean to storm
Their eyes and hearts, and not their citadel.
With sigh we'll charge our mines and counter-mines,
Dance steps shall be our scaling ladders, with
Those croquet mallets for our battering rams.
Fair flowers shall bear the only blades we wield,
Our eyes shall be our very deadliest darts,
And bon-bon crackers our artillery!
  Gama. And so you think to conquer them with sighs?
My good young gentleman, a sigh, to them,
Is simply an exceptionally marked
Contraction of the intercostal muscles!
Croquet is interesting only when
It illustrates familiar theories
Of incidental and reflecting angles.
Fair flowers, to them, are mere embodiments
Of calyx, pistil, stamina, and petal.
Expressive eyes would have their charm, no doubt—

Hilar. Of course!

Gama. But only, be it understood,
As illustrating theories of vision!
But here are letters—take them if you like—
Perhaps she's tired of disobedience,
And may admit you.

Hilde. Good : Hilarion, go ;
Take Florian and Cyril, as you say.
King Gama, we detain you pris'ner here,
As hostage for the safety of our son.

Gama. A prisoner? Why, what should I do here
At Castle Hildebrand? I am not mad!

Hilde. You can amuse yourself by fancying
That there's an execution in our house,
And you're the party in possession—or
That we are dead and you've succeeded us.
In short, suppose whatever state of things
Would offer you the greatest happiness.

Gama (*to* HILARION). You run a risk, my friend; so
        take good heed,
For no one knows her temper but myself :
(*To* KING.) Since her betrothal, king, until the day
When she abjured all male society,
I was the only man she ever saw!

Hilar. Oh, that explains the mystery at once,
And simplifies our task—come, Florian,
And we will show these maidens what they've lost.

[*Exeunt* HILARION, FLORIAN, *and* CYRIL.

SCENE SECOND.—*The Gates of Castle Adamant.*

Enter GOBBO, *with ladies' robes on his arm.*

Gobbo. More robes for undergraduates! I suppose
Some students are expected here to-day.
No girl without a robe may pass those gates !
They are so proud of these here caps and gowns,
They hardly like to take 'em off a-night!
They even wear (or so I've heard it said)
Night-caps and night-gowns when they go to bed !

[*Exit into porter's lodge.*

Enter HILARION, CYRIL, *and* FLORIAN.

Hilar. So, here's the Princess Ida's castle?   Well,
They must be lovely girls if it requires
Such walls as these to keep intruders off!
  Cyril. To keep men off is only half their charge,
And that the easier half.   I much suspect
The object of these walls is not so much
To keep men off as keep the maidens in!
  Hilar. Here lives the porter, Cyril.   I'll be bound
He's quite as learned as the rest of them,
Half Newton and half Bacon!   Here he comes.

Enter GOBBO *from lodge.*

  Cyril. Half Bacon?   No,—all Bacon, I should say!
  Gobbo. Now then, what is it?
  Hilar.   I'm a royal prince ;
These gentlemen are followers of mine :
We hold King Gama's letters, charging you
To bear us safely to the Council Hall,
In which the Princess Ida holds her state.
  Gobbo. Ho! ho! ho! ho!
  Hilar. How now?—you mock at us?   (*Draws sword.*)
  Gobbo. Mock you?   Why. bless your heart and soul
          alive,
No man may place his foot within those walls ;
It's death to disobey our Princess, sir!
  Flori. It's double death to disobey your king!   (*Draws.*)
  Cyril. It's treble death to disobey ourselves!   (*Draws.*)
  Gobbo. But, sirs, I am the only man alive
Who ever enters!
  Flori.   You?
  Gobbo.   Yes!   Once a year
I am led through their ranks that they may see
What sort of thing's a man!   " See here! " she cries.
" See—this is what you lose in losing man!
This is a courtly knight—well born, well formed! "
(I'm comely, sirs ; but, bless you, I'm no knight!)
" Look, girls," she cries, " this is a courtly knight—
A type of all that's beautiful in man! "
(*Aloud.*) And then they make me gibber, squeak, and mow ;
Then, with much deference and mock courtesy,

They bow me to my duty at the gate!

Flor. Are there no males whatever in those walls?

Gobbo. None, gentlemen, excepting letter mails!
And they are driven (as males often are
In other large communities)—by women!
If you'll believe me, gentlemen, I swear,
She's so confoundedly particular,
She'll scarcely suffer Dr. Watts's hymns;
And all the animals she owns are " hers"!
The ladies rise at cockcrow every morn——

Hilar. Oh, then they have male poultry!

Gobbo.   Not at all.
(*Confidentially.*) The crowing's done by an accomplished
   hen!

Cyril. And what are these? (*Looking at robes in lodge.*)

Gobbo.   The academic robes,
Worn by the lady undergraduates
When they matriculate.

Hilar. I'll try one on. (*Does so.*)
Why, see—I'm covered to the very toes!
Ha! I've a proposition!

Flori.   State it, then.

Hilar. Suppose we dress ourselves as girls, and claim
Admission to this University?
It is a thing we've often done at home
In amateur theatricals. You know
How well I play viragos in burlesque!

Flori. My Cleopatra, too—remember that!

Cyril. My Mrs. Bouncer, too, in " Box and Cox"!

Hilar. Wilt play the woman, then?

Cyril.   Of course! What knight
Would hesitate to " take a woman's part"?

Quartette.—HILARION, CYRIL, FLORIAN, *and* GOBBO, *as
   they dress themselves in women's clothes.*

   " *Les Trois Cousines* " (*La Périchole*).

Flori.   If we are hailed with any query,
                Say we are nice young ladies, three;
            Who of the world terribly weary,
                Enter a University.
            Such lovely girls, ha, ha, ha ha!

All.   Such lovely girls, ha, ha, ha, ha!

Cyril. We will declare to them that lately,
We have been bored with suitors stately,
And we prefer young ladies greatly—
Sorry to say that that's too true!
All. Sorry to say that that's too true!
Hilar. We must take care when we are talking,
Never our manly tastes to show;
Hold up our dresses thus in walking,
Showing an inch of ankle—so!
All. Showing an inch of ankle—so!
Such lovely girls, ha, ha, ha, ha!
Such lovely girls, ha, ha, ha, ha!
Gobbo (in terror). But, gentlemen, observe—if you
do this,
What's to become of me?
Hilar. I do not know
What will become of you if we do this;
But I can read the fate in store for you
If you presume to interfere with us.
Now, porter, say to whom we should apply
To gain admission.
Gobbo (in tears). Why, to Lady Blanche
Or Lady Psyche.
Flori. Which is prettier?
Gobbo. Well, *I* like Lady Blanche by far the best.
Flori. Then we declare for Lady Blanche at once,
Gobbo. You see, she's more my age—the other one
Is young and pretty! (*Contemptuously.*)
Cyril. Bah! Then I retract;
We will be Psyche's interesting charge!
So go and summon her. (GOBBO *rings, and then exit.*)
Flori. But stop a bit,
What will your father think of such a scheme?
Cyril. Oh, he be—dashed!
Hilar. Extremely shocked I am!
Cyril. I meant my sire——
Hilar. I thought you meant your "dam"!

Enter LADY PSYCHE *from gate, attended.*

Psyche. Who summons us?
Hilar. Three would-be students, ma'am—
Three noble ladies, ma'am, of good estate,
Who wish to join this University. (*They curtsey.*)

Psyche. If, as you say, you wish to join our ranks,
And will conform with all our rules, 'tis well;
But understand—you must adapt yourselves
To all the regulations now in force,
In Princess Ida's University.
   Hilar. To all its rules we cheerfully subscribe.
   Flori. (aside to HILARION). Here's a catastrophe, Hila-
     rion!
This is my sister! She'll remember me,
Though years have passed since she and I have met!
   Hilar. No matter, hide your face—she'll know you not.
   Psyche. You say you're noblewomen—well, you'll find
No sham degrees for noblewomen, here—
Or other cruel contrivances to draw
An arbitrary line 'twixt rich and poor.
No butteries, or other institutes,
To make poor students feed rich cooks—no tufts
To mark nobility; except such tufts
As indicate nobility of brain.
As to your fellow-students, mark me well—
There are five hundred maidens in these walls
All good, all learned, and all beautiful.
You must select your intimates from these;
They are prepared to love you; will you swear
You'll do your best to love them in return?
   Flori. Upon our words and honours, ma'am, we will!
   Psyche. And will you swear that if, by any chance,
You're thrown into a man's society,
You'll not allow your thoughts to stray from us,
But, at the earliest opportunity,
You'll give up his society for ours?
   Cyril. All this, dear madam, cheerfully we swear.
   Psyche. But we go further: will you undertake
That you will never marry any man?
   Flori. Indeed we never will!
   Psyche.   Consider well,—
You must prefer our maids to all mankind!
   Hilar. To all mankind we much prefer your maids!
   Cyril. We should be dolts, indeed, if we did not,
Seeing how fair——
   Hilar. (aside to CYRIL). Take care, that's rather strong!
(*Aloud.*) We have seen men of wealth—ay, princes, too—
Whose beauty has been so remarkable,
That half the maidens in our monarch's court

                                 L

Have pined away and died for love of them!
These men—Apollos in their manly grace,
Indeed in everything (except in that
They wore a proper quantity of clothes)—
We think of with profound indifference,
But, when we see a woman who excels
In virtue, scholarship, and loveliness,
We long to lay our heads upon her breast,
And join our lives with hers!

    Psyche.   Why, that's well said;
But have you left no lovers at your home,
Who may pursue you here?

    Hilar.   No, madam, none—
We're homely ladies, as no doubt you see,
And we have never fished for lover's love—
We smile at girls who deck themselves with gems,
False hair, and meretricious ornaments,
To chain the fleeting fancy of a man;
But do not imitate them. What we have
Of hair is all our own—our colour, too,
Unladylike, but not unwomanly,
Is but the glow of rugged, boisterous health:
Our gait, untrammelled by the influence
Of high-heeled boots, small waists, and Grecian bends,
May seem undignified—but then we walk
As Nature meant us to—and man has learnt
To reckon Nature an impertinence!

    Psyche. I know how coldly men regard a girl,
Whose beauty is her poorest excellence;
But beauty goes for nothing in these walls.
You'll find yourselves appreciated here:
If what you say is true, you'll spend with us
A happy, happy time!

    Cyril.   If, as you say,
Five hundred lovely maidens wait within
To welcome us with smiles and open arms,
I think there's very little doubt we shall!

                          [Exeunt into Castle

SCENE THIRD.—*Grounds of Castle Adamant; Waterfall
and Stream, crossed by rustic bridge;* GIRL-STUDENTS
*discovered grouped about the stage, occupied with phi-
losophical instruments, etc.*

Ada. I shall be quite alone, dear, in my rooms,
So come and spend a long, long evening—do!
And bring your steam-engine!
   Chloe.   Oh, that I will!
And you shall show me all your nice new things—
That quadrant—and the anemometer;
And oh, that darling, darling dumpy-level
I've heard so much about!
   Lydia.   My love, I see
You've got another new theodolite.
(*Aside to* CHLOE.) That's the fifteenth this month! The
      one I used
Went out of fashion half a year ago!
Oh, I've a bit of scandal! What d'you think?
Melissa found a *billet-doux*, concealed
In that Egyptian mummy we unrolled
Last night. Just think of that!

    Enter MELISSA, *from bridge, running.*

   Melissa.   I say, my dear,
I have *such* news for you! I've just been shown
The robe for doctors of divinity.
Oh, it's the sweetest thing!—Magenta silk,
Trimmed with chinchilla, *bouillonné* behind,
Gored to the figure, though; and on the skirt,
Two rows of Cluny lace as deep as that!
   Chloe. Oh my! how lovely!
   Melissa.   Then the trencher cap
Is amber satin, trimmed with Cluny lace
And rows of pearls; and round the outer edge
The tiniest, tiniest rosebuds in the world!
   Ada (*to* CHLOE). It's much more lovely than the legal
      gown—
Green grenadine, with rûchings down the front,
That we shall wear.
   Chloe (*pouting*). I shall give up the law

And go into the church !   I've always felt
A serious longing for a parson's life ;
Besides, I'm dark, and look a fright in green !
    Sacha. Take care, here's Lady Blanche.   How stern she
      looks !

Enter Lady Blanche, l.   Girls *study vigorously.*

    Blanche. Attention, ladies, while I read to you
The Princess Ida's list of punishments :
The first is Sacharissa.   She's expelled.
    All. Expelled !
    Blanche.   Expelled—because, although she knew
No man of any kind may see these halls,
She dared to bring a set of chessmen here !
    Sacha. (*in tears*). I meant no harm—they're only men
      of wood !
    Blanche. They're men with whom you give each other
      mate—
And that's enough !   The next is Sylvia——
    Sylvia.   Oh !
    Blanche. Sylvia is rusticated for a month
Because, in spite of all our college rules
Upon the point, she dared to put three rows
Of lace insertion round her graduate's gown !
Phyllis will lose three terms, for yesterday,
When, looking through her drawing-book, I found
A sketch of a perambulator !
    All (*shocked*).   Oh !
    Blanche. Double perambulator, shameless girl !
That's all at present.   Now, attention, please ;
Your principal, the Princess, comes to give
Her usual inaugural address,
To those young ladies who joined yesterday.

March.—Enter the Princess, *over bridge, attended by eight
  "daughters of the plough."* (*All curtsey profoundly.*)

    Princess. Women of Adamant—fair neophytes,
Who pant for the instruction we can give,
Attend, while I unfold a parable :
The elephant is stronger than the man,
Yet man subdues him.   Why ?   The elephant
Is elephantine everywhere but here (*tapping forehead*).

And Man, whose brain is to the elephant's
As Woman's brain to Man's—that's rule of three—
Conquers the foolish giant of the woods,
As Woman, in her turn, shall conquer Man.
In mathematics Woman leads the way !
The narrow-minded pedant still believes
That two and two make four ! Why, we can prove—
We women, household drudges as we are—
That two and two make five—or three—or seven—
Or five and twenty, as the case demands !
Finance ? Why, I've heard clever men declare,
Their bankers' balance being overdrawn,
They don't know where to turn for ready cash,
Yet wilfully ignoring all the while
That remedy unfailing—draw a cheque !
Diplomacy ? The wily diplomate
Is absolutely helpless in our hands :
He wheedles monarchs—Woman wheedles him !
Logic ? Why, tyrant man himself admits
It's waste of time to argue with a woman !
Then we excel in social qualities—
Though man professes that he holds our sex
In utter scorn, I'll undertake to say,
If you could read the secrets of his heart,
He'd rather be alone with one of you
Than with five hundred of his fellow-men !
In all things we excel. Believing this,
Five hundred maidens here have sworn to place
Their foot upon his neck. If we succeed,
We'll treat him better than he treated us ;
But if we fail—oh, then let hope fail too !
Let no one care one penny how she looks !
Let red be worn with yellow—blue with green,
Crimson with scarlet—violet with blue !
Let all your things misfit, and you yourselves
At inconvenient moments come undone !
Let hair-pins lose their virtue ; let the hook
Disdain the fascination of the eye,—
The bashful button modestly evade
The soft embraces of the button-hole !
Let old associations all dissolve,
Let Swan secede from Edgar—Grant from Gask,
Sewell from Cross—Lewis from Allenby—
In other words, let Chaos come again !

Who lectures in the Upper Hall to-day?
   Blanche. I, madam, on Abstract Philosophy.
There, I propose considering at length
Three points—the Is, the Might Be, and the Must.
Whether the Is, from being actual fact,
Is more important than the vague Might Be,
Or the Might Be, from taking wider scope,
Is, for that reason, greater than the Is,
And lastly, how the Is and Might Be stand
Compared with the inevitable Must.
   Prin. The subject's deep—how do you treat it, pray?
   Blanche. Madam, I take three Possibilities,
And strike a balance then between the three,
As thus—the Princess Ida Is our head—
The Lady Psyche Might Be—Lady Blanche—
Neglected Blanche—inevitably Must.
Given these three hypotheses—to find
The actual betting against each of them!
Come, girls!   [*Exeunt* LADY BLANCHE *and* STUDENTS.
   Prin. (looking after her). Ambitious fool. And do you
      think you can
Provide this college with a head? Go, go!
Provide yourself with one—you want it more!

Enter LADY PSYCHE, *over bridge, conducting* HILARION,
        FLORIAN, *and* CYRIL.

   Lady P. Here is the Princess Ida's favourite grove,
And here's the Princess. (*To* PRINCESS.) These are ladies
      three
Who join our College.
   Hilar. (aside to CYRIL). Gods! how beautiful!
   Prin. What special study do you seek, my friend?
   Hilar. (enraptured). Madam, I come that I may learn
      to live,
For, if I come not here, I die!
   Prin. (laughing).   Indeed?
Your case is desperate! We welcome you.
We meet at luncheon—until then, farewell!
                  [*Exit* PRINCESS.
   Flori. (aside to HILARION). When Psyche sees my face,
      I'm confident
She'll recognize her brother Florian.
Let's make a virtue of necessity,

And trust our secret to her gentle care.

(HILARION *assents.*)

(*Aloud*) Psyche! Why, don't you know me—Florian?

(PSYCHE *amazed.*)

Psyche. Why, Florian!

Flori. My sister!

Psyche. Oh, my dear,
What are you doing here—and who are these?

Hilar. I am that Prince Hilarion to whom
Your Princess is betrothed—I come to claim
Her promised love—your brother Florian, here,
And Cyril—come to see me safely through.

Psyche. The Prince Hilarion!—Cyril too! How strange!
My earliest playfellows!

Hilar. (*astonished*). Why, let me look!
Are you that learned little Psyche who
At school alarmed her mates because she called
A buttercup "ranunculus bulbosus"?

Cyril. Are you indeed that Lady Psyche, who
At children's parties drove the conjuror wild,
Explaining all his tricks before he did them?

Hilar. Are you that learned little Psyche, who
At dinner parties brought into dessert
Would tackle visitors with "you don't know
Who first determined longitude—I do—
Hipparchus 'twas, B.C. one sixty three!"
Are you indeed that little Psyche, then?

Psyche. That small phenomenon in truth am I!
But, gentlemen, 'tis death to enter here—
My vow will make me speak. What shall I do?
This palace is a rat-trap—we the bait—
And you the foolish victims!

Cyril. Be it so—
A prisoned rat, before he dies the death,
Has liberty to nibble at the bait! (*Kisses her.*)

Psyche. Forbear, sir—pray—you know not what you
do!
We have all promised to renounce mankind.

Hilar. But on what grounds do you, fair Psyche, base
This senseless resolution?

Psyche. Senseless? No!
It's based upon the grand hypothesis,
That as the Ape is undeveloped Man
So Man is undeveloped Woman.

Hilar.　　　　　　　　　　Then,
This, of all others, is the place for us!

    Enter MELISSA *unperceived, at back; she listens in*
        astonishment.

If Man is only undeveloped Woman,
We men, if we work very hard indeed,
And do our utmost to improve ourselves—
May in good time *be* woman! Though I own
Up to this point (as far as I'm aware)
The metamorphosis has not commenced.
    Melissa (coming down). Oh, Lady Psyche!—
    Psyche (startled).　　　　What—you heard us, then
Oh, all is lost!
    Melissa.　　　　Not so; I'll breathe no word.
        (Advancing in astonishment to FLORIAN.)
How marvellously strange! And are you then,
Indeed, young men?
    Flori.　　　　　　Well, yes—just now we are;
But hope, by dint of study, to become,
In course of time, young women!
    Melissa (eagerly).　　　　　　No! no! no!
Oh, don't do that! Is this indeed a man?
I've often heard of them, but till this day
Never set eyes on one. They told me men
Were hideous, idiotic, and deformed!
They're quite as beautiful as women are!
(Patting FLORIAN'S *cheek.)* Their cheeks have not that
       pulpy softness which
One gets so weary of in womankind!
Their features are more marked,—and oh! their chins—
              (feeling his chin)
How curious!
    Flori.　　　　I fear it's rather rough.
    Melissa. Oh, don't apologize—I like it so!
But I forgot; my mother, Lady Blanche,
Is coming—and her eyes are very keen—
She will detect you, sir!
    Hilar.　　　　　　Oh, never fear!
We saw her ladyship an hour ago;
She seemed to have suspicions of our sex,
And showed us robes, and gave us needlework,
As though to test us. Well, we did the work

Like seamstresses—and named the various stuffs,
As if we'd spent a full apprenticeship
At Swan and Edgar's!

Enter LADY BLANCHE. *Exeunt the three* GENTLEMEN *with*
LADY PSYCHE.

Blanche (aside to MELISSA). Here, Melissa—hush!
Those are the three new students?
    Melissa (confused).   Yes, they are—
They're charming girls!
    Blanche (sarcastically). Particularly so!
So graceful, and so very womanly;
So skilled in all a girl's accomplishments!
    Melissa (confused). Yes, very skilled!
    Blanche.   You stupid little fool!
Awhile ago, I placed before their eyes
Some Cluny lace—*they called it Valenciennes*—
Hemming is stitching—so at least they say—
A gusset is a gore—a tuck's a flounce—
Merino's cotton—linen's calico—
Poplin is silk, and rep is corduroy!
I bade them hem a pocket handkerchief—
They placed their thimbles on their forefingers!
And set about their work as clumsily
As if they had been men, in girls' disguise!
    Melissa (trembling). You surely wrong them, Mother
        dear, for see—(*picking up a case from floor*)
Here is an *étui* dropped by one of them—
Containing scissors, needles, and——
    Blanche (taking it from her, and opening it). Cigars!!!
Why, these *are* men! And you knew this, you cat!
    Melissa. Oh, spare them—they *are* gentlemen, indeed,
The Prince Hilarion—betrothed long since
To Princess Ida—with two trusted friends!
Consider, Mother, he's her husband now!
And has been, twenty years! Consider, too (*insidiously*),
You're only second here—you should be first—
Assist the Prince's plan, and when he gains
The Princess Ida's hand, you *will* be first!
You will design the fashions—think of that!
And always serve out all the punishments!
The scheme is harmless, Mother—wink at it

Blanche. The prospect's tempting! Well, well, well,
 I'll try—
Though I've not winked at anything for years!
'Tis but one step towards my destiny—
The mighty Must! Inevitable Shall!

 [Exit LADY BLANCHE.
Melissa. Saved for a while, at least!

Enter FLORIAN.

Flori. Melissa here?
 Melissa. Oh, sir, you must away from this at once,
My Mother guessed your sex—it was my fault;
I blushed and stammered so, that she exclaimed:
" Can these be men ? " (then seeing this) " Why, these——"
" *Are men !* " she would have added, but " *are men* "
Stuck in her throat! She keeps your secret, sir,
For reasons of her own ; but fly from this,
And take me with you—that is—no, not that!
 Flori. I'll go—but not without you. (*Bell.*) Why,
 what's that?
 Melissa. The luncheon bell.
 Flori. I'll wait for luncheon, then.
See, here's Hilarion with the stern Princess,
And Cyril with my sister Psyche, too.

Enter CYRIL *with* PSYCHE, *and* HILARION *with* PRINCESS,
 LADY BLANCHE, *also all the other* GIRLS, *over bridge,
 bearing luncheon, which is spread. They all sit down
 and eat,* CYRIL *drinking freely.*

 Prin. You say you know the Court of Hildebrand?
There is a prince there—I forget his name.
 Hilar. Hilarion?
 Prin. Exactly. Is he well?
 Hilar. If it is well to droop and pine and mope—
To sigh, " Oh, Ida! Ida! " all day long—
" Ida! my love! my life! Oh, come to me! "—
If it is well, I say, to do all this,
Then Prince Hilarion is very well.
 Prin. He breathes *our* name? Well, it's a common
 one!
And is the booby comely?
 Hilar. Pretty well.

I've heard it said that if I dressed myself
In Prince Hilarion's clothes (supposing this
Consorted with my maiden modesty),
I might be taken for Hilarion's self,
But what is this to you or me, who think
Of all mankind with unconcealed contempt?
   Prin. Contempt? Why, damsel, when I think of man,
Contempt is not the word!
   Cyril (getting tipsy).   I'm sure of that;
Or, if it is, it surely should not be!
   Hilar. (to CYRIL). Be quiet, idiot, or they'll find us out!
   Cyril. The Prince Hilarion's a goodly lad!
   Prin. You know him, then?
   Cyril.   I rather think I do!
We were inseparables.
   Prin.   Why, what's this?
You loved him, then? *(horrified).*
   Cyril.   We did—and do—all three!
And he loves us sincerely in return!
   Hilar. (confused). Madam, she jests—*(aside to* CYRIL)
Remember where you are!
   Cyril. Jests? Not at all—why, bless my heart alive,
You and Hilarion, when at the Court,
Rode the same horse!
   Prin.   Astride?
   Cyril.   Of course—why not?
Wore the same clothes—and once or twice, I think,
Got tipsy in the same good company!
   Prin. Well, these are nice young ladies, on my word—
   Cyril (to FLORIAN). Don't you remember that old laugh-
     ing song,
That he and we would troll in unison,
At the Three Pigeons—just when daylight broke?
I'll give it you!

Song, CYRIL; *Air—Laughing Song from "Manon Lescaut."*

   A young and earnest reader,
   Once with a special pleader,
     Was reading for the bar,
       Ha! ha! ha! ha!
   A budding luminary,
   Particularly wary,

As lovers often are,
　　Ha! ha! ha! ha!
He met a lady bright, ha! ha;
'Twas very late at night, ha! ha
　　There shone no moon nor star,
　　Ha! ha! ha! ha!
Her head lay on his shoulder,
And what d'you think he told her?—
　　You'll never guess, I know.
I scarcely like to tell you,
For fear it should repel you—
　　Come, whisper, whisper low!
　　　No! no! no! no! no! no! no! no!
　　　Ha! ha! ha! ha! ha! ha! ha! ha!
They threaded many mazes,
Of buttercups and daisies,
　　They wandered very far,
　　Ha! ha! ha! ha!
So amiable he found her,
He put his arms around her,
　　And she opposed no bar,
　　Ha! ha! ha! ha!
He squeezed her little fin, ha! ha!
He chucked her little chin, ha! ha!
　　And christened her his star,
　　Ha! ha! ha! ha!
Her head lay on his shoulder,
And what d'you think he told her?—
　　You'll never guess, I know.
I'll hazard it and tell you,
Although it may repel you—
　　Come, whisper, whisper low!
　　　No! no! no! no! no! no! no! no!
　　　Ha! ha! ha! ha! ha! ha! ha! ha!

　　　　　(*After song he lights a cigarette.*)

Prin. Infamous creature—get you hence away!
Hilar. Dog! Here is something more to sing about!
　　　　　　　　　　　　(*Strikes him.*)
Cyril (*sobered*). Hilarion—are you mad?
Prin. (*astonished*).　　　　　Hilarion? Help!
Why, these are men! Lost! Lost! betrayed! undone!
　　　　　　　　　　　(*Running on to bridge.*)
Girls get you hence—man-monsters, if you dare

Approach one step—I—ah! (*loses balance and falls*).
Psyche.   Oh! save her, sir!
Blanche. It's useless, sir; you'll only catch your death.
                   (HILARION *springs in.*)

Sacha. He catches her—
Melissa.   And now he lets her go—
Again she's in his grasp—
Psyche.   And now she's not!
He seizes her back hair—
Blanche.   And it comes off!
Psyche. No—no—she's saved! She's saved! She's saved!
     She's saved!
     (HILARION *is seen swimming with the* PRINCESS *in one*
     arm—he swims to a bank and the PRINCESS *and he*
     are brought to land.)
Prin. You've saved our lives and so have saved your
     own,
But leave this palace—men in women's clothes!

         Enter LYDIA, *running.*

Why, what's the matter now?
Lydia.   King Hildebrand,
Holding your father captive, sends to say
That if Hilarion suffers any harm,
Your father's life will pay the penalty;
Moreover—if you do not yield yourself,
According to the tenor of your oath,
He will attack you ere to-morrow's dawn—
And force compliance!
Prin.   Will he so, indeed?
We'll teach these men a lesson. (*To* HILARION.) Get you
     gone!
You saved our lives—we thank you for it—go!
Arm, Amazons! We'll show these gentlemen
How nobly Woman vindicates her claim
To equal individuality!
Arm! Arm! This is our opportunity.

The three GENTLEMEN *are thrust forth by the* AMAZONS.
            Tableau.

SCENE FOURTH.—*Hildebrand's Camp before Ida's Castle.*

Enter HILDEBRAND *and* GAMA.

Hilde. The Princess Ida still holds out, although
Our camp is fairly pitched before her walls.
King Gama, if Hilarion comes not back
All safe and sound, you'll surely suffer death!
Your head for his!
    Gama.   The stakes are poorly matched:
It's Lombard Street against a China orange!
    Hilde. In the mean time, pray make yourself at home.
Direct my army as it were your own.
On every matter that concerns the state,
Your orders give;—they will not be obeyed,
But that don't matter!
    Gama.   Don't it?
    Hilde.   Not a jot!
The ecstasy of absolute command
Is seriously dashed when you reflect,
That for all consequences that ensue,
You by the world are held responsible!
But here, where all are bound to hear your word
With every outward token of respect,
They systematically disobey it,
Your power of high command is just as great,
The consequences absolutely *nil.*

Enter ATHO.

    Atho. My liege, three gentlemen await without,
Attended by a troop of soldiery. (*Gives note.*)
    Gama (*reads*). "The Princes Arac, Guron, Scynthius,
King Gama's sons, desire that you will set
Their father free." (*To* ATHO.) Admit these gentlemen.
                            [*Exit* ATHO
My sons! That's brave!

Enter ARAC, SCYNTHIUS, *and* GURON.

    Hilde.   What would you, gentlemen?
    Arac. What would we? Why, look you, King Hilde-
        brand—

You hold our father in unkingly bonds,
Our sister you beleaguer in her home,
You threaten to lay waste our richest lands,
And then you coolly ask us, " What would we ? "
   Guron. We come to claim our father at your hands.
   Scynthius. We come to save our sister Ida from
The rude assault of savage soldiery.
Why, they are girls—mere girls—and should be stormed
As other girls are stormed, if stormed at all !
   Hilde. As other girls are stormed so shall they be ;
We'll use no cannon, bayonet, or sword,
For such ungentlemanly arguments—
Convincing though they be—would but convince
These women 'gainst their will ! We'll witch them forth
With love songs, odes, and idle fripperies,
Such as a woman cannot long withstand.
Stay, you shall see——

Enter ATHO.

   Atho.   All is prepared, my liege,
To storm the walls——
   Hilde.   Then let the siege commence !

Enter FIRST OFFICER.

Who leads the serenading party, eh ?
   First Officer. Sir Michael Costa.
   Hilde.   Good ! the light guitars
Fall in at six—the King's own baritones,
Led by Sir Santley.
   First Officer.   He's not knighted, sir !
   Hilde. He shall be, then. They will parade at five.
                      [*Exit* FIRST OFFICER.

Enter SECOND OFFICER.

   Second Officer. Who leads the scaling party, sir ?
   Hilde.   Of course
The first light tenors ; they can highest go.
                   [*Exit* SECOND OFFICER.
   Atho. And who shall first climb up the outer wall,
And reconnoitre what goes on within ?
   Hilde. Some tenor, fool, who can " go up to see ! "
                         [*Exit* ATHO.
Let all be furnished with their photographs,

And scatter them among these Amazons.
Bid the director of the poets direct
And post five hundred valentines, and see
They get them by to-night's delivery.
Go, tell the gallant lady, who commands
The horse brigade of royal milliners,
To place five hundred toilet tables out
Within full view of Princess Ida's walls.
Upon them place five hundred mirrors; then
Lay out five hundred robes of French design;
And if they still hold out they're more than women!
   [*Exeunt* OFFICERS, GAMA, ARAC, SCYNTHIUS, *and* GURON.
    King. If all this fails, I have a deadlier scheme:
Five hundred waltzing bachelors—tried men,
Who can waltz forwards—backwards—anyhow—
Shall twirl and twist before their dazzled eyes,
Thrumming soft music on a light guitar.

Song, KING HILDEBRAND; *Air,* "*Largo al Factotum.*"

Like a teetotum with a guitar—
      Just so!
   La, la, la, la!
Bachelors spin at 'em, thus from afar—
      Just so!
   La, la, la, la!
Oh, tickle their vanity;
  Oh, never be chary,
  Oh, flatter your fairy,
  Ever unwary,
    Tickle it, ah!
Bravo bravissimo,
Generalissimo.
    Serve her it, ah!
Flatter her beauty,
With an acute eye,
Say it's your duty,
    Call her a star!
Sneer at another,
Coddle her mother,
Butter her brother,
   Ever so far!
  La, la, la, la!
Load her with frippery,

Glovery, slippery,
Cleverly planned, no going too far !
Marabout feather,
    Gossamer airy,
Fastened together,
    Give to your fairy.
      La, la, la, la !
Oh, tickle her vanity,
    Oh, never be chary,
    Oh, flatter your fairy,
    Ever unwary,
      Tickle it, ah !
Marry her merrily,
Change it all, verily ;
Snapping and wrangling,
Jingling and jangling,
Snarling and snapping,
Rubbing and rapping.
" Why are you mum to me ?
" Why don't you come to me ?
" Why are you mum to me ?
" Why don't you come to me ?
" Quicker, oh ! quicker, oh ! quicker, oh ! "
My goodness ! my gracious !
    A row, sir !
Pucker your brow, sir,
    Pucker it, ah !
    Pucker it, ah !
Lick her, oh, no more !
Quicker, oh, " The door ! "
    Set it ajar !
    Light a cigar !
    Set it ajar !
    Light a cigar !
    Give her a sou !
    Bid her adoo !
    Give her a sou !
    Bid her adoo !
Bravo bravissimo,
Finish your capering.
Like a teetotum
    With a guitar !
    With a guitar !
    With a guitar !

M

Bravo bravissimo,
Generalissimo!
Take her and marry her
Worry her, harry her;
Oh, you may carry her
Ever so far!
Just like a teetotum
With a guitar!

Enter ATHO.

Atho. My liege, I bring good news: your plan succeeds.
Three ladies of the Princess Ida's band
Are coming towards your camp.
    Hilde.   The mirrors did it!
Admit them.

Enter HILARION, CYRIL, *and* FLORIAN, *still in women's clothes.*

    Why—Hilarion! Cyril too!
And Florian! dressed as women. Ho! ho! ho!
                      (All jeer them.)
    Hilar. We gained admission to fair Ida's halls
By this disguise. We were detected, though.
And should have suffered death, but that she knew,
In killing us, she killed her father too!
    Gama (in high glee). Here, set me free! Hilarion safe
    again—
Is this indeed Hilarion?
    Hilar.   Yes, it is.
    Gama. Why, you look handsome in your women's
    clothes.
Stick to 'em—man's attire becomes you not!
(To FLORIAN *and* CYRIL.) And you, young ladies, will you
    please to pray
King Hildebrand to set me free again?
Hang on his neck and gaze into his eyes,
Bring all your woman's wiles to bear on him.
He never could resist a pretty face!
    Cyril. You dog! Though I wear woman's garb, you'll
    find
My sword is long and sharp.
    Gama.   Hush, pretty one

Here's a virago!   Here's a termagant!
If length and sharpness go for anything,
You'll want no sword while you can wag your tongue.
   Flori. What need to talk of swords to such as he?
He's old and crippled.   (*To* GAMA.)   Oh, if you were
      young,
And tolerably straight—and I could catch
You all alone, I'd—Ah!
   Gama (*bashfully*).   Oh, go along,
You naughty girl—why, I'm a married man!
But I've three sons—see, ladies—here they are—
Fine fellows—young and muscular and brave.
They'll meet you, if you will.   Come, what d'ye say?
   Arac. Ay, pretty ones, engage yourselves with us,
If three rude warriors who have spent their lives
Hacking at enemies, affright you not!
   Hilar. (*to* GAMA).   Old as you are, I'd wring your
      shrivelled neck
If you were not the Princess Ida's father.
   Gama. If I were not the Princess Ida's father,
And so had not her brothers for my sons,
No doubt you'd wring my neck—in safety too!
   Hilar. Enough! I speak for Florian and Cyril.
Arac, we take your challenge—three to three—
So that it's understood that Ida's hand
Depends upon the issue.
   Arac.   There's my hand;
If she consents not—sister though she be
We'll raze her castle to the very ground!

                         [*Exeunt.*

SCENE FIFTH.—*Inner Gate of Castle Adamant.*

All the LADY STUDENTS *discovered—the eight* SERVANTS *as
Amazons—the others all around.   Flourish—Enter*
PRINCESS IDA, *followed by* LADY BLANCHE.

   Prin. Is all prepared for war?   We have to meet
Stern bearded warriors in fight to-day.
Wear nought but what is necessary to
Preserve your dignity before their eyes,
And give your limbs full play.
   Blanche.   One moment, ma'am:

Here is a paradox we should not pass
Without inquiry.   We are prone to say,
"This thing is Needful—that Superfluous
Yet they invariably co-exist!
We find the Needful comprehended in
The circle of the grand Superfluous;
While the Superfluous cannot be bought
Unless you're amply furnished with the Needful
These singular considerations are——

  Prin. Superfluous, yet not Needful—so, you see,
These terms may independently exist.
Women of Adamant, we have to show
These men how they have underrated us.
Now is the time to prove our titles to
The highest honours they monopolize.
Now is the time to prove our theory
That woman, educated to the work,
Can meet man face to face on his own ground,
And beat him there.   Now let us set to work!
Where is our lady surgeon?

  Sacha.   Madam, here!

  Prin. We shall require your skill to heal the wounds
Of those that fall.

  Sacha.   What! heal the wounded?

  Prin.   Yes!

  Sacha. And cut off real live legs and arms?

  Prin.   Of course!

  Sacha. I wouldn't do it for a thousand pounds!

  Prin. Why, how is this?   Are you faint-hearted,
   girl?
You've often cut them off in theory.

  Sacha. In theory I'll cut them off again
With pleasure, and as often as you like—
But not in practice!

  Prin.   Coward, get you hence!
I've craft enough for that, and courage too.
I'll do your work!   My Amazons, advance!
Why, you are armed with spears—mere gilded toys!
Where are your muskets, pray?

  Ada.   Why, please you, ma'am,
We left them in the armoury, for fear
That, in the heat and turmoil of the fight,
They might go off.

  Prin.   "They might!"   Oh, craven souls,

Go off yourselves!   Thank Heaven, I have a heart
That quails not at the thought of meeting men.
I will discharge your muskets.   Off with you!
Where's my bandmistress?
    Chloe.   Please you, ma'am, the band
Do not feel well, and can't come out to-day!
    Prin. Why, this is flat rebellion!   I've no time
To talk to them just now!   But happily
I can play several instruments at once,
And I will drown the shrieks of those that fall
With trumpet music such as soldiers love.
How stand we with respect to gunpowder?
My Lady Psyche—you who superintend
The lab'ratory, where your class compounds
That hideous chemical—are you prepared
To blow these bearded rascals into shreds?
    Psyche. Why, madam——
    Prin.   Well?
    Psyche.   Let us try gentler means—
Treat them with the contempt that they deserve.
We can dispense with fulminating grains,
While we have eyes with which to flash our rage.
We can dispense with villainous saltpetre,
While we have tongues with which to blow them up.
We can dispense, in short, with all the arts
That brutalize the practical polemist.
    Prin. (*contemptuously*).   I never knew a more dispensing
        chemist!
Away! away!   I'll meet these men alone,
For all my women have deserted me!

Enter MELISSA.

    Melissa. Madam, your brothers crave an audience.
    Prin. My brothers?   Why, what do they here?
    Melissa.   They come
To fight for you.
    Prin.   Admit them!
    Blanche.   Infamous!
One's brothers, ma'am, are men!
    Prin.   So I have heard;
But all my women seem to fail me when
I need them most: in this perplexity
Even one's brothers may be turned to use.

Enter Arac, Guron, *and* Scynthius.

Arac. My sisters!
Prin.   Arac, Guron, Scynthius, too!
                       (*They embrace.*)
  Arac. We have arranged that Prince Hilarion
And his two followers shall fight us here;
And if we fall, we've promised him your hand.
  Prin. (*sighing*). So be it, Arac; brothers though you be,
With all your faults you're brave, as brutes are brave.
So be it—fight them here, but (*aside and bashfully*) oh,
       my brother,
Kill whom you will, but spare Hilarion!
He saved my life!
  Melissa (*aside to* Arac). Oh, save me Florian,
He is her brother! (*indicating* Psyche).
  Psyche (*aside to* Arac). Oh, spare Cyril, sir,
You've no idea what jolly songs he sings!
  Arac. Bah! I can spare them all—I want them not!
But here they come: stand back, the lists prepare—
Get you within those walls, poor trembling ones.
And see that no one interferes with us.

Enter Hilarion, Cyril, *and* Florian, *with* Kings Gama
     and Hildebrand—Princess *and* Ladies *retire within*
     outer wall, and group themselves on battlements.

  Gama. Come, boys, we've all prepared; begin! begin!
Why, you lack mettle!—Gad, I'll spur you up!
(*To* Arac.) Look, Arac—there's the son of that vile king,
Who, when he held me as his prisoner,
Tormented me with tortures worse than death.
I hadn't anything to grumble at!
He found out what particular meats I loved,
And gave me them—the very choicest wine—
The costliest robes—the richest rooms were mine.
He suffered none to thwart my simplest plan,
And gave strict orders none should contradict me
He made my life a curse! Go in at them!
Avenge your father's wrongs! (*To* Hilarion.) And as
     for you——
(*Pointing to his sons*) Here are three princes, sirs, who
     stand between

You and your happiness—so cut them down!
Give them no mercy, they will give you none
Come, Prince Hilarion, begin, begin!
You've this advantage over warriors
Who kill their country's enemies for pay,
You know what you are fighting for—look there!
　　　　(*Pointing to* LADIES *on battlements.*)

Hilar. Come on!
Arac.　　　　　Come on!
Cyril.　　　　　　　Come on!
Scyn.　　　　　　　　　Come on!
Flori.　　　　　　　　　　　Come on!

　　(*Desperate fight—at the end,* HILARION, CYRIL, *and*
　　FLORIAN *wound* ARAC, GURON, *and* SCYNTHIUS.

Prin. (*entering through gate*). Hold! stay your hands!
—we yield ourselves to you.
Ladies, my brothers all lie bleeding there!
Bind up their wounds—but look the other way.
Is this the end? How say you, Lady Blanche—
Can I with dignity my post resign?
And if I do, will you then take my place?
　Blanche. To answer this, it's meet that we consult
The great Potential Mysteries; I mean
The five Subjunctive Possibilities—
The May, the Might, the Would, the Could, the Should.
Can you resign? The Prince Might claim you; if
He Might, you Could—and if you Should, I Would!
　Prin. I thought as much. Then to my fate I yield—
So ends my cherished scheme! Oh, I had hoped
To band all women with my maiden throng,
And make them all abjure tyrannic Man.
　Hilde. A noble aim!
　Prin.　　　　　　You ridicule it now;
But if I carried out this glorious scheme,
At my exalted name Posterity
Would bow in gratitude!
　Hilde.　　　　　But pray reflect—
If you enlist all women in your cause,
And make them all abjure tyrannic Man,
The obvious question then arises, " How
Is this Posterity to be provided?"
　Prin. I never thought of that! My Lady Blanche,
How do you solve the riddle?

Blanche.   Don't ask me—
Abstract Philosophy won't answer it.
Take him—he is your Shall.   Give in to Fate!
  Prin. And *you* desert me! I alone am staunch!
  Hilar. Madam, you placed your trust in woman—well,
Woman has failed you utterly—try man,
Give him one chance, it's only fair—besides,
Women are far too precious, too divine
To try unproven theories upon.
Experiments, the proverb says, are made
On humble subjects—try our grosser clay,
And mould it as you will!
  Cyril.   Remember, too,
Dear Madam, if at any time you feel
Aweary of the Prince, you can return
To Castle Adamant, and rule your girls
As heretofore, you know.
  Prin.   And shall I find
The Lady Psyche here?
  Psyche.   If Cyril, ma'am,
Does not behave himself, I think you will.
  Prin. And you, Melissa, shall I find you here?
  Melissa. Madam, however Florian turns out,
Unhesitatingly I answer, No.
  Gama. Consider this, my love: if your mamma
Had looked on matters from your point of view
(I wish she had), why, where would you have been?
  Lady B. There's an unbounded field of speculation,
On which I could discourse for hours!
  Prin.   No doubt!
We will not trouble you.   Hilarion,
I have been wrong—I see my error now.
Take me, Hilarion—" We will walk the world
Yoked in all exercise of noble end!
And so through those dark gates across the wild
That no man knows! Indeed, I love thee—Come!"

Finale, from " Le Pont des Soupirs."

Cyril.   Singers know
         How sweetly at a piano
         A tenor and soprano
            Together sound.
Chorus.   Singers know, etc.

Hilar.　　This will show
　　That men and women verily
　　Can get along more merrily
　　　Together bound.

Chorus.　　This will show
　　That men and women verily
　　Can get along more merrily
　　　Together bound!
　　　Together bound!
　　　Together bound!

THE PALACE OF TRUTH.

A FAIRY COMEDY.

IN THREE ACTS.

DRAMATIS PERSONÆ.

KING PHANOR	...	...	...	...	MR. BUCKSTONE.
PRINCE PHILAMIR		...	...	...	MR. KENDAL.
CHRYSAL	...	...	...	...	MR. EVERILL.
ZORAM	...	...	...	...	MR. CLARK.
ARISTÆUS	...	...	...	...	MR. ROGERS.
GÉLANOR	...	...	...	...	MR. BRAID.
QUEEN ALTEMIRE	...	...	...	..	MRS. CHIPPENDALE.
PRINCESS ZEOLIDE		...	...	...	MISS MADGE ROBERTSON.
MIRZA	...	...	...	...	MISS CAROLINE HILL.
PALMIS	...	...	...	...	MISS FANNY WRIGHT.
AZÈMA	...	...	...	...	MISS FANNY GWYNNE.

ACT I.

GARDENS OF KING PHANOR'S COUNTRY HOUSE.

MORNING.

ACT II.

INTERIOR OF THE PALACE OF TRUTH.

NOON.

ACT III.

THE AVENUE OF PALMS.

NIGHT.

[The action of the piece takes place within the space of twenty-four hours.]

THE PALACE OF TRUTH.

ACT I.

SCENE.—*Garden of* KING PHANOR'S *Country House.* KING PHANOR *discovered with* CHRYSAL, ZORAM, ARISTÆUS, *ana* PALMIS. ARISTÆUS *is standing sulkily apart.*

As the curtain rises, KING PHANOR *is finishing a recitation which he is accompanying on a mandolin, in a very affected manner.*

Phanor. "Oh, I would not—no, I would *not* be there!"
    (ZORAM *and* CHRYSAL *applaud vigorously.*)
Chrysal. My lord, I pray you read it once again,
My ears are greedy for the golden sound.
Phan. Chrysal, you make me blush!
Chrys.   My lord, a blush
Is modesty's sole herald—and true worth
Is ever modest.   Pray you, sir, again!
Phan. It's a poor thing—a string of platitudes—
Stale metaphors—time-honoured similes.
I'm a poor poet, gentlemen!
Chrys.   I swear
There never lived a poet till now!
Zoram.   And then
The music you have wedded to the words
(I speak of this with some authority)
Shames, in its flow of rhythmic melody,
The counterpoint of Adam de la Halle!
Phan. (*bashfully*). The merit is not altogether mine.
I wrote the music—but I did not make
This dainty instrument.   Why, who could fail
To charm, with such a mandolin as this?
Zor. Believe me, the result would be the same,
Whether your lordship chose to play upon

The simple tetrachord of Mercury
That knew no diatonic intervals,
Or the elaborate dis-diapason
(Four tetrachords, and one redundant note),
Embracing in its perfect consonance
All simple, double and inverted chords!
 Phan. (*to* CHRYSAL). A wonderful musician—and a man
Of infinite good taste!
 Zor.   Why, from my birth
I have made melope and counterpoint
My favourite study.
 Phan.   And you really care
To hear my work again, O melodist?
 Zor. Again, my lord, and, even then again!
 Phan. (*recites*). "When pitch-encrusted night aloft
   prevails;
" When no still goddess through the mid-air sails;
" When scorpions vomit forth their poisonous scum;
" When to the demon tryst gaunt witches come;
" When noisome pestilence stalks through the glen,
" Bellowing forth its enmity to men;
" When ghastly toads scream loudly through the air;
" Oh, I would not—no, I would *not* be there!"
 Chrys. (*in raptures*). Why, where's the cunning of the
   sorcerer
Placed by the magic of such words as these?
" *When pitch-encrusted night aloft prevails;* "
Why, there's an epithet might make day night,
And shame the swallows to their couching place!
" *When no still goddess through the mid-air sails!* "
Why, here's a blackness, Zoram, so intense
It scares the very deities away!
 Phan. (*explaining*). "Still goddess" means the moon.
 Chrys.   The moon—my lord?
Of course—the moon! See how, in ignorance,
We seek upon the surface of the wave
For pearls that lie uncounted fathoms deep.
The darkness frightens e'en the moon away!
The metaphor is perfect!
 Phan. (*annoyed*).   No, no, no!
The moon has not yet risen, sir! The moon
Frightens the darkness—darkness don't fright *her*!
Why sits the genial Aristæus there
All solitary? How d'you like my work?

(*Aside to* CHRYSAL.) We'll have some fun with him.
    (*Aloud.*) Your verdict, come!
  Arist. I'm blunt and honest. I can't teach my tongue
To lie, as Zoram here, and Chrysal do.
I tell the truth, sir. If you want to know
My estimate of what you've given us,
I think your poetry contemptible—
Your melody, my lord, beneath contempt.
  Phan. That's rather strong.
  Arist.   It's strong, my lord, but true.
I'm blunt—outspoken. If I've angered you,
So much the worse; I always speak the truth.
  Chrys. Heed not the yelping of this surly cur;
Nought satisfies him, Phanor!
  Arist.   There you're wrong,
For I was satisfied to hear it once;
'Twas you that wanted it a second time!
  Chrys. Back to your kennel, sham Diogenes!
  Arist. I'm no Diogenes. *He* spent his life
Seeking an honest man. *I* live in courts.
  Zor. My lord, I pray you send the fellow hence,
For he and we are always out of tune.
An inharmonious bracketing of notes,
Whose musical extremes don't coalesce:
He's sharp and we are flat.
  Arist.   Extremely flat!
  Chrys. He's vinegar, my lord, and we are oil.
  Arist. Oil is a sickening insipid food
Unless it's qualified with vinegar.
I'm rough and honest. If I've angered you,
I'll go.
  Phan. No, no, you have not angered us.
(*Aside to* ZORAM) I like the fellow's humour—he may
    rave!
I'm tired of hearing truths, so let him lie!
But where's Queen Altemire?
  Chrys.   My lord, she comes—
A perfect type of perfect womanhood.
The dew of forty summers on her head
Has but matured her beauty, by my life!
For five and thirty years, a bud—and now
A rose full blown!
  Arist.   Say over-blown.
  Phan.   What's that?

Arist. My lord, the Queen's too fat.
Phan.   Well, that may be.
But don't you tell her so.   Your insolence
Amuses me—it won't amuse the Queen :
She has no sense of humour.   So take care.
   Arist. My lord, I'm rough, but honest.   I've a tongue
That cannot frame a lie.
   Phan.   But bear in mind
Besides that very rough and honest tongue,
You have a palate, and a set of teeth,
And several delicate contrivances
That aid digestion.   Tell her she's too fat,
And she may take offence ; and, if she does,
She'll throw that apparatus out of work :
That's all.

               Enter the QUEEN *and* MIRZA.

               Good morning, Altemire, my queen.
Why, you seem sad.
   Altem.   My lord, I'm very sad.
   Palmis. The Queen is sad !   Zoram, attune your lyre
And soothe her melancholy.
   Altem.   No, no, no—
I'm not in cue for music—leave us, pray—
I would take counsel with my lord—look, sirs,
I am not well.   [*The three* COURTIERS *exeunt into house.*
   Phan. (aside to PALMIS). Palmis, what's here amiss ?
What causes this ?   Have *I* done anything ?
   Palmis. I know not, but I think it bears upon
Your daughter's troth to brave Prince Philamir.
Whenever we have spoken on the point
She has commanded silence.
   Phan.   Well, we'll see.
Chrysal awaits you—you may go to him ;
Talk to him of your pledge to marry *him*,
And he'll not silence you.   There, you may go.
                        [*Exit* PALMIS *into house.*
Now what's the matter ?
   Altem.   Oh, I'm sick at heart
With apprehension !   Our dear Zeolide
To-morrow is betrothed to Philamir,
The bravest and the most accomplished Prince
In Christendom.   Phanor, she loves him not !
   Phan. What makes you think so ?

Altem. Phanor, you are blind !
Why, see how coldly Zeolide receives'
His songs of love—his bursts of metaphor:
" I love you, Philamir," and there's an end.
She will vouchsafe her spouse-elect no more—
No tenderness—no reciprocity ;
A cold, half-sullen and half-wayward smile,
And that is all. The maiden lavishes
More love upon her horse !
    Phan. Perhaps she thinks
Her horse will bear such tokens of regard
With more discretion than her lover would !
    Altem. Phanor, I tell you she loves him not.
I am a woman, with a woman's tact.
    Phan. She *says* she loves him.
    Altem. So indeed she says,
And says no more. Phanor, had I been woo'd
With ardent songs of overwhelming love,
Framed by so fair a poet as Philamir,
It would have turned my giddy woman's brain,
And thrilled my reason to its very core !
    Phan. I never thought my wooing poetry,
Now I begin to think it may have been.
    Mirza. Oh, sir, *I* love the Princess. Pause before
You sacrifice her earthly happiness
For sordid ends of selfish policy.
The Prince is rich. What then? The girl is poor.
But what is wealth of gold to wealth of love ?
What famine's so deplorable as his
Who hungers for a love he cannot find ?
What luxury so wearisome as hers
Who's surfeited with love she values not?
King Phanor, let the Princess be released !
    Altem. My lady Mirza, you forget yourself !
    Mirza. I do forget myself, rememb'ring her;
I have her happiness at heart. The maid
Is more than life to me. Forgive me, Queen.
I could not help but speak.
    Phan. Well, say no more.
I'll question her, and if it then appears
She loves not Philamir, she shall be free.
I also love the girl—but, here she comes.
I'll find some test which shall decide the point.
        [*Exit* PHANOR *into house.*

N

Enter ZEOLIDE.

Altem. My daughter, where's the Prince?
Zeo.   I cannot say;
I saw his highness yesterday, but since
Have not set eyes on him.
Altem.   Has he returned
From hunting?
Zeo.   Yes, I heard the Prince's voice
Not half an hour ago.
Altem.   And, in return,
You made no sign to him?
Zeo.   No sign, indeed.
I heard his song—'twas very sweetly sung:
It told of love—it called for no reply.
Altem. A song of love that called for no reply?
Zeo. It asked no question, mother.
Altem.   Surely, girl,
There may be questions that are not expressed.
Zeo. And answers, mother—mine was one of them!
Altem. Come, Zeolide, I've much to say to you.
Renounce Prince Philamir ere 'tis too late!
He will release you; he is proud and brave,
And would not force a hated life on you.
Come, Zeolide, throw off this weary bond.
And marry whom you love, or marry none!
Zeo. As I am bound, dear mother, I'll remain,
So let me stay with Mirza.
Altem. (annoyed).   You can stay!
[*Exit* QUEEN ALTEMIRE *into house, glancing angrily at*
    MIRZA; ZEOLIDE *notices this with some surprise.*
Zeo. Why, Mirza, how my mother frowns at you!
How have you angered her?
Mirza.   I love you well;
And when I told her of my sister-love,
In words more passionate than politic,
The Queen rebuked me sternly.
Zeo.   Oh, for shame!
Mirza. She is your mother, and she claims your love,
And cannot brook that I should share that love.
I can forgive the noble jealousy
That comes of woman's love for woman.
Zeo.   Yes

For you are Mirza—queen of womankind—
The best, the noblest woman in the world !
   Mirza. Why, here is warmth ! and people call you cold,
Because you are so cold to Philamiir.
   Zeo. Why, Mirza, he's a man !

Enter PHILAMIR *from house—he overhears* MIRZA.

   Mirza.   A man indeed!
The bravest warrior that wields a sword ;
The rarest poet that ever penned a lay ;
An admirable knight—gay, handsome, young,
Brave, wealthy, and accomplished—with a tongue
Might shame a siren's !
   Zeo.   Hush ! a siren's tongue
Is not renowned for much sincerity.
   Mirza. He is sincere.
   Zeo.   Indeed, I hope he is !
   Phil. (coming forward). I thank you, Lady Mirza, for
     those words.
   Mirza (coldly). I little thought that they were over-
     heard.
This is ungenerous, Prince Philamir.
   [*Bows coldly and exit ;* PHILAMIR *rushes to* ZEOLIDE,
     who receives him very quietly.
   Phil. Dear Zeolide, at last we are alone !
Oh, I have longed for this !
   Zeo.   Indeed ! And why ?
   Phil. And why ? We can converse without reserve.
   Zeo. What should I say when we are quite alone
That I should leave unsaid were others here ?
I can but say, "I love you," Philamir.
   Phil. And is that all ?
   Zeo.   And is not that enough ?
   Phil. All the world knows you love me !
   Zeo.   That is why
I do not blush to own it in the world.
   Phil. But give me more—*I* love *you,* Zeolide,
As the earth loves the sun !
   Zeo.   The earth is glad
To see the sun, and asks no more than that.
You would do well to imitate the earth.
   Phil. I am content to imitate the earth—
I am content to sit and gaze at you,

Tranced in a lazy glow of happiness;
But if you speak and wake me from that trance,
Wake me, dear Zeolide, with warmer words.
" I love you!" Why, I know you love me well!
Say nothing, Zeolide, and I'm content.
If you say anything, say more than that!

 Zeo. What words could I employ which, tested in
The crucible of unimpassioned truth,
Would not resolve themselves into those three?
Now I must go—your sun's about to set—
So farewell earth!

 Phil.   And when the sun is down
The earth is inconsolable!

 Zeo.   Until
The moon appears! Perhaps there is a moon
That fills my place until I rise again?

 Phil. No more, dear Zeolide; or, if there be,
She floats in one perpetual eclipse!

 Zeo. The moon is not the less a moon because
The earth thinks fit to hide her from the sun!

 Phil. Nay; you pursue the metaphor too far.
If I, the earth, conceal a nightly moon,
Why, you, the sun, have many worlds to warm,
And some are nearer to you than this earth!

 Zeo. Hush, Philamir! I'm ready to believe
That you're an earth that knows no moon at all,
If you'll allow that I, although a sun,
Consent to warm no other world than this!

      (*Kissing his forehead, and going.*)
 Phil. Oh, do not leave me thus, dear Zeolide.
I am a beggar, begging charity;
Throw me more coin that bears the stamp of love!

 Zeo. I have one coin that bears that holy stamp—
I give you that—I have no more to give.

 Phil. Tell me its value, then, in words of love!

 Zeo. What! would you have me advertise my alms,
And trumpet forth my largess to the world?

 Phil. Not to the world, dear Zeolide—to me!

 Zeo. Ah, you would have me say, " *You* are my world!"
You see, I have the trick of ardent speech,
And I could use it, were I so disposed.
But surely, Philamir, the mendicant
Who is not satisfied to take my alms
Until he knows how much that alms be worth,

Can scarcely stand in need of alms at all!
I love you, Philamir—be satisfied.
Whose vows are made so earnestly as hers
Who would deceive you by her earnestness?
Why, if I sought to trick you, Philamir,
I should select such phrases for my end—
So passionate—and yet so delicate,
So fierce—from overflow of gentle love,
So furious—from excess of tenderness,
That even your expressions of regard,
Unbounded in their hot extravagance,
Would pale before the fury of *my* words,
And you, from very shame, would call them back,
And beg my pardon for their want of warmth!
I love you, Philamir—I'll say no more!   [*Exit.*
    Phil. Gone! But I'll follow her——(*going*).

Enter PHANOR *from house.*

Phan.   Stop, Philamir,
If, as she says, she loves you, well and good;
She'll give you proof of it in her good time;
But if she don't, why, take an old boy's word
(Who speaks of love with some authority),
She'll love you none the better for the warmth
That prompts you to perpetual persecution.
The girl has taken this road—take you that.
    [PHILAMIR *stands irresolute, then goes off slowly in the*
        direction indicated.
That's good advice!

Enter QUEEN ALTEMIRE *from house.*

Altem.   My lord, old Gélanor,
The steward of your palace, has arrived
And waits without.
    Phan.   We'll see him presently.
    Altem. (*with some hesitation*). Now, do you know, I
        often wonder why,
Possessing such a palace, furnished with
The rarest luxuries that wealth can buy,
You hold your Court in this secluded place?
I have been married to you eighteen years,
Yet I have never seen this palace, which

Stands barely twenty miles away, and which
You visit regularly once a month.
    Phan. (rather confused). There are good reasons,
    Altemire.
    Altem. (angry). No doubt!
Exceedingly good reasons! When a man
Maintains a bachelor establishment,
He has the best of reasons to decline
To take his wife there!
    Phan.   You're a jealous fool.
    Altem. Jealous I am, and possibly a fool,
But not a fool for being jealous.
    Phan.   Peace,
And I will tell you why I take you not.
That palace is enchanted. Every one
Who enters there is bound to speak the truth—
The simple, unadulterated truth.
To every question that is put to him
He must return the unaffected truth.
And, strange to say, while publishing the truth
He's no idea that he is doing so;
And while he lets innumerable cats
Out of unnumbered bags, he quite believes
That all the while he's tightening the strings
That keep them from a too censorious world.
What do you say to that?
    Altem. (amazed).   Say? Would the world
Were one such palace, Phanor!
    Phan.   If it were,
At least we all should meet on equal terms;
But to be taken from a world in which
That influence don't exist, and to be placed
Inside a fairy palace where it does
(Accompanied, moreover, by one's wife),
Might take one at a disadvantage!
    Altem.   Well
I am prepared to undergo the test
If you'll accompany me.
    Phan.   No, no, no!
You are a worthy woman, Altemire,
But, Altemire, you have your faults!
    Altem.   My lord,
I am a woman!
    Phan.   Yes, exactly so!

If you were *not* a woman, Altemire,
Or, being one, were some one else's wife,
I'd take you there to-morrow!
 Altem.   But, my lord,
Why won't you take me, being what I am?
 Phan. Because, my wife, I don't know what you are.
 Altem. You know, at least, that I'm a faithful wife.
 Phan. I think you're more than faithful. I believe
You are a perfect woman, Altemire,
A pattern as a mother and a wife—
And, so believing, why, I do not care
To run the risk of being undeceived!
 Altem. (annoyed). My lord, you are unjust! Can you
  believe
I should expose myself to such a test
Had I been guilty of unfaithfulness?
I am no perfect woman, Phanor. I have faults
That advertise themselves. No need to say
That I'm quick-tempered, jealous, over-prone
To underrate the worth of womankind—
Impetuous—unreasonable—vain—
I am a woman, with a woman's faults.
But, being woman, Phanor, I'm a wife;
And, in that I am one, I need not blush.
You have some better reason. Possibly
You dread the palace on your own account?
 Phan. I dread the palace, Altemire? No. no.
I am a child of impulse. All my faults
Lie on the surface. I have nought to hide.
Such little faults as sully me you know.
 Altem. Or guess.
 Phan.   Ha! Am I then to understand
My Queen suspects her husband?
 Altem.   Yes, you are!
 Phan. Then this decides me. You *shall* go with me.
 Altem. But——
 Phan.   Not a word—King Phanor cannot brook
The breath of jealousy. With all his faults,
His married life has been as pure as snow.
We two will go this morning.
 Altem.   Stay! A thought
Let us take Zeolide and Philamir,
They shall not know the fairy influence
To which they are subjected. If the maid

Does not love Philamir, she'll show it then,
And the betrothal can be cancelled.   If
She loves him, why, she'll show it all the more:
Then the betrothal shall be ratified.

 Phan. We *will* take Zeolide and Philamir,
Chrysal and Zoram—Aristæus too,
And Palmis—yes, and blameless Lady Mirza—
Mirza, the good, the beautiful, the pure!

 Altem. Mirza!   Eternal Mirza!   Everywhere
I hear her irritating virtues praised!
I'm weary of the woman!

 Phan.   Stop a bit,
Till we are in the palace.   Then we'll learn
Not only your opinion of her worth,
But also why you hold it.

 Altem.   Well, well, well!
The maid is young and beautiful, and I
Am envious of that youth and beauty.   See.
I can anticipate the influence
To which I'm going to subject myself.
There I was wrong.   Mirza *shall* go with us,
And by her conduct under such a test,
Prove the injustice of my estimate.
I'll go and warn the Court.

      [*Exit* QUEEN ALTEMIRE *into house.*

 Phan.   The course I take
Is rather rash, but the experiment
Will not be destitute of interest.

    Enter GÉLANOR *from house.*

Well, Gélanor, what tidings do you bring?
About our palace?

 Gélan.   Sir, the old, old tale.
Men come and go—and women come and go.
Although the palace gates are opened wide
To rich and poor alike—and rich and poor
Alike receive full hospitality
For any length of time they care to stay,
Few care to stay above a day or two.
Free entertainment in a princely home
Is little valued when it's coupled with
The disadvantage of a dwelling-place
Where every one is bound to speak the truth.

When does my lord propose to start ?
Phan.   To-day.
But this time not alone, good Gélanor.
   Gélan. And who is to accompany you, sir?
   Phan. My wife.
   Gélan.   Your wife?
   Phan.   My wife.
   Gélan.   Great heavens, my lord,
Have you reflected ?
   Phan.   Yes.
   Gélan.   To any place
Where one is bound to speak the baldest truth
Concerning all the actions of one's life,
It's hardly politic to take one's wife!
   Phan. Oh, I've the fullest confidence in her.
She's a good woman, Gélanor.
   Gélan.   Ah, sir,
I have seen married couples, by the score,
Who, when they passed within our crystal walls,
Have boldly advertised themselves prepared
To stake their souls upon each other's faith—
But who, before they've spent an hour at most
Under the castle's mystic influence,
Have separated ne'er to meet again !
Oh, have a care !
   Phan.   Queen Altemire knows all,
And knowing all, she fears not for herself,
So I've no fear for her !
   Gélan.   But *you*, my liege—
How will *you* bear yourself 'neath such a test?
You have been married nearly eighteen years:
That's a long time !

Enter MIRZA, *unobserved.*

   Phan.   Well, yes—I've thought of that.
I'm a good husband—as good husbands go.
I love my wife—but still—you understand—
Boys will be boys ! There *is* a point or two—
Say two, as being nearer to the mark—
On which I do not altogether care
To stand examination by my wife.
Perhaps I may have given out that I've
Been dining *here*—when I've been dining *there*—

I may have said " with A "—when 'twas with B—
I may have said " with *him* "—when 'twas with *her*—
Distinctions such as these, good Gélanor,
Though strangely unimportant in themselves,
Still have a value, which the female mind's
Particularly quick to apprehend.
Now here's a talisman—a crystal box—*(producing it)*.
Whoever carries this within those walls
May overcome the castle's influence,
And utter truth or falsehood as he wills.
I should do well, I think, to take this box?
   Gélan. From all accounts, my lord, I think you would!
(Sees Mirza.) Ahem! We are observed!
   Mirza.   My lord, I trust
My presence here is not inopportune?
I will withdraw.
   Phan.   No, Lady Mirza, no!
I was exhibiting to Gélanor
A curious specimen of crystal work—
He understands such things.
   Mirza (taking box).   And so do I.
How marvellously pure! No single flaw
Affects its exquisite transparency!
A perfect emblem of a spotless life!
   Gélan. But, Lady Mirza, perfect spotlessness
Is apt to smack of insipidity.
   Mirza. No—hold it to the light, and see the change!
See how its exquisite prismatic hues,
Under the influence of searching light,
Are instantly made clear and manifest.
As shines this crystal in the sun, so shines
A perfect woman in the light of truth.
The modest beauties of a spotless life
Remain unknown and unsuspected, till
A ray of truth-light starts them into life,
And shows them—all unwilling—to the world!
   Gélan. But there are hidden qualities of soul
That even truth cannot detect. Suppose
This crystal, peerless in its spotlessness,
Turned out to be a potent talisman,
With power to work all kinds of devilry?
There are such things!
   Phan. (aside).   Why, there are women, too
(I have known many such), to whom the box

Might still be very properly compared!

Mirza. Impossible, my lord. I'll not believe
That aught so beautiful could be so base.
(*Returning it.*) I thank you, sir. I've read a lesson here
That I shall take good heed to profit by.

Enter the QUEEN ALTEMIRE, *with* ZEOLIDE, PHANOR,
ARISTÆUS, ZORAM, *and* PALMIS, *from house.*

Altem. Here comes your Court, my lord.
Phan. That's well. My friends,
I have a palace, twenty miles away—
A lovely place, engirt with crystal walls;
Its grounds will show fair flowers and shady groves,
Huge forest trees, rare fountains, hill and dale.
There's hunting, fishing—eighteen years preserved!
There the sun shines unclouded all day long.
What say you—will you go?
Chrys. Go? What care I
Whether it rain or shine so that I may
Bask in the sunshine of my King and Queen!
Phan. In half an hour we start. Once there, our life
Shall be a song, and Aristæus here,
The jolly, genial, laughing Aristæus,
Shall strike the key-note!
Arist. Well, I'll do my best.
Zor. But pray consider. If the intervals
Throughout the diatonic series, sir,
Were mathematically equal, why,
It would not greatly matter, as you know,
Upon what note your melody commenced.
But as it is not so, we must respect
The intervals the melody demands.
No key-note struck by Aristæus could
Be correspondent with those intervals!
Phil. I'll give the key-note. We will pass the day
By quivering willows at the waterside,
Lapped in a lazy luxury of love!
There we'll forget the world of work-a-day,
And crown our happiness with songs of love
What say you, dearest Zeolide?
Zeo. I've said
As much as it is maidenly to say—
I love you, Philamir—be satisfied!

ACT II.

SCENE.—*Interior of the Palace of Truth.*

Enter GÉLANOR, *meeting* KING PHANOR *and* QUEEN
ALTEMIRE *and* ZEOLIDE.

Gélan. Welcome, my lord! Madam, I humbly trust
The palace realizes all the hopes
That you had entertained concerning it.
Altem. Indeed, it far exceeds them, Gélanor.
There is no lovelier abode on earth!
And so says Zeolide.
Zeo.   Indeed she does!
Why, father, I have lived near eighteen years,
And never knew until three hours ago
That you possessed so lovely a domain!
Why have I wasted eighteen years on earth,
When such a heaven as this awaited me?
Gélan. (aside to PHANOR). You have not told the
        Princess or your Court
The palace's peculiarity?
Phan. Not I. The secret is our own, as yet—
The Queen's, and yours, and mine.
Gélan.   With you and me
The secret's safe. But then—Queen Altemire—
If you have told *her* all——
Phan.   No, no—not all!
Here is a secret which is yours and mine;
                    (*producing crystal box*)
And yours and mine the secret shall remain.
Protected by this talisman, I stand,
A sturdy rock amid the shifting sands—
A salamander in a world of fire—
Achilles in a crowd of myrmidons—
Achilles, with an iron-plated heel!
Go, send my courtiers—I anticipate
No ordinary sport from watching them.
                    [*Exeunt* GÉLANOR *and* PHANOR.
Altem. What are you reading, Zeolide?
Zeo. (with scroll).   A song
Written by Chrysal set to Zoram's notes;

They gave it me before we left our home,
But in the hurry of the journey here,
I managed to mislay it—here it is.

Enter ZORAM, CHRYSAL, *and* ARISTÆUS.

Altem. And here are author and composer, too—
And Critic, teeming with humanity.
Come let us hear it.

(ZEOLIDE *sings a song. At its conclusion* CHRYSAL *and*
ZORAM *applaud.*)

*Chrys. (coming forward with all the action of a man
who is expressing extreme approval).* Oh, I protest,
my ears have never heard
A goodly song more miserably sung.
(*Clapping hands*) Oh, very poor indeed—oh, very weak ;
No voice—no execution—out of tune—
Pretentious too—oh, very, very poor ! (*Applauding as if
in ecstasies.*)
Altem. (amused). Indeed ! I think I've often heard you
say
No voice could rival Princess Zeolide's ?
Chrys. (enthusiastically). I've often said so—I have
praised her voice,
Because I am a courtier—paid to praise.
I never meant one word of what I said;
I have the worst opinion of her voice,
And so has Zoram.
Zor.   I ?   Oh, dear me, no !
I can form no opinion on the point,
I am no judge of music.
Chrys.   Eh ?
Zor.   Not I !
I hardly know the treble from the bass,
And as to harmony—I know the word,
But hang me if I guess at what it means !
Zeo. Oh, Zoram, you are jesting—why, you wrote
The air I sung !
Zor.   *I* wrote the air ?   Not I,
I paid a poor musician for his work,
And palmed it off upon you as my own.
A common trick with melodists who stand
Far higher in the world's esteem than I !

Altem. Well, Aristæus there has still to speak.
What says that rollicking philosopher?
Come, growl it out!

Arist. (gruffly, as if finding fault). It's sweetly pretty,
   ma'am,
And very nicely sung. I like it much.

Zeo. What! Aristæus pleased?

Arist. (very savagely).   Of course I am;
I'm always pleased with everything.

Altem.   Indeed!
Men look on Aristæus as a man
Whom nothing satisfies.

Arist. (with outrageous bluntness). Then men are wrong.
No child's more easily amused than I.
But, here at Court, where every one is pleased
With everything, my amiability
Would go for nought; so I have coined myself
A disposition foreign to my own,
In hopes my clumsy boorish insolence
Might please you by its very novelty;
And prove, perchance, a not unwelcome foil
To Zoram's mockery of cultured taste,
And Chrysal's chronic insincerity!
I'm rough and honest, frank—outspoken—blunt.

Chrys. Boor! when you dare to say I'm insincere
You tell the truth—there, make the most of that!

Zor. Chrysal, your hand; I'm glad to find at last
Your eyes are opened to your many faults.

Chrys. How, sir, is this intentional affront?

Zor. No, not intentional. I tried to frame
A pleasant speech, but, by some awkward slip,
The truth escaped me quite against my will.
(With great admiration.) You systematic liar!

Chrys.   Insolent!

Zor. Sir!

Chrys.   This shall cost or you or me his life.
In half an hour you shall hear from me! [*Exit* CHRYSAL.

Zor. (in terror). What *have* I said?

Altem. (aside).   These boobies must not fight.
But how to stop them? Here comes Philamir!
Now he and Zeolide can meet. But first
I must get rid of Zoram. (*To* ZORAM.) Get you hence,
I will contrive to pacify your foe.

Zor. But——

Altem.   Go !

Zor. (*piteously*). I'm sure I don't know what I've done !

     [*Exeunt* ZORAM *and* QUEEN ALTEMIRE.

Enter PHILAMIR,—ZEOLIDE *runs to him and embraces him—he turns away.*

Zeo. My love, is Philamir unhappy ?

Phil.   Yes.

I have heard people talking of our troth,
And prophesying that it will soon cease.

Zeo. Indeed ! They think you do not love me, then ?

Phil. They doubt not that—they doubt your love for me.
Some say it sleeps ; some say that it is dead ;
Some that it never lived. Oh, Zeolide,
If love for Philamir is yet unborn,
Why bring it now to light ! Where will you find
A fitter nursery for love than this ?
If that love lives, but sleeps, why, wake it now
And let it revel in these golden groves.
If it is dead, why, here's a paradise
That well might summon it to second life !

Zeo. It sleeps not, Philamir, nor is it dead ;
It lives and cannot die.

Phil.   But people say
That love should advertise itself in words
More fervid than the weary formula,
" I love you, Philamir." You love your friends.
Why, Zeolide, I think I've heard you say
You love your horse !

Zeo.   Unjust ! You ask me, then,
To limit my illimitable love,
And circle, with a boundary of words,
A wealth of love that knows no bounds at all !
There is a love that words may typify—
A mere material love—that one may weigh
As jewellers weigh gold. Such love is worth
The gold one pays for it—it's worth no more.
Why, Philamir, I might as well attempt
To set a price upon the universe—
Or measure space—or time eternity,
As tell my love in words !

Phil. (*astonished*).   Why, Zeolide,
At last you speak ! Why, this, indeed, is love

Zeo. (aside). What have I said? (*Aloud and coldly.*)
Indeed, I'm glad to think
My words have pleased you!
   Phil. (with enthusiasm). Pleased me? They've done
      more—
They've gratified my vanity, and made
Me feel that I am irresistible!
   Zeo. Indeed!
   Phil.   Indeed, dear Zeolide, they have.
Why, how you frown!
   Zeo. (coldly).   If such a love as mine
Serves but to feed your sense of vanity,
I think it is misplaced.
   Phil.   My vanity
Must needs be fed, and with such love as yours.
I have worked hard to gain it, Zeolide!
You are not nearly as attractive as
Five hundred other ladies I could name,
Who, when I said I loved them, stopped my lips——
   Zeo. (astonished). I'm glad they did!
   Phil.   With kisses, ere I could
Repeat the sentence; and it hurt me much
That you, who are comparatively plain,
Should give me so much trouble, Zeolide.
   Zeo. (aside.) What can he mean? (*Aloud*) Oh, you are
      mocking me——
   Phil. Mocking you, Zeolide? You do me wrong!
(*With enthusiasm.*) Oh, place the fullest value on my
   words,
And you'll not overvalue them! I swear,
As I'm a Christian knight, I speak the truth!
   Zeo. Why, Philamir, you've often told me that
You never loved a woman till we met!
   Phil. (with all the appearance of rapture). I always
     say that. I have said the same
To all the women that I ever woo'd!
   Zeo. And they believ'd you?
   Phil.   Certainly they did.
They always do! Whatever else they doubt,
They don't doubt that! (*He tries to embrace her.*)
   Zeo. (horror-struck). Away, and touch me not!
   Phil. What? Has my earnestness offended you,
Or do you fear that my impassioned speech
Is over-coloured? Trust me, Zeolide,

If it be over-charged with clumsy love,
Or teem with ill-selected metaphor,
It is because my soul is not content
To waste its time in seeking precious stones,
When paste will answer every end as well!

Zeo. Why, Philamir, dare you say this to me?

Phil. All this, and more than this, I dare to say.
I dare to tell you that I like you much,
For you are amiable, refined, and good—
Saving a little girlish diffidence
I have no serious fault to find with you!

Zeo. You're very good!

Phil.   Indeed, I think I am,
But let that pass. In truth I like you much.
At first I loved you in an off-hand way!

Zeo. At first?

Phil.   Until the novelty wore off,
And then, receiving but a cold response
To all the seeming fury of my love,
My pride was nettled, and I persevered
Until I made you tell me of your love,
In words that bore comparison with mine.
I've done that, and I'm amply satisfied.

Zeo. (*in blank astonishment*). And this is Philamir, who
        used to breathe
Such words of passion and such songs of love!
Those words that fiercely burnt with such false fire,
Those songs that sung so lovingly of lies,
Bore unsuspected fruit—I gathered it
And garnered it away. Oh, Philamir,
As misers store up gold, I stored my love
In all the inmost corners of my heart,
Dreading to speak or look at Philamir,
Lest some unguarded word or tell-tale glance
Should give a clue to all the wealth within!
I laughed within myself, as misers laugh,
To find my hoard increasing day by day,
And now—the coin I hoarded up is base—
The flowers that decked my life are worthless weeds—
The fruit I plucked is withered at the core—
And all my wealth has faded into air!

Phil. Faded? Why, Zeolide, what do you mean?
I do not love you as a lover should,
Yet you reproach me! Oh, you are unjust.

o

Zeo. Indeed, I'll not reproach you! Let me go.
My grief shall be as silent as my love.
Farewell!   [*Exit*
  Phil. That woman's mad! Unquestionably mad!
My show of love has sent her brain adrift.
Poor girl! I really like her very much.
I tell her that I love her—and in words
Which never yet were known to miss their mark
When uttered by Prince Philamir—in words
So charged with passion that they well might charm
The very proudest maid in Christendom;
And off she bounces as indignantly
As if I'd told the very plainest truth!

Enter CHRYSAL.

  Chrys. Your Royal Highness seems disturbed.
  Phil.   I am!
I'm much annoyed with Princess Zeolide.
You know how coldly she has hitherto
Received the protestations of my love?
  Chrys. (*politely*). I do indeed. You've been the
            laughing-stock
Of all the Court for months on that account.
  Phil. (*amazed*). Oh, have I so?
  Chrys.   Upon my soul, you have.
  Phil. You're candid, sir.
  Chrys. (*still as if paying a compliment*). I can afford to be
Extremely candid with Prince Philamir.
But let that pass. You were reminding me
How coldly Princess Zeolide received
Your vows. What then?
  Phil.   Why, not ten minutes since
Her manner changed, and all her pent-up love
Burst from her lips in frenzied eloquence.
I was astounded!—I, of course, began
To echo all her sentiments tenfold.
I picked the very fairest flowers that grow
Upon the dreamy plains of metaphor,
And showered them upon her. White with **rage**
She started from me—telling me, with tears,
Her dream of love had melted into air!
I see you don't believe me, Chrysal——
  Chrys.   Well,
I half believe you. I can scarcely think

The Princess spoke with rapture of your love;
But I can quite believe that when you spoke
In what you're pleased to think is metaphor,
The well-bred Princess shrank instinctively
From such a florid prince as Philamir
(with a respectful bow).

    Phil. (*haughtily*). This form of compliment is new to
      me!
    Chrys. My lord, my speciality consists
In framing novel forms of compliment.
But who comes here?—a modest little maid—

Enter AZÈMA—*she starts on seeing* PHILAMIR *and* CHRYSAL.

And rather pretty, too.
    Phil. (*angrily*).   She hears you, sir!
(*Politely to* AZÈMA.) I fear we've frightened you?
    Azèma.   Oh no, indeed,
I am not frightened, though I seem to be.
    (AZÈMA'S *manner is characterized by the extremest modesty*
      and timidity throughout this scene.)
    Chrys. But why affect a fear you do not feel?
    Azèma (*with extreme timidity*). Because, although I
      entered here to seek
Prince Philamir, I'm anxious he should think
This meeting is a simple accident.
Do not suppose that this is modesty;
'Tis but an artifice to make you think
That I am timid as a startled fawn!
    Chrys. (*aside to* PHILAMIR). This is a character. I'll
      open fire,
And storm her weakest point—her vanity.
Now, my artillery of compliments,
A salvo, if you please. (*Aloud, with the air of one who is*
    paying an elaborate compliment.) I have remarked
That you've a certain girlish prettiness,
Although your nose is sadly underbred.
(*Aside.*) That's rather neat!
    Azèma.   Are you Prince Philamir?
    Chrys. Not I, indeed, fair lady. This is he—
The most conceited coxcomb in the world (*with an elaborate*
    bow to PHILAMIR, *who starts angrily*).
No thanks—indeed 'tis true.
    Azèma (*to* CHRYSAL).   Then go your way—
I don't want you! I only want the prince.

'Twas Philamir I came to captivate.
   Chrys. Here's candour if you like!
   Azèma.   Oh, leave us, sir!
Find some excuse to go, that he and I
May be alone together.
   Phil.   Leave me, sir.
I'll give your tongue a lesson ere the night!
   Chrys. How has my tongue offended?—Oh, I see—
Exactly—don't explain! (*Aside.*) Poor Zeolide!   [*Exit.*
   Phil. Insolent scoundrel! (*following him*).
   Azèma.   Oh, don't follow him.
I want you here alone. You can begin—
I am not shy, though I appear to be.
Indeed, I entered here ten minutes since,
Because I heard from those outside the gates,
That you, Prince Philamir, had just arrived.
   Phil. Then you're a stranger here?
   Azèma.   I am, indeed!
The people told me any one was free
To enter.
   Phil. Yes, quite right. Did they say more?
   Azèma. Oh yes, much more. They told me then that
      you
Received but sorry treatment at the hands
Of Princess Zeolide. They told me, too,
That your betrothal might ere long collapse;
(*With extreme modesty.*) So, thought I, as I am beyond
      dispute
The fairest maid for many a mile around—
And as, moreover, I possess the gift
Of feigning an enchanting innocence
I possibly may captivate the prince,
And fill the place once filled by Zeolide.
                 (*Sits; her ankle is exposed.*)
   Phil. The Princess has a candid enemy!
I beg your pardon, but the furniture
Has caught your dress.
   Azèma (*re-arranging her dress hastily*). Oh, I arranged
      it so,
That you might see how truly beautiful
My foot and ankle are (*as if much shocked at the exposé*).
   Phil.   I saw them well;
They're very neat.
   Azèma.   I now remove my glove

That you may note the whiteness of my hand.
I place it there in order that you may
Be tempted to enclose it in your own.

   Phil. To that temptation I at once succumb.
     (*Taking her hand—she affects to withdraw it angrily.*)
   Azèma (*with affected indignation*). Go on! If you had
     any enterprise,
You'd gently place your arm around my waist
And kiss me. (*Struggling to release herself.*)
   Phil.   It might anger you!
   Azèma.   Oh no!
It's true that I should start with every show
Of indignation, just in order to
Maintain my character for innocence—
But that is all.
   Phil. (*puts his arm round her and kisses her*). There,
     then—'tis done!
   Azèma (*starting, with a great show of rage*). How, sir?
I think it's time that I should take my leave.
(*Very indignantly.*) I shall be in the Avenue of Palms.
At ten o'clock to-night. I mention this
That you may take the hint and be there, too! (*going.*)
   Phil. One moment, pray. Let me assure you now,
That such an unmistakable coquette,
And one who shows her cards so candidly,
Will not supplant the Princess Zeolide!
   Azèma (*surprised*). Supplant the Princess Zeolide?
     Why, sir,
By what authority do you imply
That I have cherished any such design?
   Phil. Your own admission.
   Azèma.   Oh, impossible!
(*Indignantly.*) But as it seems that I've no chance with you,
I'll try the gentleman who left us here.
He comes!

        Enter CHRYSAL.

     Oh, sir, I crave a word with you!
Are you a wealthy man? (*with extreme delicacy of
     manner.*)
   Chrys.   I am, indeed.
   Azèma. And you've a title?
   Chrys.   Yes, of highest rank.

Azèma. A bachelor.

Chrys.   A bachelor as yet,
Betrothed to Palmis.

Azèma (shrinking). Oh! *(Hopefully.)* But possibly
You do not love her much?

Chrys. (with enthusiasm). Oh, not at all !

Azèma. You'll do—give me your arm.   *(He does so—*
      she shrinks.) Oh, sir, indeed——

(Impatiently to CHRYSAL, *who hesitates)* Do take my hand
      and put it through your arm.

(He does so.) That's it! Oh, sir, indeed I know you not !

[*Exeunt* CHRYSAL *and* AZÈMA,—AZÈMA *affecting to try*
      and release herself. PHILAMIR *stands astounded for*
      a moment.

Phil. I've found a clue that solves these mysteries!
This palace is enchanted ground ! It's plain
That there's some subtle influence at work,
Affecting everybody here—but me !
Chrysal, the honey-tongued, turns out to be
A blunt and scurrilous outspoken boor ;
Zoram, the musical enthusiast,
Can hardly tell the treble from the bass ;
Then Aristæus, surly, blunt, and gruff,
Turns out to be the gentlest soul alive ;
And, most inexplicable change of all,
The amiable but prudish Zeolide
Becomes a foolish vixen, blind with love,
Maddened with jealous and unreasoning rage !
Then comes a girl—a commonplace coquette—
Who, while she lays her plans with practised skill,
Explains their aim, and holds them to the light
That all may see their arrant hollowness !
It's evident there's some enchantment here
That shows up human nature as it is,
And I alone resist its influence !
Ah, here is Mirza—lovely paragon—
I'll notice how it operates on her.

Enter MIRZA.

Mirza (starts). I beg your pardon. I was looking for
My diary ; I've dropped it hereabouts.

Phil. Allow me to assist you in your search ?

Mirza (hastily). No, no ; that must not be. My diary
Must ne'er be seen by other eyes than mine !

Phil. Indeed! and why?

Mirza.   My very inmost thoughts—
The secret utterances of my heart—
Are there inscribed. I would not for my life
That any eyes but mine should rest on it.

Phil. Can Lady Mirza harbour any thought
That all the world may not participate?
I'll not believe it.

Mirza (eagerly). Hush—I charge you, sir!
Ask me no questions here—for I have learnt
That this is fairy ground, where every one
Is bound, against his will, to speak the truth.
If you interrogate me, I am bound
To answer truly. I need say no more
To such a courteous knight as Philamir.

Phil. (aside). It is then as I thought! (*Aloud.*) I
         guessed the truth—
This palace doubtless *is* enchanted ground,
And I alone resist its influence!

Mirza. Indeed!

Phil.   I had occasion some time since
To feign unbounded love for Zeolide
(For whom I don't particularly care):
Well, notwithstanding my indifference,
I spoke with all my usual gush of love,
From which I venture to conclude that I
Am unaffected by this magic power.

Mirza. You do not love the Princess Zeolide?
You who professed unutterable love?

Phil. I liked her well enough at first, but now
I'm weary of my liking. She displays
So much unreasonable petulance,
Such causeless anger—such unbridled wrath,
That I'm resolved to break the weary link
That binds us. I'll be free to love again.
                    (*Taking* Mirza's *hand.*)

Mirza (releasing herself). Oh, Philamir! Oh, shame
         upon you, sir.
She loves you! You are loved by Zeolide!
Why, there's a heaven opened to your eyes,
And you'll not enter, Philamir! Oh, shame
To blight so true a heart as hers! Oh, fool,
To throw aside in wrath so fair a prize!

Phil. But listen—I've a fairer prize in view.

Mirza—I love *you!*
 Mirza (shuddering with terror). Spare me, sir, I pray!
 Phil. Now by this castle's mystic influence,
I challenge you to answer truthfully—
Do you love me?
 Mirza (shrinking from him). Have pity, Philamir!
Withdraw your question, I beseech you, sir!
If you insist, I must perforce reply—
I charge you, on your knighthood, press me not!
   (Philamir *pauses, struggling with his feelings.*)
 Phil. (releasing her). My Lady Mirza, you are free to go.
          [*Exit* Mirza *hastily.*
How subtly works the mystic influence,
That all seem subject to,—excepting me!
And from the fearful ordeal only one
Of all the women here comes out unscathed.
The peerless Mirza—good, and wise, and pure,
Most excellent and unapproachable!
To know that Mirza loves me, is to know
That she is mortal—that I knew before.
To know that Mirza's worthy of my love,
And that, despite the searching influence
That I alone resist—oh, this indeed
Is happiness!—I'm sure she loves me well!

    Enter Zeolide.

 Zeo. Indeed she does! If half an hour ago
She spoke abruptly to her Philamir,
She bitterly repents it. Oh, my love,
Forgive me, for in truth I love you well!
 Phil. (embracing her fondly). But my remark did not
      apply to you;
I spoke of Lady Mirza.
 Zeo. (recoiling).   Mirza?
 Phil.   Yes,
I'm quite convinced she loves me!
 Zeo.   Philamir,
You should not jest with such a sacred word.
You've played your joke upon me, and you've seen
How readily I fell into the trap;
Let that content you. There—I'm not annoyed—
I'll not be caught again!
 Phil. (earnestly).   Dear Zeolide,

Indeed I do not jest—nor did I when
You left me in unwarrantable rage.
I love the Lady Mirza—she loves me.
    Zeo. (horrified). She told you so?
    Phil.   Well, no.   I'm bound to say
She did not tell me so in open words:
Her love for you restrained her. She's too good—
Too pure—too honourable—to allow
A passion for her dearest friend's betrothed
To master her. You should have heard her plead
Your hopeless cause. She struggles with her love,
And tries to keep it down—but still she loves.
    Zeo. (astounded). And you return this love?
    Phil.   Most heartily.
(*With affectionate gesture.*) I'm getting weary of you, and
    I wish
That I could find sufficient argument
To justify me in releasing you. (*She shrinks from him.*)
Why, now you frown again! Oh, Zeolide,
This wilfulness is insupportable!
    Zeo (enraged). Support it then no longer, Philamir!
There—you are free—our bond is at an end;
Choose your path, I'll choose mine. Our roads diverge.
We part and may not meet again. Farewell!
(*Changing her manner.*) Oh Philamir, heed not my words;
    I spoke
In reckless haste—I spoke my death-warrant!
Philamir, do not leave me, let me live;
See how I love you! I am at your feet—
I, Zeolide, whom once you thought so cold—
I, Zeolide, who am not wont to kneel!
Oh, give me till to-night, and pass the hours
That intervene in marshalling the past,
And let that plead my cause! You loved me once,
You asked me for my love—I gave my life,
For I must die if you abandon me!
Have mercy on me! Give me till to-night!
There's some enchantment in this fearful place.
This is not Philamir—it is his shape,
But does not hold his soul. Before the night
I'll seek my father, and I'll gain from him
The key that solves this fearful mystery.
Go now—nay, do not speak—no—not a word—
I'll not believe that this is Philamir.

Go, leave me now—and we will meet to-night!

> [*He hesitates ; then exit*

Oh, Philamir, my love, my love, my love! (*She falls sobbing
on couch.*)

Enter PALMIS.

Palmis. What ? Zeolide in tears ? Has Philamir
Been too emphatic in his vows of love ?
Have pity on him!
    Zeo.   Palmis, pity *me*—
He loves me not!
    Palmis.   Indeed !
    Zeo.   He told me so.
    Palmis (relieved). Oho ! He told you so ?
    Zeo.   Most openly.
    Palmis. Then there is hope for you. Come, dry your
    eyes ;
When men are over head and ears in love.
They cannot tell the truth—they must deceive,
Though the deception tell against themselves !
Here Chrysal comes—(*astonished*) a lady on his arm !

Enter CHRYSAL *and* AZÈMA—*he leaves* AZÈMA *abruptly on seeing* PALMIS.

    Palmis.   Why, Chrysal, who is this ? Where have
    you been ?
    Chrys. (*affectionately*). I have been wandering through
    shady groves
With that exceedingly attractive girl.
    Palmis. You have been flirting, sir ?
    Chrys. (*putting his arm round her waist*). Exceedingly !
I always do when I'm away from you.
    Palmis (*to* AZÈMA). Oh, you're a brazen woman !
    Azèma (*with great modesty*).   That I am !
An ordinary every-day coquette
Who lives on admiration, and resolves
To gain it by whatever means she can.
    Zeo. (*aside to* PALMIS). Palmis, there's some enchant-
    ment in this place—
I know not what—it influences all.
Do not dismiss him yet, until we learn
Its nature !

Chrys. (with affection). Yes, my Palmis, wait awhile,
Do not dismiss me yet; although it's true
I never loved you, yet I want your love
Because you have much influence at Court,
And have it in your power to help me on
To further favour.

    Palmis (astounded). Chrysal, are you mad?
You never loved me?

    Chrys. (enthusiastically). Never, on my soul!
In point of fact, I always hated you,
And mean to tell you so when I have won
The highest rank your mistress can confei.
In the mean time, however, I am fain
To make you think that I adore you still.
Observe the heaving of my swelling heart;
My fervid manner—my ecstatic gaze—
It's all assumed!

    Palmis.   Oh, miserable man!
Go—get you hence, sir.

    Chrys. (astonished).   Palmis, what on earth
Possesses you?

    Palmis.   Don't speak to me again;
I can't endure you!

Re-enter ZORAM.

    Zor.   I am glad of this.
Dear Palmis, I for many a weary day
Have sought to win your love from Chrysal here,
By every mean, contemptible device
That my unequalled cunning could suggest.

    Chrys. (amazed). And you admit this to my very face?

    Zor. (cordially). With pleasure, Chrysal. I have sought
       in vain,
By daily blackening your character,
To sicken pretty Palmis of her love.
I've told her you're an unexampled rake,
A gambler and a spendthrift, mean, poor, base,
Selfish and sordid; cruel, tyrannical;
But all in vain, she loves you all the more.
(*Taking his hand.*) Forget the angry words you spoke
       to-day;
In the glad glow of hope that I shall gain
Your Palmis' love, I freely pardon you.

Chrys. (*in furious rage*). This evening, in the Avenue of Palms,
I shall await you, sir.
   Zor. (*in blank astonishment*). Oh dear, oh dear,
What *have* I said?

Enter GÉLANOR.

Gélan.   Hush, gentlemen—the Queen.

Re-enter QUEEN ALTEMIRE *hastily.*

Altem. (*in a rage*). Where is the King?   Go, send him
   here to me.
Oh, Zeolide, go, get you hence away,
For I have words for Phanor that 'twere best
His daughter did not hear.
   Zeo.   My father comes.

Re-enter PHANOR *and* MIRZA.

Altem. Now, sir, I've every reason to believe,
From what I've heard, that you're deceiving me!
I'll question you—oh, infamous old man!
   Phan. (*aside*). The Queen is jealous. Where's my talis-
   man? (*Finds it.*)
All right—it's well I have it with me now.
(*Aloud.*) Interrogate me. Conscious innocence
Has little fear of palaces of Truth!
   Altem. You have been walking in the shrubbery;
What were you doing there?
   Phan. (*with great show of love for* ALTEMIRE). Why,
   making love
To Mirza. I invariably do
Whenever I've a chance; but all in vain.
She's a good woman, and despises me.
(*To* MIRZA.) Haven't I offered love to you?
   Mirza.   You have.
   Phan. And you despise me, don't you?
   Mirza.   Heartily.
   Phan. (*to* ALTEMIRE). I told you so, and she endorses it
Believe me, I am bound to speak the truth!
   Altem. (*bitterly*). I do believe you.
   Phan. (*taking her by the hand*). Thank you, Altemire.

Altem. Stand off, don't touch me, horrible old man !
You tell me you've made love to Mirza?
 Phan. (astonished).   **No!**
Did I say that?
 Altem.   Most unmistakably.
 Phan. Oh, come, I say !
 Zor.   You did indeed, my lord!
 Phan. I said that I made love to Mirza ?
 Chrys.   Yes,
Those were the very words !
 Phan.   Oh, Mirza, come,
You can deny this!
 Mirza.   Would, my lord, I could.
To spare the Queen I would be silent, but
Some unknown power masters me, and makes
Me own, against my will, that it was so !
 Altem. There, sir—you hear her words!
 Phan. (aside to GÉLANOR).   Why, Gélanor,
How's this ? The talisman is out of gear !
      (*Showing box to* GÉLANOR.)
 Gélan. Let me examine it. (*Takes it and returns it.*)
   A forgery !
A clever imitation ; virtueless !
It lacks the small inscription on the hinge !
     (PHANOR *falls breathless into a chair.*
 Phan. To-morrow morning we go home again !

ACT III.

SCENE.—*The Avenue of Palms—night.* CHRYSAL *dis
covered with a drawn sword in his hand.*

Enter GÉLANOR.

Gélan. Chrysal, alone! And with a naked sword !
Chrys. I'm waiting Zoram. I have challenged him.
He meets me here—the Avenue of Palms.
 Gélan. Has he offended you?
 Chrys.   Most grievously.
You heard the words he used to me to-day ?
 Gélan. I did.

Chrys.   Then blood must flow. I am a knight,
My knightly honour claims this sacrifice.
I've been insulted—one of us must die!
    Gelan. You are a valiant man, if one may judge
By your demeanour.
    Chrys. (very valiantly). My demeanour? Bounce!
Mere idle empty froth and nothing more.
Why, notwithstanding that I look so brave,
I'd give the riches of a universe
To find some decent means of backing out;
But, no, my honour must be satisfied!
If I endured with patience Zoram's taunts,
I should deserve to have my knightly spurs
Struck from my heels! 'Sdeath, sir, I'm bound to fight!
    Gelan. Is Zoram a good swordsman?
    Chrys.   Not at all.
I'm far more skilled—but still I can't repress
A certain sense of terror. Accident
May give him victory.
    Gelan.   Apologize!
    Chrys. (indignantly). To Zoram? Never! Would you
        have me stain
My hitherto untarnished 'scutcheon? Shame!
Stand back—he comes!

Enter ZORAM, *with drawn sword.*

                            Well, sir, you've kept your word.
    Zor. Of course I have!
    Chrys. (very sternly). I'm very much surprised—
I may say disappointed—to remark
That you're prepared to fight and do not show
The signs of terror that I hoped to see.
    Zor. (very bravely). Oh, sir, I pray you don't deceive
        yourself!
My valiant manner hides an inward fear
That almost robs me of the power of thought!
Chrysal, you've grievously insulted me ;
My sense of honour forces me to fight!
But I would rather have my hand cut off
(Could that be done without inflicting pain)
Than measure swords with you!
    Chrys.   You craven hound!
    Zor. Craven yourself!

Chrys. (*furiously*).   I am, but you don't know it,
You musical impostor!
   Zor.   Ha, what's that?
I can stand much abuse and never flinch,
But when you twit me with my ignorance
Of musical expressions, blood alone
(Unless we're interrupted) can extract
The venom of the insult! Come! On guard!
                          (*They fight.*)
   Gelan. (*aside*). These donkeys must not fight! (*Aloud.*)
      Come—let me try
To reconcile you.
   Chrys.   Reconcile us? No!
But you can interfere to stop the fight! (*They desist.*)
   Zor. (*looking reproachfully at* GÉLANOR). I little thought
      when I called Chrysal on,
That such a venerable gentleman
Would suffer two impetuous headstrong youths
To cut each other's throats.
   Gélan.   Come, come—desist.
   Chrys. This hound abused me!
   Zor.   He insulted me;
   Both. Our honour *must* be satisfied!
                      (*They cross swords.*)
   Gélan.   No, no—
Attend to me. Within these crystal walls
A strange mysterious influence prevails:
All men are bound to speak the plainest truth!
And this they do, without suspecting it.
(*To* ZORAM.) When Chrysal spoke the words that angered
     you
He did not mean to speak them. He believed
That he was paying you a compliment.
(*To* CHRYSAL.) When Zoram said that he considered you
A systematic liar, mean, poor, base,
Selfish, and sordid, cruel, tyrannical,
'Twas what he *thought*—not what he would have *said!*
   Chrys. I see—if that was only what he *thought,*
It makes a difference.
   Gélan.   What *could* he say?
He was compelled, you know, to speak the truth.
   Chrys. Of course, I understand. Zoram, your hand!
   Zor. With pleasure. (*Shaking hands with* CHRYSAL.)
      Chrysal, I should like to say

That I esteem you—but indeed I can't.
My detestation of you knows no bounds.
   Chrys. How, sir?   A fresh affront?
   Zor.   What can I do?
I try my best to say agreeable things,
But you're so utterly contemptible!
I'd put it more politely, but I can't!
I'm bound against my will to speak the truth!
I'd not insult you openly, for worlds—
Indeed, it's only what I *think* of you!
   Chrys. If it is only what you *think* of me,
Why, say no more ; give me your hand again—
My knightly honour's amply satisfied!
      [*They sheathe their swords, then exeunt arm in arm*
   Gélan. So dies that breeze away!   Oh, honour, honour!
Let no one take you at the estimate
Your self-elected champions price you at!
More harm is worked in that one virtue's name,
Than springs from half the vices of the earth!

     Enter Queen Altemire, *in violent rage.*

   Altem. Why, Gélanor, this is no spot for you,
You'd better go—the King will wish you gone.
   Gélan. Indeed!   And why?
   Altem.   I'll tell you, Gélanor,
His majesty has an appointment here.
Oh, Gélanor, I've been alone with him
This afternoon, and I have learnt such things!
Why, even here—despite the castle's charm,
Despite the sacred influence of the place,
He prosecutes his infidelities!
At first he persecuted Mirza, but
Failing to find much favour in her eyes,
He looked for other game.   Why, Gélanor,
He meets some woman called Azèma here,
At ten o'clock to-night!
   Gélan.   The deuce he does!
   Altem. Then I resolved to know the very worst.
I locked him in my room and questioned him
For full three hours about his married life.
Oh, I elicited such fearful things!
Why, Gélanor, there's not a woman's name
In all the long baptismal catalogue

That's not identified with his intrigues!
Tall, short, stout, slender, fair, dark, old and young,
High, low, rich, poor, good, bad, maid, widow, wife,
Of every country and of every clime!
All's fish that his nets catch!
    Gélan.   And a king's net
Is very comprehensive. Here she comes!

Enter AZÈMA.

Altem. Is this the woman? Tell me, who are you?
Azèma. I am Azèma.
Altem.   And *I* am the Queen!
Azèma (bowing). Then, madam, you're extremely in the
    way.
Altem. How so?
Azèma.   I've an appointment with the King,
Of which you are entirely unaware;
But though I'm much annoyed to find you here,
I'm glad to find you here with Gélanor.
Altem. And why?
Azèma.   If our intrigue should come to light,
We can retaliate by giving out
That you and Gélanor are just as bad.
Altem. Upon my word!
Gélan.   Oh, this is past belief!
Altem. Infamous hussy, you shall pay for this!
Azèma. Why, madam, how have *I* offended you?
Altem. How?—you are here to meet the King, alone;
At night—by pre-arrangement—in the dark!
Azèma. Oh, madam, this indeed is terrible!
That poor Azèma should be charged with this!
It's true I've an appointment with the King,
But as you're not aware of it, your words
Are utterly unjustifiable.
These flashing eyeballs and this angry blush
(At least I hope I'm blushing) represent
The noble rage of outraged innocence.
I'll to the King, and let him know at once
How, as I wandered through the grove, alone,
I found you here with wicked Gélanor,
At night—by pre-arrangement—in the dark.
Oh, shame upon you—shame upon you, Queen!
[*Exit* AZÈMA—ALTEMIRE *and* GÉLANOR *stand confounded.*
P

Gélan. Your majesty, I think I'd better go.
Altem. Absurd! the notion is preposterous!
You're old enough to be my father.
 Gélan.   Quite!
And wise enough to know that proper folk
Will only say " that makes the matter worse!"
 Altem. But surely here, in this enchanted home,
Where all are bound to speak the truth, our word
Will guarantee our perfect innocence!
 Gélan. Yes, if the King is pleased to take our word;
But, as you've brought a charge against the King,
Analogous to that which will be brought
Against ourselves, he may ignore the fact
That truth is truth. No, no, upon the whole,
I think, your majesty, I'd better go! [*Exit* GÉLANOR.

   Enter PALMIS *and* ZEOLIDE, ZEOLIDE *weeping.*

 Palmis. Nay, do not weep, dear mistress.
 Zeo.   Ah, my friend,
What comfort can *you* offer me?
 Palmis.   I've heard
That when one is oppressed with weight of woe,
Some solace may be found in dwelling on
The grief of one more sorely laden still.
 Zeo. More sorely laden? Where will Zeolide
Find one whose misery outweighs her own?
 Palmis. Your misery, though great, is but a grain
When balanced in the scales with mine!
 Zeo.   With yours?
 Palmis. Yes; Philamir respects you. He esteems
Your moral excellence, although no doubt
He does not love you as a lover should;
But Chrysal always hated me, and sought
To gain that love I gave so willingly
To hasten his promotion at the Court.
Your case and mine are different. Besides,
You angered Philamir. I never gave
My Chrysal any reason for his hate.
 Zeo. How did I anger him?
 Palmis.   Your petulance
Annoyed him.
 Zeo.   Petulance! He told me that
He only liked me!

Altem. (*coming forward*). True, but you forget
He was compelled to speak the plainest truth,
And knew not that he spoke it. He believed
(While he was telling you he loved you not)
That he was breathing ardent words of love;
Believing this, your reasonable rage
Seemed in his eyes irrational caprice,
And changed his waning love to sheer dislike.

 Zeo. Is this the truth, then?

 Altem.   Yes, I think it is.
The test has been exceedingly severe.

 Zeo. I'll wed no man who cannot stand this test.

 Palmis. Then, Zeolide, you'll surely die a maid!

 Altem. Come, come, be reasonable. Philamir
Is but a man—a vain and idle one,
But under this veneer of coxcombry
There's sterling stuff. The man is honest gold,
And vanity has silver-plated him.

 Palmis. At all events, you know he *likes* you well.
How many maidens when they wed a man
Have reason to be sure of half as much!

 Zeo. But then his love for Mirza!

 Altem.   Idle pique!
No doubt he hoped—as other lovers hope—
In the fierce whirlpool of a new-born love
To drown remembrance of the love just dead.
Here comes the Lady Mirza! We will go,
And leave you with her. Tell her everything;
She is a noble lady—wise and pure!
She will not rob you of your Philamir.
There—tell her all!

 Zeo.   Forgive me, mother dear,
My heart is softened. I have been unjust.

      [*Exeunt* ALTEMIRE *and* PALMIS.

    Enter MIRZA.

 Mirza. Oh, Zeolide, I know what you would say.
Say on, dear Zeolide, and have no fear.

 Zeo. Mirza, for three long years we two have been
As sisters are, and I would speak to you
As younger sister speaks to elder-born.
Give me your counsel, Mirza; it will be
As pure, as true, as honest as those eyes.

Mirza. If counsel such as mine can serve you aught,
'Tis thine, dear Zeolide. My sister, speak.
   Zeo. With all my soul I love Prince Philamir.
A lady—good and beautiful and wise—
Unwittingly hath robbed me of my love;
She is too pure, too gentle, too divine,
To seek a love that rightly is not hers.
No, no, this lady hath not sought his love—
Of that I'm certain, yet she hath his love!
Oh, Mirza, when my Philamir declared
His love for me, I cast away the world
To enter Paradise. Now, Philamir
Has led this lady (all unwillingly)
Within its gates, and I am left without—
A lonely wanderer 'twixt earth and heaven.
Mirza, dear sister, say—what shall I do?
Give me thy counsel—I'll abide by it.
   Mirza. No need to speak to me in parable.
I am that lady whom you over-praise—
That most unhappy woman, Zeolide!
Despite myself, I must admit the truth,
I do love Philamir—shrink not from me.
Mine is no idle love. Four years ago,
Ere you had ever seen Prince Philamir,
I was a lady of his father's Court.
He loved me even then, and I loved him—
No need to tell you, dearest Zeolide,
The nature of that love; you know too well
How women love who love Prince Philamir!
We were betrothed, but secretly. Alas!
I was a humble waiting lady, he
A mighty Prince—so we concealed our love.
Then it was rumoured that he sought your hand,
That policy, the curse of kings, required
That he should marry you. Then I fell ill—
(*Struggling with her emotion*) Pass over that. Let it
    suffice that I
Released him—for I loved him passing well!
   Zeo. (*amazed*). I never knew of this!
   Mirza.   No, Zeolide,
I've learnt to bear my sorrow silently.
But for the sacred genius of this spot,
Whose influence no mortal can resist,
My secret would have passed away with me.

But I was true to you; for though I saw
How coldly you received his vows of love——
   Zeo. (rising, astonished). Coldly! Why, every word he
     spoke to me
Rang through my brain, and would have waked up love
Had love been dead !
   Mirza.   I thought you loved him not.
But though I grieved for him, yet when he spake
(As he at times would speak) of our old love,
I checked him with a simulated scorn,
For then, dear Zeolide, I loved you both !
   Zeo. You love me still?
   Mirza.   Most heartily !
   Zeo.   Why, then,
Have mercy on me, give me Philamir——
He is the soul and essence of my life !
Dear sister Mirza, give him back to me.
Oh, rather take my life than take my love,
And leave me here to linger on, alone !
   Mirza. Fear not, dear Zeolide, I love him well,
But I will never see his face again !
   Zeo. Promise me this—swear to renounce his love !
   Mirza. As there's a shining sun in heaven I swear!
See, I am brave, and I will fight my love
As I have fought ere this. Take courage, dear ;
I'll leave this place to-night, and Philamir
Shall ne'er set eyes upon my face again.
There, go—I'll tell him this. He's coming now——
Go, dry your eyes—he should not see them so.
Come back again when they are at their best.
                          [*Exit* Zeolide.

            Enter Philamir.

   Phil. Mirza—I have some words to say to you—
The diary you lost to-day ?
   Miraz (eagerly).   Well, sir,
And have you found it ?
   Phil.   Mirza, I have found
A portion of it—one loose leaf—behold ! (*Producing page.*)
   Mirza. And you have read it, Philamir ?
   Phil. (guilty).   I have!
   Mirza. Oh, shame upon you—shame upon you, sir !
You gave your knightly word—you are forsworn !

Phil. But, Mirza, hear me out, ere you condemn.
I saw a paper tossed before the wind
And little dreaming 'twas your diary,
I picked it up. I knew not what it was
Till I began to read it. Then I knew,
And knowing so much, burnt to know still more!
    Mirza. But when you knew it held my secret thoughts,
You read no further?
    Phil. (abashed).   Mirza, I read on!
    Mirza. Lost! lost! Give me that leaf, Prince Philamir:
You have deceived me, sir—I trusted you.
    Phil. But, Mirza, where's the knight who would have
        stopped
When of himself he read such words as these?—
(*Reads*) " I still love Philamir, but I must strive
To battle with my love. Oh, give me grace
To fight this fight."
    Mirza.   I charge you read no more!
    Phil. " By day his every look—his every word—
Renews some mem'ry that should be long dead ;
By night the phantom of my loved one's face
Burns in my eyes and robs me of my rest!"
    Mirza. My secret has gone forth. I strove to keep
That love as silent as my silent heart;
But it was not to be. You now know all!
Yet no—not all!
    Phil.   Then, Mirza, tell me all.
Speak openly—hide nothing from me now.
    Mirza. I will speak openly. I love you, sir
And, loving you, I leave the Court to-night,
That I may never see your face again.
    Phil. Recall those words!—we will not—must not part!
                        (*He detains her.*)

Enter ZEOLIDE, *unobserved.*

    Mirza. Release me, Philamir, and let me go!
I love you! Let me hide myself away.
I love you! Leave me with myself alone.
I love you! Show me gratitude for this,
And leave me free to sanctify my vow,
For I have sworn to see your face no more!
    Phil. To whom have you sworn this?
    Mirza.   To Zeolide,

Whom you once loved so well—who still loves you.

Phil. I never loved her, Mirza—who is she,
That she should come between me and my love?
She loves me not, and I have done with her.

   Mirza. Oh, this will kill her, sir!

   Zeo.   No—Mirza—no!

It will not kill me. I can bear this blow.

                        (*Coming forward.*)

Prince Philamir, we two have been betrothed—
Your word is plighted—well, I set you free.
Mirza, you swore to leave Prince Philamir—
Your word is plighted—well, I set you free.

    (*She takes* Mirza's *hand and places it in* Philamir's.)

Oh, Philamir—this is indeed the end!
Be true to her—such sacred love as hers
Should purify its object—oh, be true!
I'm but a chapter in your book of life,
I who had thought to be the book itself!
The chapter's ended, and to Zeolide
The book is closed for ever! Philamir,
When you are tempted to do Mirza wrong,
Turn to that chapter—read it through and through—
And let the tale of all that I have borne
Warn you from fresh inconstancy; my grief
May thus be Mirza's safeguard to the end.
Mirza—my sister—he will love you well—
Here, in the home of truth, he tells you so.
May you be happy in his new-born love,
May he be worthy of such love as yours—
(*To* Philamir.) Speak not, but let me go.

               (*Kisses* Mirza's *forehead.*)

               Farewell—farewell!

[*Exit* Zeolide, *weeping*—Philamir *and* Mirza *stand for
   a moment gazing at each other—then they fall into
   each other's arms.*

   Phil. Mirza, my own! At last—at last my own!

   Mirza. Oh, Philamir! I am so cruelly racked
By sentiments I cannot reconcile;
I know not whether this is joy or grief!
True, when I think of Philamir, the air
Seems charged with music, and the earth I tread
All flowers. When I remember Zeolide
I could go mad with sorrow!

   Phil.   Then, my love,

Think not of Zeolide!
 Mirza.   Ah, Philamir,
You speak as men speak of a worn-out love.
You only know one kind of love, you men!
My love for Zeolide is otherwise,
Unselfish, generous, a sister's love.
Yet have I stolen from her gentle heart
That which in all the world she loved the best!
 Phil. You are too sensitive. Say rather, she
Hath freely given that she prizes least.
 Mirza. Oh, Philamir, indeed you do her wrong,
And may perchance wrong me, as you wronged her.
 Phil. (rising). Impossible! For if the words I breathe
Were dashed with any mockery of love,
I should, against my will, confess it now.
Mirza, I love you! These are idle words
When spoken in the unenchanted world,
But, spoken here, they bear significance
That rivals in its worth a life-long test!
Let us exchange some trinket which shall serve
As evidence of this our solemn troth.
Here is my pledge. (*Giving a ring.*)
 Mirza.   My love, what can I give?
I have no trinkets—I am very poor!
 Phil. A handkerchief—a glove—no matter what!
(*She feels in pocket and takes out handkerchief—the
 crystal box falls out with it—he picks it up and
 retains it.*)
This crystal box—nay, give it me, 'twill serve
To chronicle——
 Mirza (hastily). No, no, Prince Philamir!
Not that—not that! it is a talisman!
 Phil. Then I will steal it as I stole your heart,
And I will keep it while I keep that heart.
 Mirza. Give me that box, or I must own the truth—
That I am miserably false in all!
     (*Throwing herself at his feet.*)
That my morality is all assumed!
That I am mean, and base, and treacherous!
A shameless schemer! heartless—impudent!
Give me that box, or I must own that I
Abstracted it from Phanor's cabinet,
And substituted one that I possessed
Exactly like it. I must own to you

That I'm unutterably infamous—
A hypocrite—a traitress to my friend—
All this, and more, I must admit, if you
Retain that talisman! Oh, give it me,
And let this locket testify our love!
The King! The King! The King! I am undone!

[*Exit* Mirza *hastily.*

Phil. Gone, gone!—and Philamir, who thought he knew
The ways of women well, had still to learn
That in one woman's body there is place
For such a goodly show of purity,
And such unequalled treachery of heart!
Oh, Zeolide, for how much infamy
Have I rejected thine unequalled love?

Enter Phanor *with* Chrysal *and* Zoram.

Phan. Congratulate me, I'm half mad with joy;
Azèma comes to tell me that she found
The Queen and Gélanor together here—
Alone—at night!
    Phil.   Well, sir, and what of that?
    Phan. Nothing at all, my boy! Why, that's the joke.
Old Gélanor has dandled Altemire
Upon his aged knee five hundred times!
    Phil. What—lately?
    Phan.   No! I won't commit myself
By telling you how many years ago,
But long before her majesty was weaned.
    Phil. (*shrugging his shoulders*). I see no reason to con-
      dole with you,
Because her majesty and Gélanor
Were here together—neither do I see
Why you should be congratulated, sir!
    Phan. You're very dull! The Queen has just found out
That I had an appointment in this grove
To meet Azèma—don't you understand?
I can retort and take indignant ground.
What was she doing here with Gélanor?
You'll see! (*Sees box.*) Hallo! what's that?
    Phil.   A talisman.
It fell from Mirza's pocket as you came.
    Phan. The deuce it did! Allow me; this is mine!

(*Taking it.*)

    Phil. I know: she stole it from your cabinet;

She owned as much!
   Phan.   Confound her impudence!
   Phil. Oh, I have been deceived!
   Phan.   And so have I
Most seriously deceived! Hush, here's the Queen,
And with that gay deceiver, Gélanor!
The talisman has turned up just in time.

Enter ALTEMIRE *and* GÉLANOR, *with* AZÈMA *and* MIRZA.

So, madam, I've detected you!
   Altem. (*indignantly*).   How, sir?
   Phan. Never mind how—and you too, Gélanor.
Oh, I'm ashamed of you! (*Crossing to* GÉLANOR.)
   Gélan.   Your majesty,
I don't know what you mean.
   Phan.   You bad old man!
(*Affecting to weep*) You whom I trusted so! (*Aside.*)
        Don't be alarmed,
I'm not in earnest. (*Aloud.*) Oh, it's infamous!
Why, let me see—how old are you?
   Gélan.   My lord,
If you imply——
   Phan.   Imply! (*Aside.*) Don't be a fool,
I'm not in earnest; I have found the box!
(*Aloud.*) Explain this conduct!
   Altem.   Sir, is this a joke?
   Phan. Well, not exactly, madam; you've been found
Philandering at night with Gélanor.
Being within the influence of these walls,
You're bound to speak the truth. If you can say
Your meeting's innocent, I'm satisfied.
   Altem. As innocent as truth itself, I swear.
   Phan. I'm satisfied! Your hand——
   Altem.   Nay, hear me first.
I charge you with appointing here to meet
Azèma; you are bound to tell the truth,
Being within the influence of these walls.
If you can unreservedly deny
This charge, I also shall be satisfied.
   Phan. Emphatically I deny the charge!
   Altem. (*astounded*). You do?
   Phan.   I do! (*Piously.*) This is the Home of Truth,
And all are subject to its influence.

Altem. (*puzzled*). But you admitted it when you
    confessed
Your gallantries to me this afternoon!
  Phan. Oh, you've been dreaming!
  Altem.   Do I understand
That you deny that you confessed all this?
  Phan. Distinctly! (*Piously.*) This is the Abode of
  Truth.
  Altem. I *have* been dreaming! Phanor, there's my
  hand.
I've deeply wronged you.
  Phan.   Altemire, you have!
But say no more—we are good friends again.
  Altem. Then you forgive me?
  Phan.   Heartily I do!
  Altem. I'll never be a jealous fool again.
  Phan. I'm very glad indeed to hear you say so.

Enter ZEOLIDE—ALTEMIRE *retires with* GÉLANOR *and con-*
    verses with ZEOLIDE—PHILAMIR, *seeing* ZEOLIDE, *comes*
    down abashed.

  Phan. (*to* PHILAMIR). Well, and what's wrong with
    you?
  Phil.   I've been a fool,
A madman, and a true-born idiot!
  Phan. By the mysterious influence of this place,
I can believe it!
  Phil.   I have given up
The noblest woman that I ever knew,
For that abominable cockatrice
Who quitted me as you arrived.
  Phan.   Well! well!
You may regain her yet.
  Phil.   Impossible!
  Phan. Oh, not at all! there—take this talisman.
             (ZEOLIDE *overhears this speech.*)
With this you're proof against the influence
That rules this place; you can declare to her
That you adore the very ground she walks,
And wallow in the foolish flummery
That used to make you so ridiculous.
She will believe it all—there, take it, boy,
And make good use of it to win her back.

Phil. I'll use it, Phanor, and I'll use it well!

Zeo. (*aside*). He takes the box. And thus he thinks
     to win
The hand of his forsaken Zeolide!
Oh, Philamir, this is contemptible.
I think I could have loved you, but for this!

Phil. Dear Zeolide, I hold a talisman,
Enabling me to counteract the charm
That reigns within these walls. With this in hand
I can tell truth or falsehood as I please,
And you must needs believe me. Zeolide,
I've learned to set a value on your love
Transcending all the riches of the earth;
Yet would I rather live without that love—
A life of self-reproach without that love—
Repentant and alone without that love—
Than stoop to gain it by such treachery.
Here is the talisman. (ZEOLIDE *takes it.*) No longer
     armed
Against the sacred influence of Truth,
I tell you of my sorrow and my love
With all the warmth of a repentant heart!
     (*He presses* ZEOLIDE *to his heart and kisses her.*)

Altem. (*indignantly*). Give me that talisman! (*Takes it.*)
     I have a clue
To much that was a mystery : Behold!
     (*She breaks it—a loud crash—all come forward.*)

Enter ARISTÆUS.

Gelan. You know not what you've done! The castle's
     charm
Is bound up with that mystic talisman!
Now that the box is broken, these fair walls
Are disenchanted!

Phan.   P'raps it's quite as well.
Now that the place has lost its influence
We shall get on much better. We have learnt
A lesson that should last us till we die—
We've learnt how matrimonial constancy
By causeless jealousy is sometimes tried—
     (*Looking reproachfully at* ALTEMIRE.)

Altem. How jealousy is sometimes justified—
     (*Looking reproachfully at* PHANOR.)

Chrys. How Zoram—music's vaunted pioneer—
Don't even know his notes—and has no ear!
Even his cant expressions are the wrong ones!
    Zor. I *have* an ear!
    Phan. (shaking his hand). You have—two very long
      ones!
    Palmis. You've learnt to doubt the love that those
      profess,
Who by such love gain temporal success—
                     (Looking angrily at CHRYSAL.*)*
    Zor. That surly misanthropes, with venom tainted—
    Arist. Are often not as black as they are painted!
    Azèma. To doubt all maids who of their virtue boast:
That they're the worst who moralize the most!
                     (Looking at MIRZA.*)*
    Mirza. That blushes, though they're most becoming,yet
Proclaim, too oft, the commonplace coquette!
                     (Looking at AZÈMA.*)*
I can declare, with pardonable pride,
I never blush!
    Azèma.   You couldn't if you tried!
    Phil. Under the influence that lately reigned
Within these walls I breathed my love unfeigned;
Now that that power no longer reigns above,
I ratify the accents of my love.
Forgive me, Zeolide, my life, my bride!
    Zeo. (very demurely). I love you, Philamir—be satisfied!

TRIAL BY JURY.

A DRAMATIC CANTATA.

IN ONE ACT.

DRAMATIS PERSONÆ.

THE LEARNED JUDGE ... ... MR. F. SULLIVAN.
COUNSEL FOR THE PLAINTIFF.
THE DEFENDANT ... ... MR. W. FISHER.
FOREMAN OF THE JURY ... ... MR. CAMPBELL.
USHER ... ... MR. KELLEHER.
THE PLAINTIFF ... ... MISS BROMLEY.

BRIDESMAIDS, GENTLEMEN OF THE JURY, ETC.

TRIAL BY JURY.

SCENE.—*A Court of Justice.*

BARRISTERS, ATTORNEYS, *and* JURYMEN *discovered with*
USHER.

Chorus.

Hark, the hour of ten is sounding!
Hearts with anxious fears are bounding;
Hall of Justice crowds surrounding,
    Breathing hope and fear—
For to-day in this arena,
Summoned by a stern subpœna,
Edwin, sued by Angelina,
    Shortly will appear.

(*The* USHER *marshals the* JURY *into Jury-box.*)

Solo, USHER.

Now, Jurymen, hear my advice—
All kinds of vulgar prejudice
    I pray you set aside:
With stern judicial frame of mind,
From bias free of every kind,
    This trial must be tried.

Chorus.

From bias free of every kind
This trial must be tried.

(*During Choruses,* USHER *says, fortissimo,* " *Silence in
Court!* ")

Q

Usher.

Oh, listen to the plaintiff's case:
Observe the features of her face—
　　The broken-hearted bride.
Condole with her distress of mind—
From bias free of every kind
　　This trial must be tried!

Chorus.

From bias free, etc.

Usher.

And when amid the plaintiff's shrieks,
The ruffianly defendant speaks—
　　Upon the other side;
What *he* may say you needn't mind—
From bias free of every kind
　　This trial must be tried.

Chorus.

From bias free, etc.

Enter Defendant.

Defendant (*recit.*).

Is this the Court of the Exchequer?

All.

It is!

Defendant (*aside*).

Be firm, my moral pecker,
Your evil star's in the ascendant!

All.

Who are you?

Defendant.

I'm the Defendant!

Chorus of JURYMEN (*shaking their fists*).

Monster, dread our damages!
We're the jury,
Dread our fury!

DEFENDANT.

Hear me, hear me, if you please,
  These are very strange proceedings—
For, permit me to remark,
  On the merits of my pleadings,
You're at present in the dark.

(DEFENDANT *beckons to* JURYMEN—*they leave the box,
  and gather round him as they sing the following*):—

Ha! ha! ha!
That's a very true remark—
On the merits of your pleadings,
We're entirely in the dark!
Ha! ha!—ha! ha!

Song, DEFENDANT.

When first my old, old love I knew,
  My bosom swelled with joy;
My riches at her feet I threw—
  I was a love-sick boy!
No terms seemed extravagant
  Upon her to employ—
I used to mope, and sigh, and pant,
  Just like a love-sick boy!

But joy incessant palls the sense;
  And love, unchanged, will cloy,
And she became a bore intense
  Unto her love-sick boy!
With fitful glimmer burnt my flame
  And I grew cold and coy,
At last, one morning, I became
  Another's love-sick boy!

Chorus of JURYMEN (*advancing stealthily*).

Oh, I was like that when a lad ;
A shocking young scamp of a rover !
I behaved like a regular cad ;
But that sort of thing is all over.
I'm now a respectable chap
And shine with a virtue resplendent,
And therefore I haven't a scrap
Of sympathy with the defendant !
   He shall treat us with awe,
   If there isn't a flaw,
Singing so merrily—Trial-la-law!
Trial-la-law—Trial-la-law !
Singing so merrily—Trial-la-law !

Recit. USHER.

Silence in Court, and all attention lend.
Behold your Judge ! In due submission bend !

Enter JUDGE *on Bench.*

Chorus.

All hail, great Judge !
 To your bright rays
We never grudge
 Ecstatic praise.
   All hail !
May each decree
 As statute rank,
And never be
 Reversed in banc.
   All hail !

Recit. JUDGE.

For these kind words accept my thanks, I pray !
A Breach of Promise we've to try to-day :
But firstly, if the time you'll not begrudge,
I'll tell you how I came to be a judge.

ALL.

He'll tell us how he came to be a judge!

JUDGE.

Let me speak.

ALL.

Let him speak.

JUDGE.

Let me speak.

ALL.

Let him speak.   Hush! hush!! hush!!!
(*fortissimo*) He'll tell us how he came to be a judge!

Song, JUDGE.

When I, good friends, was called to the bar,
   I'd an appetite fresh and hearty,
But I was, as many young barristers are,
   An impecunious party:
I'd a swallow-tail coat of a beautiful blue—
   A brief which I bought of a booby—
A couple of shirts and a collar or two,
   And a ring that looked like a ruby!

Chorus.

A couple of shirts, etc.

JUDGE.

In Westminster Hall I danced a dance,
   Like a semi-despondent fury;
For I thought I should never hit on a chance
   Of addressing a British jury—
But I soon got tired of third-class journeys,
   And dinners of bread and water;
So I fell in love with a rich attorney's
   Elderly, ugly daughter.

Chorus.

So he fell in love, etc.

JUDGE.

The rich attorney he jumped with joy,
  And replied to my fond professions:
"You shall reap the reward of your pluck, my boy
  At the Bailey and Middlesex Sessions.
You'll soon get used to her looks," said he,
  "And a very nice girl you'll find her!
She may very well pass for forty-three
  In the dusk, with a light behind her:"

Chorus.

"She may very well," etc.

JUDGE.

The rich attorney was good as his word:
  The briefs came trooping gaily,
And every day my voice was heard
  At the Sessions or Ancient Bailey.
All thieves who could my fees afford
  Relied on my orations,
And many a burglar I've restored
  To his friends and his relations.

Chorus.

And many a burglar, etc.

JUDGE.

At length I became as rich as the Gurneys.
  An *i*ncubus then I thought her,
So I threw over that rich attorney's
  Elderly, ugly daughter.
The rich attorney my character high
  Tried vainly to disparage—
And now, if you please, I'm ready to try
  This breach of promise of marriage!

Chorus.

Aud now, if you please, etc.

JUDGE.

For now I am a Judge!

ALL.

And a good Judge too?

JUDGE.

Yes, now I am a Judge!

ALL.

And a good Judge too?

JUDGE.

Though all my law is fudge,
Yet I'll never, never budge,
But I'll live and die a Judge!

ALL.

And a good Judge too!

JUDGE (*pianissimo*).

It was managed by a job!

ALL.

And a good job too!

JUDGE.

It was managed by a job!

ALL.

And a good job too!

JUDGE.

It is patent to the mob,
That my being made a nob
Was effected by a job.

ALL.

And a good job too!

Enter COUNSEL *for* PLAINTIFF.

COUNSEL (*recit.*).

Swear thou the Jury!

USHER.

Kneel, Jurymen, oh! kneel!

(*All the Jury kneel in the Jury-box, and so are hidden from
audience.*)

USHER.

Oh, will you swear by yonder skies,
Whatever question may arise
'Twixt rich and poor—'twixt low and high,
That you will well and truly try?

JURY (*raising their hands, which alone are visible*).

To all of this we make reply,
By the dull slate of yonder sky:
That we will well and truly try.

(*All rise with the last note, both hands in air.*)

Recit. USHER.

This blind devotion is indeed a crusher!
Pardon the tear-drop of the simple Usher!

(*He weeps.*)

Recit. COUNSEL.

Call the plaintiff!

Recit. USHER.

Oh, Angelina! Angelina!! Come thou into Court.

Enter the BRIDESMAIDS, *each bearing two palm branches, their arms crossed on their bosoms, and rose-wreaths on their arms.*

Chorus of BRIDESMAIDS.

Comes the broken flower—
Comes the cheated maid—
Though the tempest lower,
Rain and cloud will fade!
Take, O maid, these posies:
Though thy beauty rare
Shame the blushing roses,
They are passing fair!
Wear the flowers till they fade:
Happy be thy life, O maid!

(*The* JUDGE, *having taken a great fancy to* FIRST BRIDES-
MAID, *sends her a note by* USHER, *which she reads,
kisses rapturously, and places in her bosom.*)

Solo, ANGELINA.

O'er the season vernal
Time may cast a shade;
Sunshine, if eternal,
Makes the roses fade!
Time may do his duty;
Let the thief alone—
Winter hath a beauty
That is all his own.
Fairest days are sun and shade:
I am no unhappy maid!

(*By this time the* JUDGE *has transferred his admiration to*
ANGELINA.)

Chorus of BRIDESMAIDS.

Comes the broken flower, etc.

(*During Chorus* ANGELINA *collects wreaths of roses from*
BRIDESMAIDS *and gives them to the* JURY, *who put
them on, and wear them during the rest of the piece.*)

JUDGE (*to* ASSOCIATE).

Oh, never, never, never, since I joined the human race,
Saw I so exquisitely fair a face.

The JURY (*shaking their forefingers at* JUDGE).

Ah, sly dog!   Ah, sly dog!

JUDGE (*to* JURY).

How say you, is she not designed for capture?

FOREMAN (*after consulting with the* JURY).

We've but one word, my lord, and that is—Rapture!

PLAINTIFF (*curtseying*).

Your kindness, gentlemen, quite overpowers!

The JURY.

We love you fondly, and would make you ours!

The BRIDESMAIDS (*shaking their forefingers at* JURY).

Ah, sly dogs!   Ah, sly dogs!

COUNSEL *for* PLAINTIFF (*recit.*).

May it please you, my lud!
Gentlemen of the Jury!

Aria.

With a sense of deep emotion,
    I approach this painful case;
For I never had a notion
    That a man could be so base,
Or deceive a girl confiding,
Vows, *etcœtera*, deriding.

ALL.

He deceived a girl confiding,
Vows, *etcœtera*, deriding.

(PLAINTIFF *falls sobbing on* COUNSEL's *breast, and remains there.*)

COUNSEL.

See my interesting client,
  Victim of a heartless wile!
See the traitor all defiant
  Wears a supercilious smile!
Sweetly smiled my client on him,
Coyly woo'd and gently won him!

ALL.

Sweetly smiled, etc.

COUNSEL.

Swiftly fled each honeyed hour
  Spent with this unmanly male!
Camberwell became a bower,
  Peckham an Arcadian Vale,
Breathing concentrated otto!—
An existence *à la* Watteau.

ALL.

Bless us, concentrated otto! etc.

COUNSEL (*coming down with* PLAINTIFF, *who is still sobbing on his breast*).

Picture, then, my client naming
  And insisting on the day:
Picture him excuses framing—
  Going from her far away;
Doubly criminal to do so,
For the maid had brought her *trousseau!*

ALL.

Doubly criminal, etc.

COUNSEL (*to* PLAINTIFF, *who weeps*).

Cheer up, my pretty—oh, cheer up!

JURY.

Cheer up, cheer up, we love you!

(COUNSEL *leads* PLAINTIFF *fondly into Witness-box; he takes a tender leave of her, and resumes his place in Court.*)

(PLAINTIFF *reels, as if about to faint.*)

JUDGE.

That she is reeling
Is plain to me!

FOREMAN.

If faint you're feeling,
Recline on me!

(*She falls sobbing on to the* FOREMAN'S *breast.*)

PLAINTIFF (*feebly*).

I shall recover
If left alone.

ALL (*shaking their fists at* DEFENDANT).

Oh, perjured lover,
Atone! atone!

FOREMAN.

Just like a father
I wish to be.   (*Kissing her.*)

JUDGE (*approaching her*).

Or, if you'd rather,
Recline on me!

(*She staggers on to bench, sits down by the* JUDGE, *and falls sobbing on his breast.*)

COUNSEL.

Oh! fetch some water
From far Cologne!

ALL.

For this sad slaughter
Atone! atone!

JURY (*shaking fists at* DEFENDANT).

Monster, monster, dread our fury—
There's the Judge, and we're the Jury!

Song, DEFENDANT.

Oh, gentlemen, listen, I pray,
 Though I own that my heart has been ranging,
Of nature the laws I obey,
 For nature is constantly changing.
The moon in her phases is found,
 The time and the wind and the weather,
The months in succession come round,
 And you don't find two Mondays together.
  Consider the moral, I pray,
   Nor bring a young fellow to sorrow,
  Who loves this young lady to-day,
   And loves that young lady to-morrow.

BRIDESMAIDS (*rushing forward, and kneeling to* JURY).

Consider the moral, etc.

You cannot eat breakfast all day,
 Nor is it the act of a sinner,
When breakfast is taken away,
 To turn your attention to dinner;
And it's not in the range of belief,
 That you could hold him as a glutton,
Who, when he is tired of beef,
 Determines to tackle the mutton.
  But this I am ready to say,
   If it will appease their sorrow,
  I'll marry one lady to-day,
   And I'll marry the other to-morrow.

BRIDESMAIDS (*rushing forward as before*).

But this he is ready to say, etc.

JUDGE (*recit.*).

That seems a reasonable proposition,
To which I think your client may agree.

ALL.

Oh, Judge discerning !

COUNSEL.

But, I submit, my lord, with all submission,
To marry two at once is Burglaree !

(*Referring to law book.*)

In the reign of James the Second,
It was generally reckoned
As a very serious crime
To marry two wives at one time.
    (*Hands book up to* JUDGE, *who reads it.*)

ALL.

Oh, man of learning !

Quartette.

JUDGE.

A nice dilemma we have here,
That calls for all our wit :

COUNSEL.

And at this stage it don't appear
That we can settle it.

DEFENDANT.

If I to wed the girl am loth
A breach 'twill surely be !

PLAINTIFF.

And if he goes and marries both
It counts as Burglaree !

ALL.

A nice dilemma, etc.

Duet, PLAINTIFF *and* DEFENDANT.

PLAINTIFF (*embracing* DEFENDANT *rapturously*).

I love him—I love him—with fervour unceasing,
    I worship and madly adore ;
My blind adoration is always increasing,
    My loss I shall ever deplore.
Oh, see what a blessing—what love and caressing
    I've lost, and remember it, pray,
When you I'm addressing are busy assessing
    The damages Edwin must pay.

DEFENDANT (*repelling her furiously*).

I smoke like a furnace—I'm always in liquor,
    A ruffian—a bully—a sot.
I'm sure I should thrash her—perhaps I should kick her,
    I am such a very bad lot!
I'm not prepossessing, as you may be guessing,
    She couldn't endure me a day !
Recall my professing when you are assessing
    The damages Edwin must pay !

(*She clings to him passionately ; he drags her round stage, and
flings her to the ground.*)

JURY.

We would be fairly acting,
But this is most distracting !

JUDGE (*recit.*).

The question, gentlemen, is one of liquor,
    You ask for guidance—this is my reply :
If he, when tipsy, would assault and kick her,
    Let's make him tipsy, gentlemen, and try !

COUNSEL.

With all respect
I do object !

ALL.

With all respect
We do object!

DEFENDANT.

I don't object!

ALL.

We do object!

JUDGE (*tossing his books and papers about*).

All the legal furies seize you!
No proposal seems to please you;
I can't stop up here all day,
I must shortly go away.
Barristers, and you, attorneys,
Set out on your homeward journeys;
Put your briefs upon the shelf,
I will marry her myself!

(*He comes down from Bench to floor of Court. He embraces
Angelina.*)

Finale.

PLAINTIFF.

Oh, joy unbounded!
With wealth surrounded,
The knell is sounded
        Of grief and woe

COUNSEL.

With love devoted
On you he's doated:
To castle moated
        Away they go!

DEFENDANT.

I wonder whether
They'll live together
In marriage tether
      In manner true ?

USHER.

It seems to me, sir,
Of such as she, sir,
A judge is he, sir,
      A good judge too.

Chorus.

It seems to me, sir, etc.

JUDGE.

Oh yes, I am a Judge.

ALL.

And a good Judge too!

JUDGE.

Oh yes, I am a Judge.

ALL.

And a good Judge too;

JUDGE.

Though homeward as you trudge,
You declare my law is fudge,
Yet of beauty I'm a judge.

R

ALL.

And a good judge too!

(JUDGE *and* PLAINTIFF *dance back on to the Bench—the*
    BRIDESMAIDS *take the eight garlands of roses from*
    behind the Judge's desk (where one end of them is
    fastened) and draw them across floor of Court, so
    that they radiate from the desk. Two plaster Cupids
    in bar wigs descend from flies.   Red fire.)

IOLANTHE;

OR,

THE PEER AND THE PERI.

DRAMATIS PERSONÆ.

THE LORD CHANCELLOR.

EARL OF MOUNTARARAT.

EARL TOLLOLLER.

PRIVATE WILLIS (*of the Grenadier Guards*).

STREPHON (*an Arcadian Shepherd*).

QUEEN OF THE FAIRIES.

IOLANTHE (*a Fairy, Strephon's Mother*).

CELIA ⎫
LEILA ⎬ *Fairies.*
FLETA ⎭

PHYLLIS (*an Arcadian Shepherdess and Ward in Chancery*).

Chorus of DUKES, MARQUISES, EARLS, VISCOUNTS, BARONS AND FAIRIES.

ACT I.
AN ARCADIAN LANDSCAPE.

ACT II.
PALACE YARD, WESTMINSTER.

IOLANTHE;

OR,

THE PEER AND THE PERI

ACT I.

Scene.—*An Arcadian Landscape. A river runs around the back of the Stage.*

A rustic bridge crosses the river.

Enter Fairies, led by Leila, Celia, *and* Fleta. *They trip around the stage singing as they dance.*

Chorus.

Tripping hither, tripping thither,
Nobody knows why or whither;
We must dance and we must sing,
Round about our fairy ring!

Solo—Celia.

We are dainty little fairies,
   Ever singing, ever dancing;
We indulge in our vagaries
   In a fashion most entrancing.
If you ask the special function
   Of our never-ceasing motion,
We reply, without compunction,
   That we haven't any notion!

Chorus.

No, we haven't any notion!
   Tripping hither, etc.

Solo—Leila.

If you ask us how we live,
Lovers all essentials give—
    We can ride on lovers' sighs,
    Warm ourselves in lovers' eyes,
    Bathe ourselves in lovers' tears,
    Clothe ourselves in lovers' fears,
    Arm ourselves with lovers' darts,
    Hide ourselves in lovers' hearts.
When you know us, you'll discover
That we almost live on lover !

Chorus.

Tripping hither, etc.

(At the end of chorus, all sigh wearily.)

Celia. Ah, it's all very well, but since our Queen banished
Iolanthe, fairy revels have not been what they were !

Leila. Iolanthe was the life and soul of fairy land. Why,
she wrote all our songs and arranged all our dances ! We sing
her songs and we trip her measures, but we don't enjoy
ourselves !

Fleta. To think that five and twenty years have elapsed
since she was banished ! What could she have done to have
deserved so terrible a punishment ?

Leila. Something awful ! She married a mortal !

Fleta. Oh ! Is it injudicious to marry a mortal ?

Leila. Injudicious ? It strikes at the root of the whole fairy
system. By our laws, the fairy who marries a mortal, dies !

Celia. But Iolanthe didn't die !

Enter Fairy Queen.

Queen. No, because your Queen, who loved her with a sur-
passing love, commuted her sentence to penal servitude for life,
on condition that she left her husband and never communicated
with him again !

Leila (aside to Celia). That sentence of penal servitude she
is now working out, on her head, at the bottom of that stream !

Queen. Yes, but when I banished her, I gave her all the
pleasant places of the earth to dwell in. I'm sure I never
intended that she should go and live at the bottom of a stream !
It makes me perfectly wretched to think of the discomfort she
must have undergone !

Leila. Think of the damp! And her chest was always delicate.

Queen. And the frogs! Ugh! I never shall enjoy any peace of mind until I know why Iolanthe went to live among the frogs!

Fleta. Then why not summon her and ask her?

Queen. Why? Because if I set eyes on her I should forgive her at once!

Celia. Then why not forgive her? Twenty-five years—it's a long time!

Leila. Think how we loved her!

Queen. Loved her? What was your love to mine? Why, she was invaluable to me! Who taught me to curl myself inside a buttercup? Iolanthe! Who taught me to swing upon a cobweb? Iolanthe! Who taught me to dive into a dew-drop—to nestle in a nutshell—to gambol upon gossamer? Iolanthe!

Leila. She certainly did surprising things!

Fleta. Oh, give her back to us, great Queen, for your sake if not for ours! (*All kneel in supplication.*)

Queen (*irresolute*). Oh, I should be strong, but I am weak! I should be marble, but I am clay! Her punishment has been heavier than I intended. I did not mean that she should live among the frogs—and—well, well, it shall be as you wish—it shall be as you wish!

Invocation—Queen.

Iolanthe!
From thy dark exile thou art summoned!
Come to our call—
Come, Iolanthe!

Celia. Iolanthe!
Leila. Iolanthe!
All. Come to our call,
 Come, Iolanthe!

[IOLANTHE *rises from the water. She is clad in water-weeds. She approaches the* QUEEN *with head bent and arms crossed.*

Iol. With humbled breast
  And every hope laid low,
 To thy behest,
  Offended Queen, I bow!

Queen. For a dark sin against our fairy laws,
We sent thee into lifelong banishment;
But Mercy holds her sway within our hearts—
Rise—thou art pardoned!

Iol.   Pardoned!
All.   Pardoned!
Iol. Ah!

[*Her weeds fall from her, and she appears clothed as a fairy. The* QUEEN *places a diamond coronet on her head, and embraces her. The others also embrace her.*

Chorus.

Welcome to our hearts again,
Iolanthe! Iolanthe!
We have shared thy bitter pain,
Iolanthe! Iolanthe!
Every heart and every hand
In our loving little band
Welcome thee to fairy land,
Iolanthe!

Queen. And now, tell me, with all the world to choose from, why on earth did you decide to live at the bottom of that stream?

Iol. To be near my son, Strephon.

Queen. Bless my heart, I didn't know you had a son!

Iol. He was born soon after I left my husband by your royal command—but he does not even know of his father's existence!

Fleta. How old is he?

Iol. Twenty-four.

Leila. Twenty-four! No one, to look at you, would think you had a son of twenty-four! But that's one of the advantages of being immortal. We never grow old! Is he pretty?

Iol. He's extremely pretty, but he's inclined to be stout.

All (disappointed). Oh!

Queen. I see no objection to stoutness, in moderation.

Cel. And what is he?

Iol. He's an Arcadian shepherd—and he loves Phyllis, a ward in Chancery.

Cel. A mere shepherd! and he half a fairy!

Iol. He's a fairy down to the waist—but his legs are mortal.

All. Dear me!

Queen. I have no reason to suppose that I am more curious than other people, but I confess I should like to see a person who is a fairy down to the waist, but whose legs are mortal.

Iol. Nothing easier, for here he comes!

Enter STREPHON, *singing and dancing and playing on a flageolet. He does not see the fairies, who retire up stage as he enters.*

Song—STREPHON.

Good morrow, good mother!
  Good mother, good morrow!
By some means or other,
  Pray banish your sorrow!
    With joy beyond telling
    My bosom is swelling,
    So join in a measure
    Expressive of pleasure.
For I'm to be married to-day—to-day—
  Yes, I'm to be married to-day!

Chorus (aside). Yes, he's to be married to-day—to-day—
  Yes, he's to be married to-day!

Iol. Then the Lord Chancellor has at last given his consent to your marriage with his beautiful ward, Phyllis?

Streph. Not he, indeed. To all my tearful prayers he answers me, "A shepherd lad is no fit helpmate for a ward of Chancery." I stood in court, and there I sang him songs of Arcadee, with flageolet accompaniment—in vain. At first he seemed amused, so did the Bar; but quickly wearying of my song and pipe, bade me get out. A servile usher, then, in crumpled bands and rusty bombazine, led me, still singing, into Chancery Lane! I'll go no more! I'll marry her to-day, and brave the upshot, be it what it may! (*sees Fairies*). But who are these?

Iol. Oh, Strephon! rejoice with me, my Queen has pardoned me!

Streph. Pardoned you, mother? This is good news indeed!

Iol. And these ladies are my beloved sisters.

Streph. Your sisters! Then they are—my aunts! (*Kneels.*)

Queen. A pleasant piece of news for your bride on her wedding day.

Streph. Hush! My bride knows nothing of my fairyhood.

I dare not tell her, lest it frighten her. She thinks me mortal, and prefers me so.

Leila. Your fairyhood doesn't seem to have done you much good.

Streph. Much good! It's the curse of my existence! What's the use of being half a fairy? My body can creep through a keyhole, but what's the good of that, when my legs are left kicking behind? I can make myself invisible down to the waist, but that's of no use, when my legs remain exposed to view? My brain is a fairy brain, but from the waist downwards I'm a gibbering idiot. My upper half is immortal, but my lower half grows older every day, and some day or other must die of old age. What's to become of my upper half when I've buried my lower half I really don't know!

Queen. I see your difficulty, but with a fairy brain you should seek an intellectual sphere of action. Let me see. I've a borough or two at my disposal. Would you like to go into Parliament?

Iol. A fairy Member! That would be delightful!

Streph. I'm afraid I should do no good there—you see, down to the waist, I'm a Tory of the most determined description, but my legs are a couple of confounded Radicals, and, on a division, they'd be sure to take me into the wrong lobby. You see they're two to one, which is a strong working majority.

Queen. Don't let that distress you; you shall be returned as a Liberal-Conservative, and your legs shall be our peculiar care.

Streph. (bowing). I see your Majesty does not do things by halves.

Queen. No, we are fairies down to the feet.

ENSEMBLE.

Queen.	Fare thee well, attractive stranger.
Fairies.	Fare thee well, attractive stranger.
Queen.	Shouldst thou be in doubt or danger,
	Peril or perplexitee,
	Call us, and we'll come to thee!
Fairies.	Call us, and we'll come to thee!
	Tripping hither, tripping thither.
	Nobody knows why or whither.
	We must now be taking wing
	To another fairy ring!

[*Fairies and* QUEEN *trip off.* IOLANTHE, *who takes an affectionate farewell of her son, going off last.*

Enter PHYLLIS, *singing and dancing, and accompanying herself on a flageolet.*

Song—PHYLLIS.

Good morrow, good lover !
  Good lover, good morrow !
I prithee discover,
  Steal, purchase, or borrow,
Some means of concealing
The care you are feeling,
And join in a measure
Expressive of pleasure,
  For we're to be married to-day—to-day !
  For we're to be married to-day !

Both. Yes, we're to be married, etc.

Streph. (embracing her). My Phyllis ! And to-day we are to be made happy for ever !

Phyl. Well, we're to be married.

Streph. It's the same thing.

Phyl. I suppose it is. But, oh, Strephon, I tremble at the step I'm taking ! I believe it's penal servitude for life to marry a ward of Court without the Lord Chancellor's consent ! I shall be of age in two years. Don't you think you could wait two years ?

Streph. Two years ! Why, you can't have seen yourself ? Here, look at that (*showing her a pocket mirror*), and tell me if you think it rational to expect me to wait two years ?

Phyl. (looking at herself). No. You're quite right—it's asking too much. One must be reasonable.

Streph. Besides, who knows what will happen in two years ? Why, you might fall in love with the Lord Chancellor himself by that time !

Phyl. Yes. He's a clean old gentleman.

Streph. As it is, half the House of Lords are sighing at your feet.

Phyl. The House of Lords are certainly extremely attentive.

Streph. Attentive ? I should think they were ! Why did five-and-twenty Liberal Peers come down to shoot over your grass-plot last autumn ? It couldn't have been the sparrows. Why did five-and-twenty Conservative Peers come down to fish your pond ? Don't tell me it was the gold-fish ! No, no ; delays are dangerous, and if we are to marry, the sooner the better.

Duet—STREPHON *and* PHYLLIS.

None shall part us from each other.
  One in life and death are we :
All in all to one another—
  I to thee and thou to me !
Thou the tree and I the flower—
  Thou the idol ; I the throng—
Thou the day and I the hour—
  Thou the singer ; I the song !

All in all since that fond meeting
  When, in joy, I woke to find
Mine the heart within thee beating,
  Mine the love that heart enshrined !
Thou the stream and I the willow—
  Thou the sculptor ; I the clay—
Thou the ocean ; I the billow—
  Thou the sunrise ; I the day !

    [*Exeunt* STREPHON *and* PHYLLIS *together.*

March. Enter Procession of Peers.

Chorus.

Loudly let the trumpet bray !
    Tantantara !
  Gaily bang the sounding brasses !
    Tzing !
As upon its lordly way
  This unique procession passes,
    Tantantara ! Tzing ! Boom !
Bow, bow, ye lower middle classes !
Bow, ye tradesmen ! bow, ye masses !
Blow the trumpets, bang the brasses !
    Tantantara ! Tzing ! Boom !
We are peers of highest station,
Paragons of legislation,
Pillars of the British nation !
    Tantantara ! Tzing ! Boom !

Enter the LORD CHANCELLOR, *followed by his trainbearer.*

Song—LORD CHANCELLOR.

The Law is the true embodiment
Of everything that's excellent.
It has no kind of fault or flaw,
And I, my Lords, embody the Law.

The constitutional guardian I
Of pretty young wards in Chancery,
All very agreeable girls—and none
Are over the age of twenty-one.
    A pleasant occupation for
    A rather susceptible Chancellor!

All.   A pleasant, etc.

But though the compliment implied
Inflates me with legitimate pride,
It nevertheless can't be denied
That it has its inconvenient side.
For I'm not so old, and not so plain,
And I'm quite prepared to marry again,
But there'd be the deuce to pay in the Lords
If I fell in love with one of my wards !
    Which rather tries my temper, for
    I'm *such* a susceptible Chancellor !

All   Which rather, etc.

And every one who'd marry a ward
Must come to me for my accord,
And in my court I sit all day,
Giving agreeable girls away,
With one for him—and one for he—
And one for you—and one for ye—
And one for thou—and one for thee—
But never, oh never a one for me !
    Which is exasperating, for
    A highly susceptible Chancellor !

All.   Which is, etc.

Enter LORD TOLLOLLER.

Ld. Toll. And now, my Lords, to the business of the day.

Ld. Ch. By all means. Phyllis, who is a ward of Court, has so powerfully affected your Lordships, that you have appealed to me in a body to give her to whichever one of you she may think proper to select, and a noble lord has just gone to her cottage to request her immediate attendance. It would be idle to deny that I, myself, have the misfortune to be singularly attracted by this young person. My regard for her is rapidly undermining my constitution. Three months ago I was a stout man. I need say no more. If I could reconcile it with my duty, I should unhesitatingly award her to myself, for

I can conscientiously say that I know no man who is so well
fitted to render her exceptionally happy. But such an award
would be open to misconstruction, and therefore, at whatever
personal inconvenience, I waive my claim.

Ld. Toll. My Lord, I desire, on the part of this House, to
express its sincere sympathy with your Lordship's most painful
position.

Ld. Ch. I thank your Lordships. The feelings of a Lord
Chancellor who is in love with a ward of Court are not to be
envied. What is his position? Can he give his own consent
to his own marriage with his own ward? Can he marry his
own ward without his own consent? And if he marries his
own ward without his own consent, can he commit himself for
contempt of his own Court? And if he commit himself for
contempt of his own Court, can he appear by counsel before
himself, to move for arrest of his own judgment? Ah, my
Lords, it is indeed painful to have to sit upon a woolsack which
is stuffed with such thorns as these!

Enter LORD MOUNTARARAT.

Ld. Mount. My Lords, I have much pleasure in announcing
that I have succeeded in inducing the young person to present
herself at the Bar of this House.

Enter PHYLLIS.

Recit.—Phyllis.   My well-beloved Lord and Guardian dear,
    You summoned me, and I am here!

Chorus of Peers.   Oh, rapture, how beautiful!
    How gentle! how dutiful!

Solo—LORD TOLLOLLER.

Of all the young ladies I know,
    This pretty young lady's the fairest,
Her lips have the rosiest show,
    Her eyes are the richest and rarest.
Her origin's lowly, it's true,
    But of birth and position we've plenty;
We've grammar and spelling for two,
    And blood and behaviour for twenty!

Chorus.   Her origin's lowly, it's true,
    But we've grammar and spelling for two;
    Of birth and position we've plenty,
    With blood and behaviour for twenty!

Solo—EARL OF MOUNTARARAT.

Though the views of the House have diverged
  On every conceivable motion,
All questions of Party are merged
  In a frenzy of love and devotion;
If you ask us distinctly to say
  What Party we claim to belong to,
We reply, without doubt or delay,
  The Party I'm singing this song to!

Chorus.   If you ask us distinctly to say,
  We reply, without doubt or delay,
  That the Party we claim to belong to
  Is the Party we're singing this song to!

Solo—PHYLLIS.

I'm very much pained to refuse,
  But I'll stick to my pipes and my tabors;
I can spell all the words that I use,
  And my grammar's as good as my neighbours'.
As for birth—I was born like the rest,
  My behaviour is rustic but hearty,
And I know where to turn for the best,
  When I want a particular Party!

Chorus.   Though her station is none of the best,
  I suppose she was born like the rest;
  And she knows where to look for her hearty,
  When she wants a particular Party!

Recit.—PHYLLIS.

Nay, tempt me not.
  To rank I'll not be bound;
In lowly cot
  Alone is virtue found!

Chorus   Nay, do not shrink from us—we will not hurt you—
The Peerage is not destitute of virtue.

Ballad—LORD TOLLOLLER

Spurn not the nobly born
  With love affected,
Nor treat with virtuous scorn
  The well connected.

High rank involves no shame—
We boast an equal claim
With him of humble name
   To be respected!
Blue blood! blue blood!
   When virtuous love is sought,
   Thy power is nought,
Though dating from the Flood,
      Blue blood!

Chorus.   Blue blood! Blue blood! etc.

Spare us the bitter pain
   Of stern denials,
Nor with lowborn disdain
   Augment our trials.
Hearts just as pure and fair
May beat in Belgrave Square
As in the lowly air
   Of Seven Dials!
Blue blood! Blue blood!
   Of what avail art thou
   To serve us now?
Though dating from the Flood,
      Blue blood!

Chorus.   Blue blood! Blue blood! etc.

Recit.—PHYLLIS.

My Lord, it may not be.
   With grief my heart is riven!
You waste your words on me,
   For ah! my heart is given!

All.   Given!
Phyll.   Given!
All.   Oh, horror !!!

Recit.—LORD CHANCELLOR.

And who has dared to brave our high displeasure,
And thus defy our definite command?

Enter STREPHON—PHYLLIS *rushes to his arms.*

Streph. 'Tis I—young Strephon! mine this priceless treasure.
   Against the world I claim my darling's hand!
      A shepherd I—

All.	A shepherd he !
Streph.	Of Arcady—
All.	Of Arcadee !
Streph.	Betrothed are we !
All.	Betrothed are they—
Streph.	And mean to be—
All.	Espoused to-day !

ENSEMBLE.

Streph. A shepherd I	*The Others.* A shepherd he
Of Arcady,	Of Arcadee,
Betrothed are we,	Betrothed is he,
And mean to be	And means to be
Espoused to-day !	Espoused to-day !

Duet—Lord Mount. *and* Lord Toll. (*aside to each other*).

    'Neath this blow,
        Worse than stab of dagger—
    Though we mo-
        Mentarily stagger,
    In each heart
        Proud are we innately—
    Let's depart,
        Dignified and stately !

All.   Let's depart,
        Dignified and stately !

Chorus of Peers.

Though our hearts she's badly bruising,
In another suitor choosing,
Let's pretend it's most amusing.
    Ha! ha! ha! ha!   Tzing!   Boom!

[*Exeunt all the Peers marching round stage with much dignity.* Lord Chancellor *separates* Phyllis *from* Strephon, *and orders her off. She follows Peers. Manent* Lord Chancellor *and* Strephon.

Lord Ch. Now, sir, what excuse have you to offer for having disobeyed an order of the Court of Chancery?

Streph. My Lord, I know no Courts of Chancery; I go by Nature's Acts of Parliament. The bees—the breeze—the seas —the rooks—the brooks—the gales—the vales—the fountains and the mountains, cry, " You love this maiden—take her. we

command you!" 'Tis writ in heaven by the bright barbëd
dart that leaps forth into lurid light from each grim thunder-
cloud. The very rain pours forth her sad and sodden sympathy!
When chorussed Nature bids me take my love, shall I reply,
"Nay, but a certain Chancellor forbids it"? Sir, you are
England's Lord High Chancellor, but are you Chancellor of
birds and trees, King of the winds, and Prince of thunder-
clouds?

Lord Ch. No. It's a nice point. I don't know that I ever
met it before. But my difficulty is that at present there's no
evidence before the Court that chorussed Nature has interested
herself in the matter.

Streph. No evidence! You have my word for it. I tell you
that she bade me take my love.

Lord Ch. Ah! but, my good sir, you mustn't tell us what
she told you—it's not evidence. Now an affidavit from a
thunderstorm, or a few words on oath from a heavy shower,
would meet with all the attention they deserve.

Streph. And have you the heart to apply the prosaic rules of
evidence to a case which bubbles over with poetical emotion?

Lord Ch. Distinctly. I have always kept my duty strictly
before my eyes, and it is to that fact that I owe my advancement to my present distinguished position.

Song—LORD CHANCELLOR.

When I went to the Bar as a very young man,
   (Said I to myself—said I,)
I'll work on a new and original plan,
   (Said I to myself—said I,)
I'll never assume that a rogue or a thief
Is a gentleman worthy implicit belief,
Because his attorney has sent me a brief,
   (Said I to myself—said I!)

I'll never throw dust in a juryman's eyes,
   (Said I to myself—said I,)
Or hoodwink a judge who is not over-wise,
   (Said I to myself—said I,)
Or assume that the witnesses summoned in force
In Exchequer, Queen's Bench, Common Pleas, or Divorce
Have perjured themselves as a matter of course,
   (Said I to myself—said I!)

Ere I go into court I will read my brief through,
    (Said I to myself—said I,)
And I'll never take work I'm unable to do,
    (Said I to myself—said I.)
My learned profession I'll never disgrace
By taking a fee with a grin on my face,
When I haven't been there to attend to the case,
    (Said I to myself—said I!)

In other professions in which men engage,
    (Said I to myself—said I,)
The Army, the Navy, the Church, and the Stage,
    (Said I to myself—said I,)
Professional licence, if carried too far,
Your chance of promotion will certainly mar—
And I fancy the rule might apply to the Bar,
    (Said I to myself—said I!).
         [*Exit* LORD CHANCELLOR.

To STREPHON, *who is in tears, enter* IOLANTHE.

Streph. Oh, Phyllis, Phyllis! To be taken from you just as I was on the point of making you my own! Oh, it's too much —it is too much!

Iol. My son in tears—and on his wedding day!

Streph. My wedding day! Oh, mother, weep with me, for the Law has interposed between us, and the Lord Chancellor has separated us for ever!

Iol. The Lord Chancellor! (*aside*). Oh, if he did but know!

Streph. (*overhearing her*). If he did but know what?

Iol. No matter! The Lord Chancellor has no power over you. Remember you are half a fairy. You can defy him—down to the waist.

Streph. Yes, but from the waist downwards he can commit me to prison for years! Of what avail is it that my body is free, if my legs are working out seven years' penal servitude?

Iol. True. But take heart—our Queen has promised you her special protection. I'll go to her and lay your peculiar case before her.

Streph. My beloved mother! How can I repay the debt I owe you?

FINALE.

QUARTET.

(*As it commences, the Peers appear at the back, advancing unseen and on tiptoe.* MOUNTARARAT *and* TOLLOLLER *lead* PHYLLIS *between them, who listens in horror to what she hears.*)

Streph. (*to* IOLANTHE). When darkly looms the day,
And all is dull and grey,
To chase the gloom away
On thee I'll call !

Phyl. (*speaking aside to* MOUNT.). What was that ?

Mount. (*aside to* PHYLLIS). I think I heard him say,
That on a rainy day,
To while the time away,
On her he'd call !

Chorus.   We think we heard him say, etc.

(PHYLLIS *much agitated at her lover's supposed faithlessness.*)

Iol. (*to* STREPHON). When tempests wreck thy bark,
And all is drear and dark,
If thou shouldst need an Ark,
I'll give thee one !

Phyl. (*speaking aside to* TOLLOLLER). What was that ?

Tol. (*aside to* PHYLLIS). I heard the minx remark,
She'd meet him after dark,
Inside St. James's Park,
And give him one !

All.   The prospect's not so bad,
$\left\{ \begin{array}{c} \text{My} \\ \text{Thy} \end{array} \right\}$ heart so sore and sad
May very soon be glad
As summer sun ;
But while the sky is dark,
And tempests wreck $\left\{ \begin{array}{c} \text{my} \\ \text{thy} \end{array} \right\}$ bark,
If $\left\{ \begin{array}{c} \text{I should} \\ \text{thou shouldst} \end{array} \right\}$ need an Ark,
$\left\{ \begin{array}{c} \text{Thou'lt} \\ \text{I'll} \end{array} \right\}$ give $\left\{ \begin{array}{c} \text{me} \\ \text{thee} \end{array} \right\}$ one !

Phyl. (*revealing herself*). Ah !

(IOLANTHE *and* STREPHON *much confused.*)

Phyl.   Oh, shameless one, tremble!
                Nay, do not endeavour
                Thy fault to dissemble,
                    We part—and for ever!
                I worshipped him blindly,
                He worships another—
Streph.   Attend to me kindly,
                This lady's my mother!
Phyl.   This lady's his *what?*
Streph.   This lady's my mother!
Tenors.   This lady's his *what?*
Basses.   He says she's his mother!

(*They point derisively to* IOLANTHE, *laughing heartily at her. She for protection to* STREPHON.)

Enter LORD CHANCELLOR. IOLANTHE *veils herself.*

Lord Ch.   What means this mirth unseemly,
                That shakes the listening earth?

Lord Tol.   The joke is good extremely,
                And justifies our mirth.

Lord Mount. This gentleman is seen,
                With a maid of seventeen,
           A taking of his *dolce far niente;*
                And wonders he'd achieve,
                For he asks us to believe
    She's his mother—and he's nearly five-and-twenty!

Lord Ch. (*sternly*). Recollect yourself, I pray,
                And be careful what you say—
        As the ancient Romans said, *festina lente.*
                For I really do not see
                How so young a girl could be
        The mother of a man of five-and-twenty.

All.   Ha! ha! ha! ha! ha!

Streph. My Lord, of evidence I have no dearth—
        She is—has been—my mother, from my birth!

Ballad.

In babyhood
Upon her lap I lay,
With infant food
She moistenèd my clay :
Had she withheld
The succour she supplied,
By hunger quelled,
Your Strephon might have died!

Lord Ch. (*much moved*). Had that refreshment been denied,
Indeed our Strephon might have died!

All (*much affected*). Had that refreshment been denied,
Indeed our Strephon might have died!

Lord Mount. But as she's not
His mother, it appears,
Why weep these hot
Unnecessary tears?
And by what laws
Should we, so joyously,
Rejoice, because
Our Strephon didn't die?
Oh, rather let us pipe our eye,
Because our Strephon didn't die!

All. That's very true—let's pipe our eye
Because our Strephon didn't die!

(*All weep.* IOLANTHE, *who has succeeded in hiding her face
from the* LORD CHANCELLOR, *escapes unnoticed.*)

Phyl. Go, traitorous one—for ever we must part:
To one of you, my Lords, I give my heart!
All. Oh, rapture!
Streph. Hear me, Phyllis, ere you leave me!
Phyl. Not a word—you did deceive me!
All. Not a word—you did deceive her!

Ballad—PHYLLIS.

For riches and rank I do not long—
Their pleasures are false and vain :
I gave up the love of a lordly throng
For the love of a simple swain.

But now that that simple swain's untrue,
With sorrowful heart I turn to you—
   A heart that's aching,
   Quaking, breaking,
As sorrowful hearts are wont to do!

The riches and rank that you befall
   Are the only baits you use,
So the richest and rankiest of you all
   My sorrowful heart shall choose.
As none are so noble—none so rich
As this couple of lords, I'll find a niche,
   In my heart that's aching,
   Quaking, breaking,
For one of you two—and I don't care which!

ENSEMBLE.

Phyl. (*to* Ld. Mount. *and* Ld. Toll.). To you I give my
   heart so rich!
All. (*puzzled*).   To which?
Phyl.   I do not care!
   To you I yield—it is my doom;
All.   To whom?
Phyl.   I'm not aware!
   I'm yours for life if you but choose.
All.   She's whose?
Phyl.   That's your affair.
   I'll be a countess, shall I not?
All.   Of what?
Phyl.   I do not care!

All.   Lucky little lady!
   Strephon's lot is shady;
   Rank, it seems, is vital,
   "Countess" is the title,
   But of what I'm not aware!

Streph.   Can I inactive see my fortune fade?
     No, no!
   Mighty protectress, hasten to my aid!

Enter Fairies, tripping, headed by CELIA, LEILA, *and* FLETA,
and followed by QUEEN.

Chorus of FAIRIES.

Tripping hither, tripping thither,
Nobody knows why or whither;
　Why you want us we don't know,
　But you've summoned us, and so
　　Enter all the little fairies
　　　To their usual tripping measure！
　　To oblige you all our care is—
　　　Tell us, pray, what is your pleasure！

Streph. The lady of my love has caught me talking to
　　another—
All. 　　　　　Oh, fie！ Strephon is a rogue！
Streph. I tell her very plainly that the lady is my mother—
All. 　　　　　Taradiddle, taradiddle, tol lol lay！
Streph. She won't believe my statement, and declares we
　　must be parted,
　　Because on a career of double dealing I have started,
　　Then gives her hand to one of these, and leaves me
　　broken-hearted—
All. 　　　　　Taradiddle, taradiddle, tol lol lay！
Queen. Ah, cruel ones, to part two faithful lovers from each
　　other！
All. 　　　　　Oh, fie！ Strephon is a rogue！
Queen. You've done him an injustice, for the lady *is* his
　　mother！
All. 　　　　　Taradiddle, taradiddle, tol lol lay！
Lord Ch. (aside). That fable perhaps may serve his turn as
　　well as any other.
　　I didn't see her face, but if they fondled one another,
　　And she's but seventeen—I don't believe it was his
　　mother！
All. 　　　　　Taradiddle, taradiddle, tol lol lay！

Lord Toll. 　　I've often had a use
　　　　For a thorough-bred excuse
　　Of a sudden (which is English for " *repentè* ")
　　　　But of all I ever heard
　　　　This is much the most absurd,
　　For she's seventeen and he is five-and-twenty！

All. He says she is his mother, and he's four or five-and-
twenty!

Oh, fie! Strephon is a rogue!

Lord Mount.   Now listen, pray, to me,
For this paradox will be
Carried nobody at all *contradicente.*
Her age, upon the date
Of his birth was *minus* eight,
If she's seventeen, and he is five-and-twenty!

All. To say she is his mother is an utter bit of folly!
Oh, fie! Strephon is a rogue!
Perhaps his brain is addled, and it's very melancholy!
Taradiddle, taradiddle, tol lol lay!
I wouldn't say a word that could be construed as
injurious,
But to find a mother younger than her son is very
curious,
And that's a kind of mother that is usually spurious.
Taradiddle, taradiddle, tol lol lay!

Ld. Ch.   Go away, madam;
I should say, madam,
You display, madam,
Shocking taste.

It is rude, madam,
To intrude, madam,
With your brood, madam,
Brazen-faced!

You come here, madam,
Interfere, madam,
With a peer, madam.
(I am one.)

You're aware, madam,
What you dare, madam,
So take care, madam,
And begone!

ENSEMBLE.

FAIRIES (*to* QUEEN).	PEERS.
Let us stay, madam,	Go away, madam ;
I should say, madam,	I should say, madam,
They display, madam,	You display, madam,
Shocking taste.	Shocking taste.
It is rude, madam,	It is rude, madam,
To allude, madam,	To intrude, madam,
To your brood, madam,	With your brood, madam,
Brazen-faced !	Brazen-faced !
We don't fear, madam,	You come here, madam,
Any peer, madam,	Interfere, madam,
Though, my dear madam,	With a peer, madam.
This is one.	(I am one.)
They will stare, madam,	You're aware, madam,
When aware, madam,	What you dare, madam,
What they dare, madam—	To take care, madam,
What they've done !	And begone !

Queen (*furious*).　Bearded by these puny mortals !
　　　　　　　I will launch from fairy portals
　　　　　　　All the most terrific thunders
　　　　　　　In my armoury of wonders !

Phyl. (*aside*).　Should they launch terrific wonders,
　　　　　　　All would then repent their blunders.

Queen.　　　　Oh ! Chancellor unwary,
　　　　　　　It's highly necessary
　　　　　　　　Your tongue to teach
　　　　　　　　Respectful speech—
　　　　　　　Your attitude to vary !

　　　　　　　Your badinage so airy,
　　　　　　　Your manner arbitrary,
　　　　　　　　Are out of place
　　　　　　　　When face to face
　　　　　　　With an influential Fairy !

All the Peers (*aside*).　I never knew
　　　　　　　We were speaking to
　　　　　　　An influential Fairy !

Lord Ch.	A plague on this vagary!
	I'm in a nice quandary!
	  Of hasty tone
	  With dames unknown;
	I ought to be more chary!
	It seems that she's a fairy
	From Andersen's library,
	  And I took her for
	  The proprietor
	Of a Ladies' Seminary!

All.	$\left\{ \begin{matrix} \text{He} \\ \text{We} \end{matrix} \right\}$ took her for The proprietor Of a Ladies' Seminary!
Queen.	When next your Houses do assemble, You may tremble!
Celia.	Our wrath, when gentlemen offend us, Is tremendous!
Leila.	They meet, who underrate our calling, Doom appalling!

Queen.	Take down our sentence as we speak it,
	  And *he* shall wreak it!
	              (*Indicating* STREPHON.)

Queen.	Henceforth, Strephon, cast away Crooks and pipes and ribbons so gay— Flocks and herds that bleat and low; Into Parliament you shall go!

Fairies.	Into Parliament he shall go!
	  Backed by our supreme authority,
	  He'll command a large majority!
	Into Parliament he shall go!

Queen.	In the Parliamentary hive, Liberal or Conservative— Whig or Tory—I don't know— But into Parliament you shall go!
Fairies.	Into Parliament, etc.
Peers.	Ah, spare us!

QUEEN (*speaking through music*).

Every Bill and every measure
That may gratify his pleasure,
Though your fury it arouses,
Shall be passed by both your Houses !
You shall sit, if he sees reason,
Through the grouse and salmon season !
He shall end the cherished rights
You enjoy on Wednesday nights :
He shall prick that annual blister,
Marriage with deceased wife's sister !
Titles shall ennoble, then,
All the Common Councilmen :
   Peers shall teem in Christendom,
    And a Duke's exalted station
   Be attainable by Com-
    Petitive Examination !

PEERS.	FAIRIES *and* PHYLLIS
Oh, horror !	Their horror ! They can't dissemble Nor hide the fear that makes them tremble !

ENSEMBLE.

PEERS.	FAIRIES, PHYLLIS, *and* STREPHON.

Young Strephon is the kind of
   lout
We do not care a fig about !
   We cannot say
   What evils may,
Result in consequence.
	With Strephon for your foe, no
	   doubt,
	A fearful prospect opens out,
	   And who shall say
	   What evils may
	Result in consequence ?

But lordly vengeance will
   pursue
All kinds of common people who
   Oppose our views,
   Or boldly choose
To offer us offence.
	A hideous vengeance will
	   pursue
	All noblemen who venture to
	   Oppose his views
	   Or boldly choose
	To offer him offence.

He'd better fly at humbler
  game,
Or our forbearance he must
  claim
    If he'd escape
    In any shape
  A very painful wrench!

'Twill plunge them into grief
  and shame;
His kind forbearance they
  must claim
    If they'd escape
    In any shape
  A very painful wrench.

Your powers we dauntlessly
  pooh-pooh:
A dire revenge will fall on you,
    If you besiege
    Our high *prestige*—
(The word "*prestige*" is
French).

Although our threats you now
  pooh-pooh,
A dire revenge will fall on you,
    Should he besiege
    Your high *prestige*—
(The word "*prestige*" is
French).

Peers.   Our lordly style
        You shall not quench
        With base *canaille!*
Fairies.   (That word is French.)
Peers.   Distinction ebbs
        Before a herd
        Of vulgar *plebs!*
Fairies.   (A Latin word.)
Peers.   'Twould fill with joy,
        And madness stark
        The οἱ πολλοί!
Fairies.   (A Greek remark.)

PEERS.

You needn't wait:
  Away you fly!
Your threatened hate
  We thus defy!

FAIRIES.

We will not wait:
  We go sky-high!
Our threatened hate
  You won't defy!

Fairies.   Your lordly style
        We'll quickly quench
        With base *canaille!*
Peers.   (That word is French!)
Fairies.   Distinction ebbs
        Before a herd
        Of vulgar *plebs!*
Peers.   (A Latin word.)

Fairies.	'Twill fill with joy And madness stark The οἱ πολλοί!
Peers.	(A Greek remark.)

PEERS.	FAIRIES.
You needn't wait :	We will not wait :
Away you fly !	We go sky-high !
Your threatened hate	Our threatened hate
We won't defy !	You won't defy !

[*Fairies threaten Peers with their wands. Peers kneel as begging for mercy.* PHYLLIS *implores* STREPHON *to relent. He casts her from him, and she falls fainting into the arms of* LORD MOUNTARARAT *and* LORD TOLLOLLER.*

END OF ACT I.

ACT II.

SCENE.—*Palace Yard, Westminster.   Westminster Hall, Clock tower up* R.C.

PRIVATE WILLIS *discovered on sentry,* R.   *Moonlight.*

Song—WILLIS.

When all night long a chap remains
    On sentry-go, to chase monotony
He exercises of his brains,
    That is, assuming that he's got any.
Though never nurtured in the lap
    Of luxury, yet I admonish you,
I am an intellectual chap,
    And think of things that would astonish you.
        I often think it's comical—Fal, lal, la !
        How Nature always does contrive—Fal, lal, la !
            That every boy and every gal,
                That's born into the world alive,
            Is either a little Liberal,
                Or else a little Conservative !
                Fal, lal, la !

When in that House M.P.'s divide,
  If they've a brain and cerebellum, too,
They've got to leave that brain outside,
  And vote just as their leaders tell 'em to.
But then the prospect of a lot
  Of dull M.P.'s in close proximity,
All thinking for themselves, is what
  No man can face with equanimity.
      Then let's rejoice with loud Fal lal—Fal, lal, la !
      That Nature wisely does contrive—Fal, lal, la !
      That every boy and every gal,
        That's born into the world alive,
      Is either a little Liberal,
        Or else a little Conservative !
         Fal, lal, la !

Enter Fairies, with CELIA, LEILA, *and* FLETA. *They trip round stage.*

Chorus of FAIRIES.

Strephon's a Member of Parliament !
  And carries every Bill he chooses.
To his measures all assent ;—
  Showing that fairies have their uses.
    Whigs and Tories
    Dim their glories,
Giving an ear to all his stories—
Lords and Commons are both in the blues:
Strephon makes them shake in their shoes !
    Shake in their shoes !
    Shake in their shoes !
Strephon makes them shake in their shoes !

Enter Peers from Westminster Hall.

Chorus of PEERS.

Strephon's a Member of Parliament !
  Running a-muck at all abuses.
His unqualified assent
  Somehow nobody now refuses.
    Whigs and Tories
    Dim their glories,
Giving an ear to all his stories—

Carrying every Bill he may wish :
Here's a pretty kettle of fish!
Kettle of fish!
Kettle of fish!
Here's a pretty kettle of fish !

Enter LORD MOUNTARARAT *and* LORD TOLLOLLER *from Westminster Hall.*

Celia. You seem annoyed.

Ld. Mount. Annoyed? I should think so! Why, this ridiculous *protégé* of yours is playing the deuce with everything! To-night is the second reading of his Bill to throw the Peerage open to Competitive Examination!

Ld. Toll. And he'll carry it, too!

Ld. Mount. Carry it? Of course he will! He's a Parliamentary Pickford—he carries everything !

Leila. Yes. If you please, that's our fault !

Ld. Mount. The deuce it is!

Celia. Yes; we influence the members, and compel them to vote just as he wishes them to.

Leila. It's our system. It shortens the debates.

Ld. Toll. Well, but think what it all means. I don't so much mind for myself, but with a House of Peers with no grandfathers worth mentioning, the country must go to the dogs!

Leila. I suppose it must!

Ld. Mount. I don't want to say a word against brains—I've a great respect for brains—I often wish I had some myself—but with a House of Peers composed exclusively of people of intellect, what's to become of the House of Commons?

Leila. I never thought of that !

Ld. Mount. This comes of women interfering in politics. It so happens that if there is an institution in Great Britain which is not susceptible of any improvement at all, it is the House of Peers !

Song—LD. MOUNT.

When Britain really ruled the waves—
(In good Queen Bess's time)
The House of Peers made no pretence
To intellectual eminence,
Or scholarship sublime;
Yet Britain won her proudest bays
In good Queen Bess's glorious days !

Chorus.　　　　Yes, Britain won, etc.

When Wellington thrashed Bonaparte,
 As every child can tell,
The House of Peers, throughout the war,
Did nothing in particular,
 And did it very well :
Yet Britain set the world a-blaze
In good King George's glorious days !
Chorus. Yes, Britain set, etc.

And while the House of Peers withholds
 Its legislative hand,
And noble statesmen do not itch
To interfere with matters which
 They do not understand,
As bright will shine Great Britain's rays,
As in King George's glorious days!
Chorus. As bright will shine, etc.

Leila (who has been much attracted by the Peers during this song). Charming persons, are they not?

Celia. Distinctly. For self-contained dignity, combined with airy condescension, give me a British Representative Peer!

Ld. Toll. Then pray stop this *protégé* of yours before it's too late. Think of the mischief you're doing!

Leila (crying). But we *can't* stop him now. (*Aside to* CELIA) Aren't they lovely! (*Aloud.*) Oh, why did you go and defy us, you great geese!

*Duet—*LEILA *and* CELIA.

Leila. In vain to us you plead—
    Don't go!
  Your prayers we do not heed—
    Don't go!
   It's true we sigh,
    But don't suppose
   A tearful eye
    Forgiveness shows.
     Oh, no!
  We're very cross indeed—
    Don't go!
   It's true we sigh, etc.

T

Celia.   Your disrespectful sneers—
                        Don't go!
                Call forth indignant tears!
                        Don't go!
                You break our laws—
                    You are our foe!
                We cry because
                    We hate you so!
                            You know!
                You very wicked Peers!
                        Don't go!

FAIRIES.   LORDS MOUNT. *and* TOLL.

You break our laws—   We break their laws—
    You are our foe!   They are our foe!
We cry because   They cry because
    We hate you so!   They hate us so!
        You know!   Oh, ho!
You very wicked Peers!   If that's the case, my dears,
    Don't go!   We'll go!

Exeunt MOUNTARARAT, TOLLOLLER, *and Peers. Fairies gaze wistfully after them. Enter* FAIRY QUEEN.

Queen. Oh, shame—shame upon you! Is this your fidelity to the laws you are bound to obey? Know ye not that it is death to marry a mortal?

Leila. Yes, but it's not death to *wish* to marry a mortal!

Fleta. If it were, you'd have to execute us all!

Queen. Oh, this is weakness! Subdue it!

Celia. We know it's weakness, but the weakness is so strong!

Leila. We are not all as tough as you are!

Queen. Tough! Do you suppose that I am insensible to the effect of manly beauty? Look at that man (*referring to sentry*). A perfect picture! (*To sentry*) Who are you, sir?

Willis (coming to "attention"). Private Willis, B Company 1st Grenadier Guards.

Queen. You're a very fine fellow, sir.

Willis. I am generally admired.

Queen. I can quite understand it. (*To Fairies.*) Now here is a man whose physical attributes are simply god-like. That man has a most extraordinary effect upon me. If I yielded to a natural impulse, I should fall down and worship that man. But I mortify this inclination: I wrestle with it, and it lies beneath my feet! That is how I treat my regard for that man!

Song—FAIRY QUEEN.

Oh, foolish fay,
    Think you, because
His brave array
    My bosom thaws,
I'd disobey
    Our fairy laws?
Because I fly
    In realms above,
In tendency
    To fall in love
Resemble I
    The amorous dove?
(*aside*) Oh, amorous dove!
      Type of Ovidius Naso!
        This heart of mine
        Is soft as thine,
      Although I dare not say so!

Chorus.   Oh, amorous dove, etc.

On fire that glows
    With heat intense
I turn the hose
    Of common sense,
And out it goes
    At small expense!
We must maintain
    Our fairy law;
That is the main
    On which to draw—
In that we gain
    A Captain Shaw!
(*aside*) Oh, Captain Shaw!
      Type of true love kept under!
        Could thy Brigade
        With cold cascade
      Quench my great love, I wonder!

Chorus.   Oh, Captain Shaw! etc.

[*Exeunt Fairies and* FAIRY QUEEN, *sorrowfully*

Enter PHYLLIS.

Phyl. (*half crying*). I can't think why I'm not in better spirits! I'm engaged to two noblemen at once. That ought to be enough to make any girl happy. But I'm miserable! Don't suppose it's because I care for Strephon, for I hate him! No girl *could* care for a man who goes about with a mother considerably younger than himself!

Enter LORD MOUNTARARAT *and* LORD˙ TOLLOLLER.

Ld. Mount. Phyllis! My darling!

Ld. Toll. Phyllis! My own!

Phyl. Don't! How dare you? Oh, but perhaps you're the two noblemen I'm engaged to?

Ld. Mount. I am one of them.

Ld. Toll. I am the other.

Phyl. Oh, then, my darling! (*to* MOUNTARARAT). My own! (*to* TOLLOLLER). Well, have you settled which it's to be?

Ld. Toll. Not altogether. It's a difficult position. It would be hardly delicate to toss up. On the whole we would rather leave it to you.

Phyl. How can it possibly concern me? You are both Earls, and you are both rich, and you are both plain.

Ld. Mount. So we are. At least I am.

Ld. Toll. So am I.

Ld. Mount. No, no!

Ld. Toll. I am indeed. Very plain.

Ld. Mount. Well, well—perhaps you are.

Phyl. There's really nothing to choose between you. If one of you would forego his title, and distribute his estates among his Irish tenantry, why, then I should then see a reason for accepting the other.

Ld. Mount. Tolloller, are you prepared to make this sacrifice?

Ld. Toll. No!

Ld. Mount. Not even to oblige a lady?

Ld. Toll. No!

Ld. Mount. Then the only question is, which of us shall give way to the other? Perhaps, on the whole, she would be happier with me. I don't know. I may be wrong.

Ld. Toll. No. I don't know that you are. I really believe she would. But the awkward part of the thing is that if you rob me of the girl of my heart, one of us must die. It's a family tradition that I have sworn to respect. It's a painful position, for I have a very strong regard for you, George.

Ld. Mount. (much affected). My dear Thomas !

Ld. Toll. You are very dear to me, George. We were boys together—at least *I* was. If I were to survive you, my existence would be hopelessly embittered.

Ld. Mount. Then, my dear Thomas, you must not do it. I say it again and again—if it will have this effect upon you, you must not do it. No, no. If one of us is to destroy the other, let it be me!

Ld. Toll. No, no.

Ld. Mount. Ah, yes!—by our boyish friendship I implore you!

Ld. Toll. (much moved). Well, well, be it so. But, no, no; I cannot consent to an act which would crush you with unavailing remorse.

Ld. Mount. But it would not do so. I should be very sad at first—oh, who would not be?—but it would wear off. I like you *very much*—but not, perhaps, as much as you like me.

Ld. Toll. George, you're a noble fellow, but that tell-tale tear betrays you. No, George; you are very fond of me, and I cannot consent to give you a week's uneasiness on my account.

Ld. Mount. But, dear Thomas, it would not last a week! Remember, you lead the House of Lords! on your demise I shall take your place! Oh, Thomas, it would not last a day!

Phyl. (coming down). Now I do hope you're not going to fight about me, because it's really not worth while.

Ld. Toll. (looking at her). Well, I don't believe it is!

Ld. Mount. Nor I. The sacred ties of Friendship are paramount.

Quartette—MOUNTARARAT, TOLLOLLER, PHYLLIS, *and* WILLIS.

Ld. Toll. Though p'raps I may incur your blame,
     The things are few
     I would not do
    In Friendship's name!

Ld. Mount. And I may say I think the same;
     Not even love
     Should rank above
    True Friendship's name!

Phyl.   Then free me, pray; be mine the blame;
     Forget your craze
     And go your way
    In Friendship's name,

Willis.   Accept, O Friendship, all the same,
        This sacrifice to thy dear name !

All.   Oh, many a man, in Friendship's name,
        Has yielded fortune, rank, and fame !
        But no one yet, in the world so wide,
        Has yielded up a promised bride!

[*Exeunt* MOUNTARARAT *and* TOLLOLLER, *lovingly, in one direction, and* PHYLLIS *in another.*

Enter LORD CHANCELLOR, *very miserable.*

Recit.—LORD CHANCELLOR.

Love, unrequited, robs me of my rest :
  Love, hopeless love, my ardent soul encumbers :
Love, nightmare like, lies heavy on my chest,
  And weaves itself into my midnight slumbers !

Song—LORD CHANCELLOR.

When you're lying awake with a dismal headache, and repose is taboo'd by anxiety,
I conceive you may use any language you choose to indulge in, without impropriety ;
For your brain is on fire—the bedclothes conspire of usual slumber to plunder you :
First your counterpane goes, and uncovers your toes, and your sheet slips demurely from under you ;
Then the blanketing tickles—you feel like mixed pickles—so terribly sharp is the pricking,
And you're hot, and you're cross, and you tumble and toss till there's nothing 'twixt you and the ticking.
Then the bedclothes all creep to the ground in a heap, and you pick 'em all up in a tangle ;
Next your pillow resigns and politely declines to remain at its usual angle !
Well, you get some repose in the form of a doze, with hot eye-balls and head ever aching,
But your slumbering teems with such horrible dreams that you'd very much better be waking ;
For you dream you are crossing the Channel, and tossing about in a steamer from Harwich—
Which is something between a large bathing-machine and a very small second-class carriage—

And you're giving a treat (penny ice and cold meat) to a party
of friends and relations—

They're a ravenous horde—and they all came on board at Sloane
Square and South Kensington Stations.

And bound on that journey you find your attorney (who started
that morning from Devon);

He's a bit undersized, and you don't feel surprised when he tells
you he's only eleven.

Well, you're driving like mad with this singular lad (by-the-bye
the ship's now a four-wheeler),

And you're playing round games, and he calls you bad names
when you tell him that " ties pay the dealer ; "

But this you can't stand, so you throw up your hand, and you
find you're as cold as an icicle,

In your shirt and your socks (the black silk with gold clocks),
crossing Salisbury Plain on a bicycle :

And he and the crew are on bicycles too—which they've somehow or other invested in—

And he's telling the tars, all the particu*lars* of a company he's
interested in—

It's a scheme of devices, to get at low prices, all goods from
cough mixtures to cables

(Which tickled the sailors) by treating retailers, as though they
were all *vege*ta*b*les—

You get a good spadesman to plant a small tradesman, (first
take off his boots with a boot-tree),

And his legs will take root, and his fingers will shoot, and
they'll blossom and bud like a fruit-tree—

From the greengrocer tree you get grapes and green pea,
cauliflower, pineapple and cranberries,

While the pastry-cook plant, cherry brandy will grant, apple
puffs, and three-corners, and Banburys—

The shares are a penny, and ever so many are taken by
Rothschild and Baring,

And just as a few are allotted to you, you awake with a shudder
despairing—

You're a regular wreck, with a crick in your neck, and no
wonder you snore, for your head's on the floor, and you've
needles and pins from your soles to your shins, and your
flesh is a-creep, for your left leg's asleep, and you've cramp
in your toes, and a fly on your nose, and some fluff in your
lung, and a feverish tongue, and a thirst that's intense,
and a general sense that you haven't been sleeping in
clover ;

But the darkness has passed, and it's daylight at last, and the night has been long—ditto ditto my song—and thank goodness they're both of them over !

(Lord Chancellor *falls exhausted on a seat.*)

Lords Mountararat *and* Tolloller *come forward.*

Ld. Mount. I am much distressed to see your Lordship in this condition.

Ld. Ch. Ah, my Lords, it is seldom that a Lord Chancellor has reason to envy the position of another, but I am free to confess that I would rather be two Earls engaged to Phyllis than any other half-dozen noblemen upon the face of the globe !

Ld. Toll. (*without enthusiasm*). Yes.   It's an enviable position when you're the only one.

Ld. Mount. Oh yes, no doubt—most enviable.   At the same time, seeing you thus, we naturally say to ourselves, " This is very sad.   His Lordship is constitutionally as blithe as a bird —he trills upon the bench like a thing of song and gladness. His series of judgments in F sharp, given *andante* in six-eight time, are among the most remarkable effects ever produced in a Court of Chancery.   He is, perhaps, the only living instance of a judge whose decrees have received the honour of a double *encore.*   How can we bring ourselves to do that which will deprive the Court of Chancery of one of its most attractive features ? "

Ld. Ch. I feel the force of your remarks, but I am here in two capacities, and they clash, my Lord, they clash !   I deeply grieve to say that in declining to entertain my last application, I presumed to address myself in terms which render it impossible for me ever to apply to myself again.   It was a most painful scene, my Lord—most painful !

Ld. Toll. This is what it is to have two capacities !   Let us be thankful that we are persons of no capacity whatever.

Ld. Mount. Come, come.   Remember you are a very just and kindly old gentleman, and you need have no hesitation in approaching yourself, so that you do so respectfully and with a proper show of deference.

Ld. Ch. Do you really think so ?   Well, I will nerve myself to another effort, and, if that fails, I resign myself to my fate !

Trio—LORD CHANCELLOR, LORDS MOUNTARARAT *and*
TOLLOLLER.

Ld. Mount.   If you go in
        You're sure to win—
  Yours will be the charming maidie :
    Be your law
    The ancient saw,
  " Faint heart never won fair lady ! "

All.   Faint heart never won fair lady !
      Every journey has an end—
    When at the worst affairs will mend—
    Dark the dawn when day is nigh—
    Hustle your horse and don't say die !

Ld. Toll.   He who shies
      At such a prize
  Is not worth a maravedi,
    Be so kind
    To bear in mind—
  " Faint heart never won fair lady ! "

All.   Faint heart never won fair lady !
    While the sun shines make your hay—
    Where a will is, there's a way—
    Beard the lion in his lair—
    None but the brave deserve the fair !

Ld. Ch.   I'll take heart
      And make a start—
  Though I fear the prospect's shady—
    Much I'd spend
    To gain my end—
  Faint heart never won fair lady !

All.   Faint heart never won fair lady !
    Nothing venture, nothing win—
    Blood is thick, but water's thin—
    In for a penny, in for a pound—
    It's Love that makes the world go round !

      [*Dance, and exeunt arm-in-arm together.*

    Enter STREPHON, *in very lou spirits.*

Streph. I suppose one ought to enjoy one's self in Parliament
when one leads both parties, as I do ! But I'm miserable, poor,
broken-hearted, fool that I am ! Oh Phyllis, Phyllis !—

Enter PHYLLIS.

Phyl. Yes?

Streph. (*surprised*). Phyllis! But I suppose, I should say
"My Lady." I have not yet been informed which title your
Ladyship has pleased to select?

Phyl. I—I haven't quite decided. You see *I* have no *mother*
to advise *me!*

Streph. No. I have.

Phyl. Yes; a *young* mother.

Streph. Not very—a couple of centuries or so.

Phyl. Oh! She wears well.

Streph. She does. She's a fairy.

Phyl. I beg your pardon—a what?

Streph. Oh, I've no longer any reason to conceal the fact—
she's a fairy.

Phyl. A fairy! Well, but—that would account for a good
many things! Then—I suppose *you're* a fairy?

Streph. I'm half a fairy.

Phyl. Which half?

Streph. The upper half—down to the waistcoat.

Phyl. Dear me! (*prodding him with her fingers*). There
is nothing to show it! But why didn't you tell me this
before?

Streph. I thought you would take a dislike to me. But as
it's all off, you may as well know the truth—I'm only half a
mortal!

Phyl. (*crying*). But I'd rather have half a mortal I do love,
than half a dozen I don't!

Streph. Oh, I think not—go to your half-dozen.

Phyl. (*crying*). It's only two! and I hate 'em. Please forgive
me!

Streph. I don't think I ought to. Besides, all sorts of diffi-
culties will arise. You know, my grandmother looks quite as
young as my mother. So do all my aunts.

Phyl. I quite understand. Whenever I see you kissing a
very young lady, I shall know it's an elderly relative.

Streph. You will? Then, Phyllis, I think we shall be very
happy! (*embracing her*).

Phyl. We won't wait long.

Streph. No; we might change our minds. We'll get married
first.

Phyl. And change our minds afterwards?

Streph. That's the usual course.

Streph.   If we're weak enough to tarry
        Ere we marry,
           You and I,
    Of the feeling I inspire
        You may tire
           By-and-bye.
    For Peers with flowing coffers
        Press their offers—
           That is why
    I think we will not tarry
        Ere we marry,
           You and I!

Phyl.   If we're weak enough to tarry
        Ere we marry,
           You and I,
    With some more attractive maiden,
        Jewel-laden,
           You may fly.
    If by chance we should be parted,
        Broken-hearted
           I should die—
    So I think we will not tarry
        Ere we marry,
           You and I!

Phyl. But does your mother know you're— I mean, is she aware of an engagement?

Enter IOLANTHE.

Iol. She is—and thus she welcomes her daughter-in-law! (*kisses her*).

Phyl. She kisses just like other people! But the Lord Chancellor!

Streph. I forgot him! Mother, none can resist your fairy eloquence: you will go to him, and plead for us?

Iol. (*much agitated*). No, no; impossible!

Streph. But our happiness—our very lives, depend on our obtaining his consent!

Phyl. Oh, madam, you cannot refuse to do this!

Iol. You know not what you ask! The Lord Chancellor is —my husband!

Streph. and Phyl. Your husband!

Iol. My husband and your father! (*addressing Strephon, who is much moved*).

Phyl. Then our course is plain: on his learning that Strephon is his son, all objection to our marriage will be at once removed!

Iol. No, he must never know! He believes me to have died childless, and dearly as I love him, I am bound, under penalty of death, not to undeceive him. But see—he comes! Quick—my veil! (*They retire up as Iolanthe veils herself.*)

Enter LORD CHANCELLOR.

Ld. Ch. Victory! Victory! Success has crowned my efforts, and I may consider myself engaged to Phyllis! At first I wouldn't hear of it—it was out of the question. But I took heart. I pointed out to myself that I was no stranger to myself —that, in point of fact, I had been personally acquainted with myself for some years. This had its effect. I admitted that I had watched my professional advancement with considerable interest, and I handsomely added that I yielded to no one in admiration for my private and professional virtues. This was a great point gained. I then endeavoured to work upon my feelings. Conceive my joy when I distinctly perceived a tear glistening in my own eye! Eventually, after a severe struggle with myself, I reluctantly—most reluctantly—consented!

IOLANTHE *comes down veiled*—STREPHON *and* PHYLLIS *go off on tip-toe.*

Recit.—IOLANTHE.

My Lord, a suppliant at your feet I kneel,
Oh, listen to a mother's fond appeal!
Hear me to-night! I come in urgent need—
'Tis for my son, young Strephon, that I plead!

Ballad—IOLANTHE.

He loves! If the bygone years
  Thine eyes have ever shed
Tears—bitter, unavailing tears,
  For one untimely dead—
If in the eventide of life
  Sad thoughts of her arise,
Then let the memory of thy wife
  Plead for my boy—he dies!

He dies! If fondly laid aside
  In some old cabinet,
Memorials of thy long-dead bride
  Lie, dearly treasured yet,
Then let her hallowed bridal dress—
  Her little dainty gloves—
Her withered flowers—her faded tress—
  Plead for my boy—he loves!

The Lord Chancellor *is moved by this appeal. After a pause—*

Ld. Ch. It may not be—for so the Fates decide :
    Learn thou that Phyllis is my promised bride!
Iol. (in horror).   Thy bride! No! no!
Ld. Ch.   It shall be so!
    Those who would separate us woe betide!
Iol.   My doom thy lips have spoken—
      I plead in vain!
Chorus of Fairies (without).   Forbear! forbear!
Iol.   A vow already broken
      I break again!
Chorus of Fairies (without).   Forbear! forbear!
Iol.   For him—for her—for thee
      I yield my life.
    Behold—it may not be!
      I am thy wife!
Chorus of Fairies (without). Aiaiah! Aiaiah! Willaloo!
Ld. Ch. (recognizing her). Iolanthe! thou livest?
Iol.   Aye!
    I live! Now let me die!

Enter Fairy Queen *and Fairies.* Iolanthe *kneels to her*

Queen.   Once again thy vows are broken:
    Thou thyself thy doom hath spoken!
Chorus of Fairies. Aiaiah! Aiaiah!
        Willahalah! Willaloo!
    Laloiah! Laloiah!
        Willahalah! Willaloo!
Queen.   Bow thy head to Destiny:
    Death thy doom, and thou shalt die!
Chorus of Fairies. Aiaiah! Aiaiah! etc.

The Peers and STREPHON *enter.   The* QUEEN *raises her spear.*

Leila. Hold !   If Iolanthe must die, so must we all ; for, as
she has sinned, so have we !

Queen. What !   (*Peers and Fairies kneel to her*—LORD
MOUNTARARAT *with* CELIA ; LORD TOLLOLLER *with* LEILA.)

Celia. We are all fairy duchesses, marchionesses, countesses
viscountesses, and baronesses.

Ld. Mount. It's our fault.   They couldn't help themselves.

Queen. It seems they *have* helped themselves, and pretty
freely, too ! (*After a pause.*)   You have all incurred death :
but I can't slaughter the whole company ! And yet (*unfolding
a scroll*) the law is clear—every fairy must die who marries a
mortal !

Ld. Ch. Allow me, as an old Equity draughtsman, to make a
suggestion.   The subtleties of the legal mind are equal to the
emergency.   The thing is really quite simple—the insertion of
a single word will do it.   Let it stand that every fairy shall die
who *don't* marry a mortal, and there you are, out of your
difficulty at once !

Queen. We like your humour.   Very well ! (*Altering the
MS. in pencil.*)   Private Willis !

Sentry (*coming forward*). Ma'am !

Queen. To save my life, it is necessary that I marry at once.
How should you like to be a fairy guardsman?

Sentry. Well, ma'am, I don't think much of the British
soldier who wouldn't ill-conwenience himself to save a female
in distress.

Queen. You are a brave fellow.   You're a fairy from this
moment (*wings spring from Sentry's shoulders*). And you, my
Lords, how say you ?   Will you join our ranks ?

(*Fairies kneel to Peers and implore them to do so.*)

Ld. Mount. (*to Ld. Tolloller*). Well, now that the Peers are
to be recruited entirely from persons of intelligence, I really
don't see what use *we* are, down here.

Ld. Tol. None whatever.

Queen. Good ! (*Wings spring from shoulders of Peers.*)
Then away we go to Fairyland.

FINALE.

Phyl. Soon as we may,
Off and away !
We'll commence our journey airy—
Happy are we—
As you can see,
Every one is now a fairy !
Every one is now a fairy !

Iol., Queen, and Phyl. Though as a general rule we know
Two strings go to every bow,
Make up your minds that grief 'twill bring
If you've two beaux to every string.

All. Though as a general rule, etc.

Ld. Ch. Up in the sky,
Ever so high,
Pleasures come in endless series ;
We will arrange
Happy exchange—
House of Peers for House of Peris !

All. House of Peers for House of Peris !

Ld. Ch., Mount., and Toll. Up in the air, sky-high, sky-
high,
Free from wards in Chancery,
$\left\{ \begin{array}{c} \text{I} \\ \text{He} \end{array} \right\}$ will be surely happier, for
$\left\{ \begin{array}{c} \text{I'm} \\ \text{He's} \end{array} \right\}$ such a susceptible Chancellor !

Up in the air, etc.

CURTAIN.

THE END.

PRINTED IN GREAT BRITAIN BY
WILLIAM CLOWES AND SONS, LIMITED, LONDON AND BECCLES.

Printed in the United States
76112LV00003B/90